£1

GW00776617

Nothing Prepared Me!

LANSDOWNE, 1983

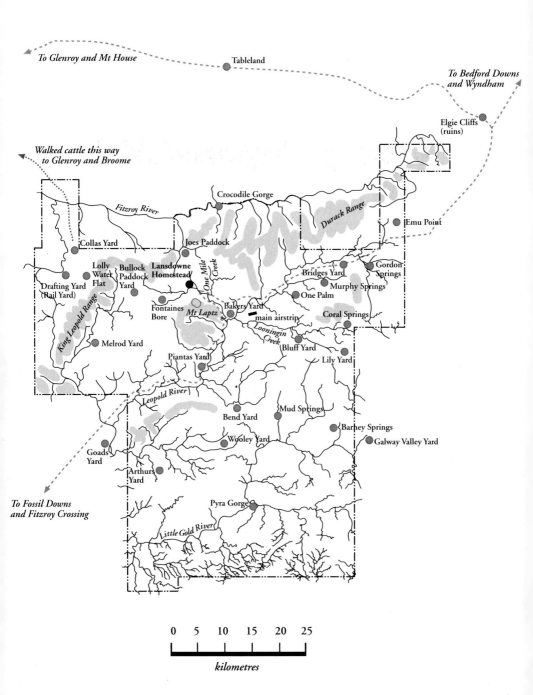

To Glenroy and Mt House

Tableland

To Bedford Downs and Wyndham

Elgie Cliffs (ruins)

Walked cattle this way to Glenroy and Broome

Crocodile Gorge

Fitzroy River

Durack Range

Emu Point

Collas Yard

Joes Paddock

Lolly Water Flat

Bullock Paddock Yard

Lansdowne Homestead

One Mile Creek

Bridges Yard

Gordon Springs

Drafting Yard (Rail Yard)

Fontaines Bore

Mt Laptz

Bakers Yard

main airstrip

Murphy Springs

One Palm

Coral Springs

King Leopold Range

Melrod Yard

Piantas Yard

Looningin Creek

Bluff Yard

Lily Yard

Leopold River

Bend Yard

Mud Springs

Goads Yard

Wooley Yard

Barhey Springs

Galway Valley Yard

Arthurs Yard

To Fossil Downs and Fitzroy Crossing

Pyra Gorge

Little Gold River

0 5 10 15 20 25

kilometres

Nothing Prepared Me!

Edna Eckford Quilty

Published by Edna Eckford Quilty
2/3 Bennett Street
Caloundra Q 4551

First published 1999
© Edna Eckford Quilty 1999
Second Edition September 1999
Reprinted November 1999
Reprinted March 2000

This book is copyright. Apart from any fair dealing for the purpose of private study, research, criticism or review, as permitted under the Copyright Act, no part may be reproduced by any process without prior written permission from the publisher.

National Library of Australia
Cataloguing-in-Publication Data

Quilty, Edna Eckford
Nothing prepared me!

ISBN 0 9577608 0 9.

1. Quilty, Edna Eckford. 2. Women ranchers - Western Australia - Lansdowne Station - Biography. 3. Ranch life - Western Australia - Lansdowne Station.
4. Beef industry -Western Australia - History.
5. Lansdowne Station (W.A.).
I. Title

636.201092

Printed by Fergies
PO Box 736
Hamilton Central Q 4007

Foreword

RM Williams

As one who has known and shared the early days of living in lonely places, it gives me great pleasure to give credit to these pages as a record of a period of Kimberley history.

Edna is one of the pioneer women of the outback. When Edna arrived in the Kimberleys it was a place of primitive communications, far distant supplies and few neighbours. It is opportune now that the story of these times is told by one who can still remember.

The Quilty family is known and respected for their contribution to the development of the Kimberleys.

R m & Williams

25 November 1998

Contents

Acknowledgments

I have many people to thank for my book. A long time ago, Frank Johnson, Editor of *Australian Shorthorn*, suggested that I write about my life in the Kimberleys. "Keep diaries," he said. I took his advice and religiously wrote up my diaries.

I started to write *Nothing Prepared Me!* long before I left *Lansdowne*. I put it aside — went back to it — and put it aside again. I am grateful to my family and friends who had faith in me and encouraged me to keep going when I felt like tossing it in.

I appreciate and thank my editor, Ben Jansen and his wife Beverley Anne who travelled many days and many miles — Ben to discuss and advise, Beverley Anne to look at hundreds of slides and photos to get it just right.

Above all, I thank my daughter-in-law, Wendy, my shining light, who kept me on track when things got rough. She sat with me for hours, questioning and wanting answers, confirming dates and places, for she was there when the changes came.

She realised that some of my words and phrases would not be understood by our city cousins or the youth of today. She patiently worked with Ben to give meaning to the expressions I used. Together they built the glossary.

Edna Eckford Quilty
Caloundra 1998

Dedication

This is a record of my life, written for my grandsons,
Matthew and Alex Quilty, Tom and Jim Wreford,
so that they may know of a way of life as I knew it.
It must be written now, before it is lost forever
in the limbo of forgotten things.

Introduction

Roger M Steele
*Northern Territory Government Advisor
and former Minister for Primary Industries*

Nothing Prepared Me! is the autobiography of Edna Eckford Quilty. Its focus is on the thirty-one years she and her husband Rod spent on *Lansdowne*, a million-acre cattle station in the Kimberley Ranges of Western Australia.

Edna grew up in Julia Creek, Queensland, where her romance with Rod began. They were married in 1952 and headed west to Lansdowne Station. The change in landscape and the hardships were dramatic.

Thrown in at the deep end, she had to cope with the traumas of life and the primitive existence of Australia's oldest residents. She lived with dirt floors, no running water and no basic infrastructure or comforts for her family.

In those early days, there were no communications except for the Flying Doctor-based two-way radio. Edna Quilty was undaunted as she became part of the exciting and traumatic events of the outback; the births and the deaths, the flooded rivers and the hardships of the lonely, timeless country of the Kimberleys.

Edna battled isolation and the lack of female company; she made friends with the Aboriginal women on the station, caring for their welfare and ministering to their piccaninnies.

Edna Quilty is a fair dinkum 'Woman of the West'. She civilised *Lansdowne* and she tells the story with quiet dignity.

The characters of the outback are disappearing but the spirit of our pioneering history lives on through this great autobiography.

Nothing Prepared Me! is a command performance of the Australian bush and a 'must read' for all Australians.

Roger Steele

Darwin, 1999

CHAPTER ONE

Great expectations

The wide Bush holds the secrets of their longing and desires,
When the white stars in reverence light their holy altar-fires,
And silence, like the touch of God, sinks deep into the breast—
Perchance He hears and understands the Women of the West.
— From Women of the West *by George Essex Evans*

My brother, three sisters and I were born into a well-to-do, middle-class Australian family — "*Upper* middle-class", my Aunt Theresa was fond of saying. With their early ties to the land, my ancestors were 'landed gentry', as they called it in those days. Mother's family (the Parkers) owned *Peak Downs* and *Lennox*, in the Clermont area of central Queensland, and Father's people (the Eckfords) also had extensive holdings, first at Maitland, in the lush Hunter Valley region of New South Wales, then *Artesian Downs*, at Richmond, western Queensland. While I was still a very young child, my parents owned *Edenvale*, in the Gulf country of Queensland.

Many years later, when living at Julia Creek, Mother would tell us of our long, hazardous journey to *Edenvale*. We travelled overland from Cloncurry — on roads of sorts. While Mother drove the heavily laden, horse-drawn wagon — with Brown Lock and Silver Side in the lead and Old Mick in the shafts — Dad rode Bay Leaf, his beautiful bay stallion. Sometimes, he would tie Bay Leaf to the back of the wagon and take the reins from Mother, as Brown Lock was skittish and hard to handle. Three small children — my baby brother Jimmie, just five months old, my sister Dadie and I — were securely tucked away in the load. Our two faithful cattle dogs trotted along beside us.

We called into *Euroka Springs*, about 60 miles (100 km) north of Julia Creek, where Mother met an old friend, Lily Byrne Quilty. Dad was also pleased to meet Lily's husband, Tom, again. Tom's parents owned *Glenore* and *Oakland Park*, in the Gulf. My father and my Uncle Joe, along with Tom Quilty and his brother Paddy, had been part of the Forest Devils, a band of wild young Gulf stockmen who excelled at the craft of poddy-dodging each other's cattle.

We spent a night at *Euroka Springs*. Mrs Quilty showed Mother to her room and arranged for my sister and me to use her babies' crib. She proudly showed off her own two babies, Rod and Pat.

Tom and Dad unhitched the horses, rubbed them down and stabled them, feeding them cracked corn and hay, their first really good feed since leaving Cloncurry, almost a month before. Ted (Tassie) Triffett, a Tasmanian who had moved to the mainland and worked his way out to western Queensland, where he spent the rest of his life, was working for the Quiltys. A clever all-round handyman, he lost no time in checking our wagon for wear and tear.

Afternoon tea, and then a well-cooked dinner, served by a young half-caste girl called Annie Fortune, were a delight to Mother. The spotless, white, starched tablecloths and shining silverware were things she missed. Dad and Tom, with a rum apiece, and Mother and Mrs Quilty with their tea, sat on the verandah after dinner and watched a storm working up. They decided to call it a day, as we were to leave again first thing the next morning. Dad wanted to keep moving — with storms about, he was worried about crossing the mighty Flinders River.

Next morning, over an early breakfast, the Quiltys tried to persuade Dad to wait until they could check the river, but he was anxious for us to push on. If the wet season was to set in earlier than usual, we would be stranded for months. After picking up some station-grown vegetables and corned beef, we resumed our trek.

When we arrived at the river, it was running a banker. The crossing seemed impossible. Dad rode up and down, trying to find a way into the fast-rising torrent. He finally decided on the best place to cross. Putting blinkers on Brown Lock and holding his rein close to the bit, my father rode beside the lead horses and urged them towards the swirling water. Brown Lock reared and tried to pull away. Mother was in the wagon, trying to help, fearful for the safety of us all. Both dogs jumped onto the top of the load. One nestled down beside my sister, brother and me; the other, excited and frightened, stood close to Mother.

Dad finally got the horses, wild-eyed and snorting, into the water. Old Mick swimming strongly in the shafts but Brown Lock and Silver Side giving a lot of trouble. The wagon started to swing away with the force of the current, throwing one of the dogs into the river, to be washed away. The horses finally settled down and started to swim for the bank.

It had taken over two hours from when we first came to the river, until we made it to the other side. We went on until Dad decided we were out of reach of the flood. We made camp, as all our possessions were soaked and had to be dried out. Dad went down-river to look for his dog, calling and whistling until dusk, but without success. Then, about 8 o'clock that night, and more dead than alive, the poor, bedraggled little thing crept into our camp.

* * *

I have no actual memories of my own of that arduous journey, or of *Edenvale*. I know my mother hated being there. The loneliness and harshness were more than she could bear. Dad was away a lot, mustering, and she missed her family. The hot sun burnt her beautiful fair skin. Water was scarce and had to be carted from the Etheridge River. Venomous snakes were a constant danger. She prayed a lot, and, after two years, finally persuaded Dad to sell up and move back to civilisation. We packed all our belongings into the same sturdy old wagon and travelled overland to Cairns. When we got there, Dad sold the wagon and the horses and we boarded a ship and steamed south for Townsville.

From Townsville, we moved to Charters Towers where my sister Coral was born. Dadie and I began school there with the good nuns of St. Columbus' Convent. When we left *Edenvale*, Dad vowed never to look another beast in the face or throw a leg over another horse, but he found the pull of the land was too great, and wanted to be back amongst stock again. He returned to the west, where he and his team of drovers lifted big mobs of *Van Rook* and *Iffley* cattle and walked them to the railhead at Gilliat. The trucking yards were later moved to Julia Creek and most of the Gulf cattle were then delivered there.

In the years just following the Great War, Julia Creek was a small town on the move. The old Cobb and Co. staging site, near the dam, was abandoned, and little general stores sprang up close to the railway line. A hotel was built, a baker's shop came and then a butcher shop. Families started to settle there.

Though he loved the land, Dad decided that, for Mother's sake, he would look for an opening for a business so he could stay at home with the family. Julia Creek was ripe for both an ice and cordial factory and a picture show. We sold the house in Charters Towers and made another move. This was to be our last for well-nigh twenty-nine years. We arrived at Julia Creek by train one bitterly cold winter's night in July, 1924.

* * *

I grew up at Julia Creek. It was a happy little town dumped down on the great blacksoil plains. Big families, small businesses, with good back-up country. My youngest sister, Meldie, was born here.

The Byrnes family owned the butcher shop. All their pretty daughters were very musical. The Kaesers owned the baker's shop; a big fun-loving family, into sport. The Wilders were early settlers; their many relations gave freely in defence of our country. The Graham clan — matriarch Granny Graham's sons and daughters populated the town into the fourth generation. I recall the Somers family, with three daughters and one son. The Triffetts, who were also very gifted. Ted, the eldest son had represented Australia in Rough Riding in America. These families were representative of the many I would come to know in Julia Creek.

The town took droughts and good seasons in its stride. It truly was the gateway to the big Gulf cattle country, although the region around Julia Creek itself, in those days, was predominantly sheep country.

I did well when I first started school — but not for long. Sport was far more interesting and my lessons suffered, however, I was happy at the little school in Julia Creek. St. Mary's Convent, Charters Towers, the boarding school where Mother sent all her daughters to 'finish', was a different kettle of fish. I hated it but knuckled down and passed my Commercial Junior — only because sport was not encouraged. I hated the discipline, the enforced silences, barley water for morning tea, "Walk — don't run!", and all the other rules that made no sense. I could hardly wait to leave school, but for Mother's sake, I stayed and finished Senior.

My school days behind me, I moved into a new exciting period of my life. I started to take a keen interest in fashion. Race meetings, balls, birthday parties, picnics and horse riding were some of my more favourite pastimes. Sport was still very important to me. No more foot races or high jumps, they belonged to my State School days. Tennis and basketball took over — while I was a good tennis doubles player, my sister, Coral, was North–West Queensland Singles Champion for three years.

We would spend days planning what we would wear to the races and the balls. Wonderful, happy, carefree days. Holidays spent in Melbourne, Sydney and Brisbane. We would travel by train to Townsville where we would board ship for those great cities. We sang "One Day in May When We Were Young and Gay". 'Gay' did not have homosexual connotations in those days. I cannot remember any great poverty. Even though there were poor families, or families not so well off as others, it made little difference to our enjoyment of life, or how we treated each other.

The Great Depression, the after-effect of the Wall Street stockmarket crash of 1929, caused mass unemployment all across the country. Hoping to find work, some men walked the dusty roads, 'humping their blueys', settling for a meal as payment for odd jobs. Others 'jumped the rattler' — illegally riding freight or stock trains. Commonly called hoboes, these men were not drifters by choice. They came in droves, travelling from town to town. The police gave them short shrift, never allowing them to stay long in any one place. After the Depression was over, the good times resumed — and we thought they would never end.

* * *

My old home at Julia Creek with stock office, dance hall, cinema and skating rink.

5

CHAPTER TWO

Decision time

The decisions we make
Are for our own sake.
They carry our dreams,
Or so it seems,
Along with us.

Matthew Quilty

My parents and the Quiltys met from time to time, whenever the Quiltys came to town. Looking back, I think there must have always been a bond between Rod Quilty and me. As small children we were close, and, in our teens, heading for a closer relationship. But it was not until 1938 that we knew we were in love. We were young and I was very happy.

The Quiltys bought *Bradshaw's Run* in the Northern Territory in 1937 or 1938. Paddy Quilty had bought it from Miller Brothers, Solicitors, of Melbourne. The Quiltys bought *Coolibah* for £3000 ($6000) in 1938. Rod and his brother Pat went with their father to the Territory. Mrs Quilty with their two daughters, Irene and Doreen, stayed at *Euroka Springs*. Rod and Pat made frequent trips back to *Euroka* to pick up gear to take to the Territory. Then came the war, and with it the sad times.

The end of 1939 brought with it global tragedy and personal grief. England declared war on Germany on 3 September. On the eve of my sister Dadie's wedding at Julia Creek, Pat Quilty died suddenly, as the result of a ruptured appendix. We left after the wedding to drive to Cloncurry for his funeral. Coral and I placed our bridesmaids' bouquets on his coffin. Rod was devastated. I hated the thought of him going

7

back to the Territory alone. We decided we would marry and I would go with him, but my parents were against an engagement, and certainly against marriage. We were too young and I would be going too far away. I listened to my parents and let Rod go. It would be eleven years before I saw him again.

The war ripped the heart out of our little town. Boys I had gone to school with rushed off to enlist. Girls left to join the Women's Auxiliary Australian Air Force, the Women's Royal Australian Naval Service, the Australian Women's Army Service and the Australian Women's Land Service. American voices were heard in our streets where once Australian slang drifted on the early night air. The stately waltz gave way to the jitterbug, and while lonely American soldiers spoke of their "Mom's apple pie", we waited for the casualty lists.

Early in September I had begun working for Australian Estates in Julia Creek as book-keeper and secretary. Though I did not know it at the time, the training I received there was to prove invaluable in the years to come.

The Quiltys sold *Bradshaw's Run* and *Coolibah* and moved to the Kimberleys in West Australia. In 1947 they bought *Mt Laptz* and *Collas* from Tommy Matthews for £1500 ($3000), running 1000 head of cattle. In 1948 they bought *Springvale* from Jimmy McAdam for £17,500 ($35,000). In 1951, they bought *Lansdowne* from Bill McDonald of *Fossil Downs* for £6000 ($12,000), with 3000 head of cattle, mostly cleanskins. *Mt.Laptz* and *Collas* became part of *Lansdowne*, and *Springvale* became the head station. Both *Lansdowne* and *Springvale* adjoined *Bedford Downs* which the Quiltys had bought in 1917 for £34,000 ($68,000).

* * *

Rod came back to Julia Creek in 1950 and we picked up the lost years as if they had never been. My parents agreed to our marriage, but with reservations. Mother asked that I visit the Kimberleys before we announced our engagement. Both she and Dad were concerned that I would be going so far away, to a life I did not know. No doubt Mother was remembering her lonely years on *Edenvale*. Rod left for the Kimberleys, and I made plans to follow him.

How confident and sure I was, and how very wrong. My sister Coral and I left Julia Creek for Mt Isa on a cold winter's afternoon in 1951. After a bitterly cold overnight stop, we left Mt Isa for a warmer Darwin early the next morning. We spent the night at the Hotel Darwin, the building still showing signs of the Japanese air raid in 1942. We left the next morning, by MacRobertson Miller Aviation (MMA), for Wyndham, where Rod met us.

Wyndham, the port for the Cambridge Gulf, was a friendly little one-street town surrounded by marsh. Along with the meatworks, a big old two-storey hotel run by the Gee family, mixed stores run by Chinese merchants, a drapery store run by Mrs Jo Flinders, a general business owned by the Davidson Brothers and a shop run by Bill Finley seemed to be the businesses of the town.

Mrs Flinders' husband carried goods and loading between Wyndham and Halls Creek. The Davidsons' mother had been a Durack, one of the most prominent pastoralist families in the area. Her son, Doug Davidson and his lovely young bride, Shirley, later moved to the family property, Dunham River Station, named after a family friend, Father Dunham.

The meatworks, Wyndham Meat, was in full swing. The *Bow River* cattle had been delivered, and Rod told us that Maggie Lilly, a part-owner of *Bow River*, was in town for the kill. Rod was so excited, wanting to show us everything and introduce us to everybody. He drove us to the Nine Mile to meet Bert Sharpe, a carrier from Wyndham. The great marsh flats were glary and steamy, governed by the tides. The Nine Mile was an extension of Wyndham town, approximately nine miles (15 km) along the only road in and out of town.

Rod began to take us through the meatworks, but the tour did not get far. Wild-eyed cattle milling around in the yards so close to where we were, the smell of blood, the noise, the slippery floors, the sound of knives being sharpened, were all too much. Frightened and confused, Coral and I quickly backed out, much to Rod's disappointment.

The next day he drove us out to the MacMicking brothers' camp. They were on the road with a mob for the meatworks and were on dinner camp before delivering that afternoon. John MacMicking later became a very efficient stock inspector, covering large tracts of country in the area. Torrence MacMicking started El Questro Station, and lived there for many years.

On the fourth day, we left Wyndham for *Springvale*. The marsh criss-crossed with wheel tracks, nobody seemed to follow a set pattern as far as a road went. We stopped at the Dunham River for lunch. After the great open plains around Julia Creek, I found the Kimberleys incredibly beautiful. The mighty Durack Range ran parallel all the way to the *Springvale*

9

turn-off. Although the country was in the throes of a severe drought, it did not have the desolate look that outback Queensland had in a drought.

We arrived at *Springvale* at 8 o'clock that evening. The Wyndham Races and Sports Day had been cancelled due to the exceptionally dry conditions, but Halls Creek was going ahead with their celebrations and we were looking forward to that. *Springvale* was a hive of activity, in preparation for the two days of races and the day of sports. Bustling order everywhere, which was to me total confusion. I simply could not understand what was going on. Rod was also excited, keen to take his little horse, Toddler, in for the 'Walk, Trot and Gallop'.

I asked Olive, Tom Quilty's second wife, if we could do some washing and was told that Daisy, one of her many well-trained lubras, would wash and iron whatever we needed. Some of the lubras helped in the kitchen, others made beds and cleaned the rooms, others worked in the flower garden and tended the lawns, while others worked in the vegetable garden. It certainly was a well-organised home.

The native boys were the station stockmen. A little half-caste boy, Gilbo, son of the previous owner, Jimmy McAdam, and a full-blood, Finnegan, whom Olive had brought over from Coolibah Station in the Northern Territory as a very small baby, were being reared as whites by the Quiltys. They shared their son Mick's room, and sometimes, on cold nights, his bed. Years later, Gilbo became an experienced stockman who managed a station; and Finnegan also became a good stockman, and very good at painting and sketching.

* * *

Having started the race and sport horses off for Halls Creek, we followed in convoy. Halls Creek was the first of my many big shocks. A little corrugated iron and mud brick town built on the banks of Halls Creek, its road sloped down to the bed of the creek. There were no streets, but the dirt highway passed along the creek bank. There was a joke that anybody who lived there for any length of time became longer in one leg than the other.

There were aborigines everywhere. There were very few lubras around, the young males walking hand in hand or sitting around in groups. They kept to themselves, away from the whites. Rod said he would drop us off at the hotel then help set up the *Springvale–Bedford* camp and stables.

The noise around the hotel was deafening, the bar being the most popular spot. Darl Smith, whose mother owned the hotel, came to show us to our room. Vivacious friendly Darl, too young to serve in the bar, was everybody's darling, and possibly the most popular girl in the district. All the young stockmen were in love with her, with the exception of Cec Watts. Head stockman on *Gordon Downs*, Cec only had eyes for pretty Dawn Johnson. Dawn's parents owned a store at Halls Creek. Cec later became Vestey's travelling manager and lived at Rockhampton.

The hotel's accommodation, separated from the dining room and the bar by an open stony courtyard, was a two-storey, galvanized iron building. With unlined walls and ceilings, the long covered-in verandah running the length of the building was partitioned off into rooms, with access through the front rooms. We weren't getting much sleep, or at least I wasn't. The continual stream of people through our room to get out to the verandah rooms disturbed me. I wasn't very happy.

The bathroom, used by both men and women, was an all-in affair with a woodchip heater that terrified me. The water we bathed in was carted from a well about half a mile from the hotel. Being accustomed, at Julia Creek, to washing in instant hot water straight from the Artesian Basin, the Halls Creek water supply was less than adequate for my liking. Coral and I would go to the bathroom together. One to stand guard at the door while the other tried to wash in cold water.

Mrs Smith did the cooking. The meals, served in the long gauzed-in dining room, were very enjoyable. Four little piccaninnies worked a punka at each end of the room. A small cement dance floor adjoined the dining room, and close up to the bar was the Bull Pen.

The Bull Pen, a small, windowless room that opened onto the bar servery, was about 6 feet by 6 feet (2 m x 2 m). It was always chock-a-block with drinkers, both male and female, with the idea that they got away from the noisy open-bar drinkers. Even when so drunk that they passed out, they could not fall down; the press of the crowd would hold them up. I was disgusted. Pious, sanctimonious me, what right had I to judge? What right indeed!

Things were getting worse and I was beginning to have doubts. Coral was having a wonderful time, but then, she was leaving. I had to think of this as a place where I might have to live.

Station people had their own camps where they set up quarters for their staff, and stables for their horses. Campfires burnt all night and stockmen young and old sat around drinking, talking and singing. Some of them had really wonderful voices. Rod's father had a strong baritone, and he knew so many old Irish songs.

The races started at 10 o'clock and went on all day. Rod would drive in every day from the *Springvale–Bedford* camp to pick us up and drive us to the racecourse. The station women, under the careful supervision of the popular Australian Inland Mission (A.I.M.) padre, Ken Beckett and his wife, Beth, would provide meals served under a spinifex bough shed.

We watched the races from our vehicles or sat under a spinifex lean-to. Everything seemed so rough and primitive. We danced to the tune of an old concertina while I thought of the balls I had been to in Queensland.

I knew I was not going to fit in. I thought of my mother at *Edenvale*. I decided to tell Rod that I would marry him, but we would have to go back to Queensland to live. With so much going on, it was hard to get much time alone with him. He was so excited and happy. I decided I would write and explain after returning to Julia Creek.

Rod put us on Connellan's plane at Halls Creek for Darwin, and so for home. I had never been on a plane as small as this, but the single seats on both sides had windows and that made up for the lack of space.

As we said our farewells, Rod gave me a letter, telling me to read it on the plane. The pages were full of plans for our wedding and settling at *Lansdowne*. He had assured me that *Lansdowne* was over the range from 'the underworld', underworld being wild rough country, with lonely, unmarked graves under almost every boab tree.

I was confused. I asked God to send me a sign. I held back from telling my parents that I didn't want to go back. Rod's mother was anxiously waiting to know what we had decided. I told her what I believed, that I simply could not live over there. We would be married but would live in Queensland. She was very upset and asked me not to take Rod away from his father. As much as it wasn't what I wanted, I decided it was probably the sign I was looking for.

I convinced my parents everything would be all right. I would be able to cope. Although I knew they were bitterly disappointed, Rod had to be my first consideration. He was very asthmatic and I could not bear to add more sadness to his already unhappy life.

* * *

Rod and me, leaning against Rod's Chev utility at
Springvale, winter 1951.

Don Steele and me at Australian Estates in Julia Creek, where I worked as a book-
keeper and secretary.

13

Eckford family,
Christmas 1944.
Standing, from left:
Uncle Joe Eckford,
Meldie, Mother,
Jim, Coral and me.
Seated, from left:
Dad nursing
granddaughter
Cathie Dawes.

From left: My sisters Meldie, Coral, Dadie, brother Jim and me at Dadie and
Peter's 50th wedding anniversary celebration, Charters Towers, 9 September 1989.

14

A studio portrait of me, taken in Brisbane for our engagement in 1951.

From left: Boss Drover Butler, Peter Dawes, Paul Beard and me, droving plant at Julia Creek.

15

CHAPTER THREE

Disastrous beginnings

They left the vine-wreathed cottage and the mansion on the hill,
The houses in the busy streets where life is never still,
The pleasures of the city, and the friends they cherished best:
For love they faced the wilderness — the Women of the West.
— from Women of the West *by George Essex Evans*

My parents announced our engagement and, on 29 January, 1952, on a lovely Townsville summer morning, we were married — thirteen years after we had first made our plans! We honeymooned in New Zealand and returned to Brisbane, where we bought a truck and some antique furniture.

I flew back to Julia Creek while Rod drove the truck. We had to wait at Julia Creek for Sammy, an electrician, and his offsider. Sammy was to travel along with us in his own vehicle to *Springvale*, where he was to install a lighting plant.

We had to pick up a complete set of batteries for the 32-volt lighting plant at *Springvale* from Lance Lewis' garage, as well as our wedding presents and the things I had gathered over the years; a beautiful silky oak chest held my linen. Rod loaded all this on, but he was very concerned about the *Springvale* batteries. They were fully charged and could cause trouble. He wanted them flat but a telegram from his father said, "You are on the spot. I want them charged."

The day came when we had to leave. I said goodbye to my brother and sisters, and, after a hard, sorrowful parting with my parents, I went to

Gannon's Hotel, where my chaperone, Mrs Gannon, and my childhood friends dried my tears as we said goodbye. Rod picked me up at the hotel. I tried hard not to let him see how upset I was, but he knew. I climbed into the truck and we left, all my possessions safely under the tarpaulin on the back.

The road was rough and corrugated and very dusty. I had my cosmetic case and Rod's small camp oven, with his spray and aspaxadrene in it, at my feet. He never went anywhere without that camp oven. His asthma attacks were frequent and the aspaxadrene, which contained adrenalin, was his only relief. Years later, research came up with a more effective treatment in the form of tablets and the Ventolin® 'puffer'.

I watched the great plains west of Julia Creek slip by, the wide open plains I loved so much. We passed through the little town of Gilliat — one hotel run by the popular Malone family, a railway station and a few houses. We stopped to say hello and goodbye to the Malones, then on again.

We crossed the dry Fullarton River and on to the "singing gate", Oorindi off to our left. How well I remember the times I had passed through that gate, how it "sang" to us as it swung on its old hinges. It is long gone now, a modern grid serves in its place. The Williams River, where my mother and her friend, Lily Quilty, had picnicked as young girls, was also dry. I, like my mother those many years ago, was on my way to a new and hard life. In the far distance, I could see the blue hills of Cloncurry. We stopped there long enough to pick up petrol, sandwiches, tinned meat and soft drink. There were so many people I would like to have seen but it was best that I did not. It was always so hard to say goodbye.

We turned off the main highway a few miles west of Cloncurry and passed through Malbon and Duchess. Rod did not want to take on the treacherous hills between Cloncurry and Mt Isa with his heavily loaded truck. We came on to the bitumen again close to Mt Isa.

I had been to Mt Isa many times but never beyond, so I was now in what, to me, was alien country — I was on edge. The sun was down low and the night, so unfamiliar and frightening, would soon be upon us. I should have had more faith in Rod.

Just before sundown we pulled into some yards. Rod said "*Yelvertoft*, we'll camp here." I had heard my father speak of *Yelvertoft*. A strange name, I never knew what it meant. Rod started to gather dry leaves, grass and wood to get the fire going. I wanted to help but he told me to go over to the trough and wash. He got my night bag down from the back of the truck, and, along with it and my cosmetic case, I headed for the water. I washed my teeth and did the best I could without benefit of a shower or plunge.

If it had not been for the campfire and voices in the darkness, I doubt I would have found my way back to the camp. The evening star was out, shining brightly in the west, other stars were beginning to join it. A gentle breeze was blowing, but I didn't see the beauty of this lovely evening. My mind was still on those I had left behind.

The billy was boiling and Rod had placed his swag close to the fire for me to sit on. The evening was getting cooler but not cold. I ate sandwiches and drank sweet billy tea. Supper over, Sammy and his man gathered more wood and then went off to their car to camp. Rod built up the fire for the night, then, clearing small rocks and stones away, he rolled out the swag beside our truck.

I looked at the swag with horror but there was nothing for it. It was to be my bed for the night and for many nights to come. I would have preferred to sleep in the cabin of the truck.

It was a bad night. I thought of my comfortable bed back home. The gentle breeze had blown up into a strong, gusty wind. Sand and grit blew in my face, my dressing gown kept blowing away. I was in two minds whether to go after it or let it go. I thought there could be wild blacks out in the dark. I was utterly miserable. Rod slept well. I don't know when I dozed off. I didn't think it was long before Rod was shaking me awake. It was dark and the stars still out. I asked, "What time is it?"

"Four o'clock," he said.

Oh dear God! I've had enough. I want to go home!

I got up, but nothing would make me go over to the trough to wash. Rod siphoned water from a 44-gallon (200 litre) drum into a tin dish and gave it to me. I washed, dressed in slacks, blouse, shoes, socks and with my cardigan, joined the men at the fire for a breakfast of bully beef, bread and strong, sweet billy tea.

I watched Rod roll up the swag and put it in the truck, while Sammy and his offsider packed the tuckerbox on the back. Rod then smothered the fire by pouring the remains of the tea on it and shovelling dry dirt on top until not a spark remained. This was my first lesson in bush lore — never leave embers or a live campfire. The passenger door of the truck had jammed so I got in and out on the driver's side, but I was pleased to climb under the steering wheel and across to my side of the truck.

Rod checked the load, petrol, oil and tyres. This was a ritual that he never failed to perform whenever we stopped. Lights on, we started to move onto the bitumen. I could see a faint glow in the east — Camooweal, our next and last Queensland town. The bitumen highway ran right through the centre of this little town, the heart of which consisted of a post office, one hotel, a general shop and a few houses scattered around. This was a typical cattle town, its existence dependent upon the success of the out-stations. Gone were the great droving days when big mobs of cattle moved across the Murranji Track, into Queensland and on to the southern states. I got out of the truck and walked about. I thought my heart would break.

A few miles on, we crossed the Northern Territory–Queensland border, and I was in the "State of the great bye and bye", my personal border of no return. To the east was Rocklands Station, managed many years later by Ray Jansen, a good friend, along with his wife Pat, with whom I shared many hard but happy times.

* * *

We crossed the Georgina and the James Rivers and stopped for dinner by the dry Ranken River. I helped gather twigs and grass to get the fire going. Rod put some heavier wood on and waited until the smoke cleared before he put the billy on. He hated smoked tea. He got the tuckerbox down and we sat under a shady tree and ate the cold roast meat and homemade bread the Camooweal publican had given us — the first time I could remember eating homemade bread. It was lovely.

We didn't dawdle. With the usual packing and checking ritual complete, we were off. The sun crept high and began to shine through the wind-screen, glary and uncomfortable, while the miles slipped by. Rod rolled up the window and hung a towel on my side of the cabin to protect me. I never took the towel down.

Rod decided he would get as close to the *Dalmore Downs* turn-off as pos-sible. Hughie Van Hey Thuysen was at *Dalmore*. Hughie worked for the Quiltys on *Coolibah*. Rod thought him to be one of the best all-round station men he had ever met. We had to keep travelling into the night to get to the turn-off. On a straight stretch of the road, the lights of an oncoming vehicle remained on high beam. Rod dimmed his, but the other driver did not. He was coming very fast. We pulled off the road to let him pass.

"That was Georgie Grantham's taxi," said Rod. "He must have a very urgent case to be driving so fast." Rod was friendly with George Grantham and Keith Jessup, two friends who had started a taxi service at Darwin. We camped a few miles further on. Night camp was much the same except that having pulled up in the dark, I had no idea what the country was like. I stayed close to the truck until the men had built the fire. I was terrified of the darkness. I was more than pleased to get into the swag and hoped to goodness it was too cold for snakes.

Although we had been late making camp, it made no difference to our 4 o'clock start next morning. We got to *Dalmore* in time for breakfast. Hughie cooked steak and eggs, station-made bread and tea with milk. While we were having breakfast, we were listening to Hughie's small wireless. A news flash announced that a Darwin taxi driver was missing. George Grantham had not been home, and his taxi had not been seen since the previous day.

Rod told Hughie that the taxi had passed us about 9 o'clock that night. They decided he would report it at Frewena. George Grantham's body was later found some miles outside Darwin, shot in the head and dumped in long grass beside the road. Two New Australians had asked him to drive them to Adelaide River. They planned to shoot him and steal his taxi. Thinking they would be safe once they crossed the the border into Queensland, they headed for Mt Isa, where they were caught and taken back to Darwin. They were tried for murder and sentenced to hang. These were the last hangings at the old Fanny Bay Gaol.

* * *

We left *Dalmore* and got back onto the bitumen. After dinner at the Frewena Roadhouse, we camped that night at a tank and trough. I felt very dirty and wanted to have a quick bath in the tank, but there I had my second lesson in bush lore — never bathe in the tanks; people use that water for drinking.

I was getting further and further away from home and I was learning things that were strange to me. Without knowing it, I was slowly but surely being initiated into what was to become my way of life for the next thirty years or so.

After the long and tiring trip from Frewena, we left the Barkly Highway at the Three Ways and came onto the Stuart Highway and headed north.

The Three Ways is simply that, where the three roads, running north, south and east, meet. Years later, a very modern roadhouse and several other buildings were erected. Access to fresh supplies of water was a problem.

Beyond the Three Ways, we were getting into hilly country. Rod stopped to show us "Churchill's Head". There was indeed a very strong resemblance to Winston Churchill. With a stick stuck there for a cigar, it truly looked like the great man. When I last saw him, in 1983, his cigar was missing, and wind and rain had started to change his appearance.

Passing through Elliott, we came to Newcastle Waters at about 4 o'clock the next afternoon. It had been a long day. Driving into Newcastle Waters, Rod said, "I saw the whole of this area under water once, just a sea of water. It was a terrific flood." I looked around and found it hard to believe. Where would all the water come from? Many years later, flying over the same area in our 182 Cessna with Rod and our pilot son, Tom, history was repeated. There wasn't a tree in sight. A great body of water covered everything.

Newcastle Waters, a small settlement typical of the Territory, with a post office, a store and a hotel, and Newcastle Waters Station close by. We stayed a couple of hours while Rod bought some groceries, loaded on another 44-gallon drum of petrol and topped up with water. He said there would be no more petrol, and very little water, until we got to Top Springs.

The hotel bar at Newcastle Waters was crowded and noisy, stockmen everywhere and they all seemed to know Rod. I sat in the cabin of our truck and read a book. Sammy and his offsider, with Rod, were enjoying themselves. Rod bought me a bottle of soft drink and we got ready to leave. The break had been good for him. He had been pushing himself very hard.

* * *

We crossed the causeway over Newcastle Creek and turned off the bitumen onto the Murranji Track. It was dusty, corrugated and *very* rough. Rod told me about the bulwaddy country; of the old-timers' stories of droving cattle through there, a hurricane light tied to the tails of their pack mules to show the way.

It was getting dark. Rod said we would push on and camp at the Nine Mile Bore. We never made it. About 9 o'clock, Rod pulled up suddenly, jumped out and ran to the back of the truck. He was back in no time, calling for me to get out quickly — the truck was on fire!

Grabbing his camp oven and my cosmetic case, I threw them as far as I could then I scrambled out. I tried to go to the back of the truck but Rod grabbed my arm and said to get as far away as possible, the petrol drums might explode. He got behind the wheel and drove the truck around in tight circles trying to throw the load off. It was impossible. He had tied it down too well. The heat was terrible.

Rod pulled an axe from behind the seat and tried to cut the ropes, but by this time the fire had burnt through the tarpaulin. It was an inferno. Rod was forced back. I ran to him as he was trying to tie a handkerchief over his mouth. His shirt was smouldering, but he still hoped he could save something.

Then the first drum exploded! I don't know if the explosion forced us to the ground or if we just collapsed, burning pieces of debris falling all around us. We got up and ran. We were still running when the second drum exploded. Rod was in a bad way, wheezing heavily, hardly able to breathe. I laid him on the ground and went looking for his camp oven. The truck was burning fiercely, lighting up a great area.

I found the camp oven and ran back to him. Aspaxadrene spilled over my hand as I put it into the phial. I sat beside him until the aspaxadrene started to work and his breathing gradually became easier. We were still sitting there when Sammy and his man arrived. They had seen the glow from a long way back but had mistaken it for our campfire. The dust haze was very thick, the dust hanging longer in the night air. We waited until the fire had burnt down and Rod was well enough to move before we went close to the wreck. Smouldering coals everywhere, small puffs of smoke going up and an occasional leap of flames. We were numb. All we had, apart from Rod's camp oven and my cosmetic case, was in ruins. Rod had us clear dead grass and twigs well back from the fire, concerned that sparks might start a bushfire — I thought we were in open country.

I never went back to the Murranji Track in daylight. Thirty-three years later, our son Tom and his wife Wendy were there, in the winter of 1985. They saw, and took photos of what still remains of the fire.

* * *

I can't remember how long we stayed there before we piled into Sammy's small car and drove back to Newcastle Waters. It was very late. It had been a night of horror, and the days that followed were a blur. Sometime during the haze of the following days, I was given a little blue cattle pup. I called him "Lucky" and loved him. I had him for only five days before he died. What of, I don't know.

Mrs Sargeant, who owned the hotel, found us rooms in which to stay. The rooms were divided by tin partitions, the walls about a foot to eighteen inches off the cement floor and about six feet high. Our neighbours talked over and passed things under the partitions. There was no privacy. Bats were bad. They came out at night and frightened me. Mrs Sargeant gave me an old tennis racquet and I did the best I could to keep them away with that.

Rod and Bill Crowson drove out and, after taking some photos with Bill's camera, towed what was left of our truck back to Elliott. Bill Crowson had managed Rosewood Station, close to the Northern Territory–Western Australia border but at that time, he and his wife Vi were living at Elliott while they negotiated for *Montejinni*, which they later bought. Vi worked at Elliott Post Office for a while.

Pressure was still on Rod to get back to start mustering. He had left his Chev utility at Biloela and arranged with a young stockman, Sammy Griffy, to drive it to Newcastle Waters. I think Newcastle Waters Station, at that time, was owned by Roy Edwards, and that he later sold it to Baillieu, Chisholm and Warriner, but I am not sure. It is now owned by Kerry Packer and ably managed by Ken Warriner, whose wife Sally is one of the Northern Territory's popular hostesses.

A priest was coming from Katherine to say mass at Newcastle Waters Station. Rod asked if I would like to go. Yes, I would. I needed closer contact with God and I wanted some answers. I thought I might get them at mass.

We were still at Newcastle Waters on Anzac Day, 1952, but our time there was drawing to an end; we were soon to leave. Sam Griffy had arrived with Rod's utility and I was booked on a bus to Julia Creek. A tea-chest had arrived from my sister, Dadie. She had sent us blankets, sheets, crockery and cutlery. What she had sent us in that tea-chest was all I had for many years on *Lansdowne*.

Early one morning, I boarded the bus to return to Julia Creek. Parting with Rod was hard but we both knew it was best. He was going to be busy for the next five or six weeks mustering *Springvale* and *Bedford* and there would be no time to settle me in at *Lansdowne*. I said goodbye to the kind-hearted and generous people at that little place. Names are forgotten. It was a long time ago but I never forgot them.

I was home for about five weeks before I flew out to join Rod again. He had finished the *Springvale–Bedford* musters and the bullocks were on the road to Wyndham. It was now time to muster *Lansdowne*, a 90%

cleanskin herd. Branding just 45 calves a year at first, we had to start a long way behind scratch in more ways than one.

Rod had been so right — his fears that the charged batteries would be a problem were justified. They had started the fire that had cost us so much. Uninsured, we had lost everything.

I flew to Mt Isa, Darwin, Wyndham, then caught Connellan's little plane on its station run to *Springvale*, where Rod met me. He borrowed an old truck from *Bedford* to take his few belongings to *Lansdowne*.

We left *Bedford* early one morning and drove all day. The country was very beautiful. The Durack, and later the King Leopold Range running parallel on our right. We travelled through valleys, past creeks and huge ghost gums, and lots of other trees I could not name, while the range threw off shades of soft mauves, blues and pale pinks. Sometimes, I could see a track that was our road, most times nothing at all. Rod had a wonderful sense of direction. We crossed the Ord, the mighty river that, some years later, would fill the great Lake Argyle Dam at Kununurra. We called into Watty Springs for dinner. The spring was named after Watty Gordon, brother-in-law of the Buchanan brothers. All these men were friends of Tom Quilty senior in Sydney.

We got to *Lansdowne* about 10 o'clock that night; it had taken us fifteen hours to drive 62 miles (103 km). Two of Rod's stockmen, Frank Bridge and Sally Malay, met us; Sally was part Malay and part Aboriginal. They had an outside fire going and the billy on. I was grateful for the mug of sweet black tea and bread spread with goat's butter, my first taste of butter made from goat's milk. The butter was strong and rather rank, and although I never liked it, there was no other option, it was that or nothing at all in those years. Tired and cold, I was pleased to get into Rod's swag where he had rolled it out on the dirt floor of my new home.

* * *

Rod and me on our wedding day, 29 January 1952.

Our truck, loaded with all our possessions, on the way to *Lansdowne*, 1952.

The remains of our truck (and all our possessions), burned out on the Murranji Track, 1952.

27

CHAPTER FOUR

Me, the lubras and the old tin shed

Friends are found in different places,
Friends are found in different races.

Matthew Quilty

My first night on *Lansdowne* was not good. With the strange sounds of dingos howling and owls hooting I couldn't sleep. I wondered if I would ever be able to settle to life here. I heard someone crying, and asked Rod, "Who's crying?"

"That's a curlew, they are hardly ever heard here."

In fact, I was only to hear that sad, mournful call once more in all the years I spent at *Lansdowne* — the night Grandma Griffin Quilty, wife of Tom Quilty senior, died. Rod was very upset when he received news of her death on the late afternoon Flying Doctor session. He was very fond of his grandmother and had trouble sleeping that night. Lying beside him, I again heard the curlew.

* * *

Rod is up long before me on this, my first morning. He gives me a mug of the sweet black tea I like so much, and steak and a fried egg on a tin plate. He also gives me a miner's tin dish and a bucket of water, telling me to wash and come out when I am ready. The men have been up for hours.

It is time to look around my new home. A long, corrugated, ex-army building — dirt floor, no partitions, doors or windows. Please God! Give me strength! The doors and windows would come later, but I was to water those dirt floors for a long time. With the help of an old lubra, I watered them three times a day with water carted in buckets from a well.

I join the men where they are unloading the truck. The tea-chest my sister had sent us, Rod's saddle and other stock gear, a tin trunk and a few other things. Some blacks are milling round. The lubras giggling and shy. I know they are talking about me but I am not ready to speak to them. I will have to ask Rod about them.

I decide I will do a tour of inspection. I need to know where the kitchen is and also the toilet and shower. There do not seem to be many buildings. A small mud hut with a tin roof and a lean-to bough shed. A little further away the vegetable garden, surrounded by a strong log fence, much like a barricade. I think of the Eureka Stockade. A well in the middle of the garden is our only water supply. What a lovely surprise the garden is. Two huge lemon trees are bowed down with fruit, tomatoes ripening on the vines, and every other vegetable I can think of growing fresh and healthy.

Frank Bridge is a keen gardener. He will teach me all I will need to know about planting and transplanting. It is hard work but a vegetable garden is absolutely necessary on a Kimberley station. Frank tells me the blacks will bandicoot the sweet potatoes, but I will never catch them at it. He is so right. The blacks love the sweet potato; it resembles their yams and is easier to get at. I have lots of dug-up and hastily replanted vines to prove it.

In the distance, about a quarter of a mile (400 metres) away, I see a small brown place with hessian walls. Three sides covered in with hessian, knee high and neck deep, and an open doorway facing into the range. A great huge pit with a kerosene box on top. The kerosene box has a round hole cut in it. This is the toilet. If you have never seen one, I can't adequately describe it. Even the Flaming Furies in Darwin are modern by comparison. I think, how in the name of heavens am I going to handle this toilet? I will have to be very careful or I will end up down that great pit.

Close by, the goat yard — much like the vegetable garden but smaller. No goats there now, milked hours before by the lubras and gone out to feed. I still have to find the bathroom and the kitchen. I hear Rod calling — time for morning tea, or 'smoko' as I was to know it from now on.

I take my mug of tea and piece of brownie up to the house and sit on the swag. I am not ready to join the men yet. I hear a soft voice calling, "Yumman?" I answer, "Yes." A young lubra, about my age, comes in, picks up my mug and plate, and leaves.

More exploring. Gunyahs down by a creek that runs at the back of the station. Some old people, piccaninnies and lots of dogs. Still no sign of a kitchen or bathroom. Nothing more to see round the house so I move towards the mud hut again. I do not know where the men are but I find the bathroom, just behind the mud hut. A three-sided affair like the toilet, open doorway facing the range; a four-gallon (18 litre) drum with perforated bottom, hanging from a limb of a gum tree, a huge flat paving stone for the floor. I give up on the kitchen. All I can see is an open fireplace.

There does not seem much else to see, so I go back to the house to unpack my suitcase and open the tea-chest. Without a wardrobe or chest of drawers, I have to sort out the clothes in my suitcase, where they are to remain. I try to imagine, looking at the bare building and the dirt floor, where we would have put the beautiful antique furniture I had insisted on buying. Rod had tried to explain how out of place it would be until he could have a home built for me, but I wanted it and he never refused me anything if he could afford it.

* * *

Lunch — cold corned beef, boiled English potatoes and sweet potatoes and lots of lovely salad. Rod sends the young lubra up with our plates, and a quart pot of tea. He joins me a few minutes later. I learn that the young lubra's name is Peggy. She became my head girl and stayed with me for many years.

Rod explains the workings of the shower: the drum is filled with water, a lever attached to a rope releases or cuts off the water as required. It seems simple enough. I will shower later that afternoon. He promises to have the boys build my own private toilet away from the existing one. It will have a proper built-up seat, thank goodness or thank Rod; however, we cannot get away from the pit.

My first shower is a total disaster. Rod had said he would get the water for me, but, about five o'clock, I decide I will try it myself. Peggy and a few lubras are fussing under the lean-to. After a lot of sign language, I get an old lubra to understand that I want water. She gets a bucket and goes to the garden well. Pouring the water into the drum, I undress, stand under the drum and pull the rope. Four gallons of ice-cold water lands on my head and shoulders. I scream with fright and frustration. Peggy grabs my towel, wraps it round me and runs me up to the house. She rubs me dry and brings some circulation back to my cold body, then rolls out the swag and makes me comfortable.

Not a good start. I hope for a better night.

As the days pass I start to cope a little better. Little Maggie and I form a team, carting water from the garden well for the house floor. She carries two buckets, chinaman fashion, with a stick across her shoulders and the buckets attached to the stick by ropes. It is all I can do to struggle up with one bucket, my hands blistering and sore. We sprinkle water on the dirt using treacle tins with holes punched in the bottom.

* * *

I experience beautiful sunny days and cold nights. I decide that, if I am to survive here, I will have to toughen up a lot and learn quickly. I will have to put my Julia Creek days far behind me.

Rod and the men are away all day, leaving early, riding into the early sunrise and not returning until just on sundown. Sensing my loneliness, the lubras start taking me with them when they go on walkabout, looking for wild fruit and sugarbag. They are not so shy with me now, but I am still a bit of a novelty to them. Rod had never lived on *Lansdowne* and I am the first white woman here.

I love the wild passionfruit and konkerberries we gather, and the sugarbag the little wild bees make. I find the oranges and apples a bit tart but not completely sour.

I am finding it harder and harder to carry the buckets of water from the well. Rod soon puts a stop to me doing that when he sees the sorry state of my hands. He puts Big Polly on to help Little Maggie. Big Polly, sullen and lazy, dodges on Little Maggie. When I tell Rod, he says I simply will have to assert my authority and learn to work with the lubras. Big Polly is the only one giving trouble, but to have order I have to take control of my house and all that goes with it. Not an easy thing for me to do by any means. The lubras work well as far as I am concerned. I am not about to interfere. They know more than I do. I learn to keep out of their way when they are working, especially when they are cooking. The lubras wash our clothes in two old-fashioned tubs set up on a plank between carpenters' trestles. I offer to help but they laughingly shake their heads.

32

I feel trapped in this valley. Great ranges and mountains all round me. I long to hear my father's voice, the touch of my mother's hand, and I miss the close contact with my brother and sisters. Afraid to go too far from the buildings, lonely and idle, I am falling into a deep depression.

With nothing to do, I look to the lubras more and more for company. Sometimes, after the evening meal, I join the men while they discuss musters, weights and numbers, cattle and more cattle. I am lost in their bush talk. Rod is happy. He has never been so relaxed and free. I know he is giving me time to adjust but I know, and he knows, things cannot go on much longer as they are.

The lubras take me to the waterholes, rivers and springs. We go swimming and I am beginning to enjoy myself. They teach me how to stay under water, breathing through a hollow bamboo stick. We play games, naked and free in the water; the water too cold for early morning or late afternoon swims, we wait until the midday sun shines down and the water, warm and clear, washes over us.

* * *

An old drover, with camels, comes to the station. He has an ugly old dog. I see the old man sitting on his swag, the dog under a tree close by. I move to go to the dog but Rod calls to me to stay clear — the dog might bite. I look at the old drover and then continue on to the dog. The dog and I immediately become friends. I watch as the drover slowly puts his revolver down. He is a kind old man but he was prepared to shoot his dog if it had attacked me. I never knew his name and I don't know where he came from. He calls his dog Boozer, and has reared him from a pup. Boozer never leaves me; with him beside me I wander further and further away from the station, no longer afraid.

The camels cause a lot of trouble. The horses go berserk whenever the camels come near or even if they can smell them on the breeze. When he leaves, the drover gives me Boozer. I know what it costs him to part with his faithful old dog, but it would have broken my heart to let him go.

Battle-scarred and ugly, Boozer is always at my side. He sleeps in the dirt beside our swag at night and stays close to me all day. Boozer had been with me for nearly three months when, going for a shower one afternoon, I nearly step on a king brown snake. Boozer rushes in and is bitten. My poor old dog died in agony. Rod buried him deep and piled stones on top. His was the first death I was to see on *Lansdowne* — I was to see many more there over the years.

* * *

MEDICAL CHEST
This Chest contains some drugs dangerous if misused and many that could be hazardous to children.
Keep all drugs in the Chest, except those marked "R" (Refrigeration).
KEEP THE CHEST LOCKED.

ROYAL FLYING DOCTOR SERVICE OF AUST

MEDICAL CHEST 1971

Item No.	Tray	Item	Amount
		St. John's First Aid Book	
* 5a.	B.	Tab. Codeine Co.	100 tabs.
8.	D.	Tincture Benz. Co. (Friars Balsam)	200 ml.
* 10.	Bottom	Tab. Phenobarbitone, 30 mg.	100 tabs.
* 11.	B.	Tab. Ipecac. and Opium (Dovers Powder), 300 mg.	50 tabs.
15a.	B.	Tab. Sodium Salicylate, 300 mg.	200 tabs.
* 18.	B.	Tab. Sulphamezathine, 500 mg.	100 tabs.
* 19.	D.	Tincture Chloroform and Morphine Co. (Chlorodyne)	25 ml. x 2
21.	D.	Potassium Citrate	150 g.
* 23a.	C.	Decicaine Solution, ½%	15 ml.
R 24a.	A.	Sulphacetamide Eye Drops, 10%	15 ml. x 2
30.	D.	Methyl Salicylate Liniment	200 ml.
31.	D.	Liquid Paraffin	200 ml.
37.	D.	Calamine Lotion	220 ml.
* 38.	D.	Tab. Quinine Sulphate, 300 mg.	100 tabs.
R* 42.	Bottom	Penicillin Procaine, 1 million units.	5 syringes
* 42a.	B.	Tab. Penicillin, 250 mg.	25 tabs. x 3
* 44.	Bottom	Tab. Pethidine Hydrochloride, 50 mg.	100 tabs.
R* 46.	A.	Neosynephrine Nose Drops, ½%	25 ml.
* 47.	B.	Tab. Stilboestrol, 5 mg.	100 tabs.
* 48.	B.	Tab. Digoxin, 0.25 mg.	100 tabs.
* 49.	B.	Tab. Ephedrine Hydrochloride, 15 mg.	100 tabs.
R 51.	C.	Sulphacetamide Eye Ointment, 10%	4 g. x 2
* 54.	Bottom	Cocaine in Olive Oil, 2%	15 ml.
58.	C.	Zinc Cream	25 g.
59.	B.	Gentian Violet Paint	25 ml.
61.	C.	Magnesium Hydroxide Mixture	180 ml.
62.	B.	Tab. Soluble Aspirin, 300 mg.	100 tabs. x 2
* 63.	Bottom	Tab. Pentobarbitone Sodium, 100 mg.	25 tabs.
* 67.	B.	Tab. Sulphamethizole (Urolucosil), 500 mg.	100 tabs.
* 68.	B.	Tab. Ergometrine Maleate, 0.5 mg.	25 tabs.
71.	C.	Compound Kaolin Powder	100 g. x 2
* 72.	B.	Cap. Tetracycline, 250 mg.	25 caps.
R* 73.	B.	Neomycin Sulphate Mixture	100 ml. x 2
* 74.	B.	Tab. Pheniramine, 10 mg.	50 tabs.
* 75.	B.	Tab. Dexchlorpheniramine (Polaramine), 2 mg.	50 tabs.

Item No.	Tray	Item	A
76.	C.	Oral Electrolyte Powder (Repalyte), 40 g. pkts.	6 pk
77.	A.	Whitfields Ointment, ½ strength	
78.	D.	Chlorhexidine Concentrate (Hibitane), 5%	100 n
79.	C.	Chlorhexidine Antiseptic Cream (Hibitane)	50
80.	B.	Tab. Paracetamol with Codeine	10(
R 81.	C.	Chloramphenicol Eye Ointment, 1%	4 g
83.	B.	Tab. Aluminium, Magnesium Hydroxide, 300 mg.-90 mg.	10
R 84.	C.	Framycetin-Gramicidin Ointment (Soframycin)	15 g
* 85.	B.	Tab. Frusemide, 40 mg.	5
* 86.	B.	Tab. Erythromycin Stearate, 250 mg.	2
* 87.	B.	Tab. Erythromycin Succinate, 200 mg.	2
* 90.	A.	Tab. Isopropamide Iodide (Tyrimide), 5 mg.	10
* 92.	A.	Tab. Glyceryl Trinitrate (Anginine), 0.6 mg.	10
* 93.	A.	Tab. Prochlorperazine (Stemetil), 5 mg.	25 ta
R* 94.	A.	Penicillin Suspension, 125 mg. per 5 ml.	
95.	A.	Neomycin-Bacitracin powder (Cicatrin)	15 g
* 96.	A.	Ampoules Morphine Sulphate, 15 mg.	5
* 97.	A.	Ampoules Prochlorperazine (Stemetil), 12.5 mg.	10
* 98.	A.	Ampoules Diazepam (Valium), 10 mg.	5
R* 99.	A.	Ampoules Adrenalin Acid Tartrate 1-1000, 1 ml.	5
R*100.	A.	Ampoules Dexamethasone (Decadron) 4 mg. per ml., 2 ml.	2
*101.	A.	Ampoules Ergometrine Maleate, 0.5 mg.	5
*102.	B.	Tab. Sulphadiazine, 300 mg.	4
R*103.	C.	Orciprenaline Aerosol Spray Pack (Alupent)	
104.	D.	Linctus Pholcodine	100 n

y	Dressings, Instruments, etc.	Amount
	Esmach Bandage (Tourniquet), 4″	1
	Thermometers	2
	Medicine Measures	2
	Eye Baths	2
	Eye Shades (right and left)	6
	Eye Droppers	6
	Disposable Syringes, 2 ml. (25 g. x ¾″)	5
	Isopropyl Alcohol Swabs	100
m	Triangular Bandages	6
m	Conforming Bandages, 2″	12
m	Conforming Bandages, 3″	12
m	Crepe Bandages, 3″	2
	Cotton Wool, 1½ oz. pkt.	6 pkts.
m	Novalind Sterile Dressing, 25 per pack	3 packs
m	Vaseline Gauze, 12 pieces per pack	3 packs
	Leukoplast Strapping, 1″	1 roll
	Leukoplast Strapping, 2″	1 roll
	Leukoflex Strapping, 3″	1 roll
	Handyplast Dressing Strip, 3″	1 pkt.
	Leukoclip Wound Closures, 10 per pkt.	3 pkts.
	Gauze Sponges, Sterile, 3″ x 3″	60 pkts.
m	Safety Pins, assorted	12
m	Scalpel	1
m	Dressing scissors, pointed	1 pair
m	Dressing Forceps	1 pair
m	Kidney dishes, 8″	1
m	Catheter, sterile 18FG. Balloon	1

ctor's orders only.

ms thus marked should be refrigerated if possible.

Inventory for our RFDS medical chest, 1971.

35

Rod has been away for days, riding with the boys, getting to know the run; where the waters are, where the cattle run, and how to get from place to place. It is so lonely without him. Before he left, he showed me how to work the battery-powered Traeger two-way radio, our contact with the outside world. I can receive and send telegrams, and when necessary, messages, through the Flying Doctor Base at Wyndham. I make lots of mistakes; it is totally different from a telephone, but Fred Ryle, the Base operator, is patient and I finally feel confident. Fred and his vivacious wife Pat are so kind and understanding; the women, in these early years, owe a lot to them.

Each day, Monday to Friday, the Flying Doctor Base held five radio sessions, approximately two hours apart. We had four telegram sessions plus one special session, which was set aside for 'medicals' only, when we could speak directly to a doctor. At the beginning of every session, the Base operator would call for any urgent medicals before he gave out or received traffic — telegrams and messages — to or from all the distant stations. Should accidents happen, or a doctor's advice be needed urgently, we simply had to wait for the next scheduled session. Over the weekends there was absolutely no contact at all with the Base or a hospital.

In the late 1950s, we were given a V-shaped whistle. By blowing on the long and short ends alternately and for a precise number of seconds, we could make radio contact with the Base between sessions and on weekends.

The whistle could be frustrating. I had trouble getting the timing right to the exact second. Rod, on the few occasions he had to use it, huffed and puffed, dropped the whistle, swore and huffed and puffed again before he got it right.

The new, modern Traeger has a button which, when pressed, makes contact with the Base or hospital, and it proved to be the most successful of all.

The Flying Doctor Service supplied all the stations with a well-stocked medicine chest. It held virtually everything needed to treat the sick or injured in an emergency. To lessen the chance of administering the wrong medicine, each of the drugs in the cabinet was labeled with a number as well as its name.

* * *

Rod, home at last, will work on the old Maple Leaf tray-back truck, to get it mobile so he can drive to a place called Rail Yard and scoop for

36

water. I am to go with him and I can take Peggy. Up early next morning, I watch the blacks pile on the back of the truck. I sit up front with Rod. No road, not even a track, we bump for hours over rocks and spinifex. One of the blacks, Old Radio, sometimes walking ahead, his arm out stiff as a poker, pointing the way. Rod says, "I hope that old bugger knows the way, because I surely don't." He need not worry; Radio is on his hunting grounds and knows exactly where he is. We pull up for dinner — cold corned beef, damper and billy tea, and arrive at Rail Yard about sundown. It has been a long rough day, but with the scenery so beautiful, I do not mind.

I wake in the morning to see Peggy sitting by the fire and the men further down the creek, already on the job. Peggy siphons water into a tin dish and I wash while she toasts a slice of damper and spreads it with treacle for my breakfast. I wander down to watch the men at work.

Sitting on a log, I notice, around a tree close to me, strands of strong, twisted wire anchoring the winch mechanism for the sand scoop. Rod does not see me there, but Paddy, a native stockman, does. He says something to Rod. Rod looks up and calls to me to move quickly. I do so. However, I have hardly moved when, with a loud 'ping', the wire breaks and rips around like an angry silver snake. Had I still been sitting near the tree, it would have cut me in two.

I watch the men gouge great scoops of sand out of the creek bed. There is a lot of water in the damp sand, but holes have to be made to allow it to seep slowly into pools. About half a mile (800 m) further up the creek, brumbies slide cautiously down the bank and begin pawing the sand.

Peggy and I go walkabout. She is looking for bush tucker — wild fruit and sugarbag. Today we come across a goanna. Picking up stones, Peggy takes off after it. I follow. It gives us a good chase as it quickly twists around the spinifex and over the rocks. Peggy's aim is good; she finally stuns it with the stones. Picking it up by the tail, she swings its head against a rock and kills it. I feel a little sick, but Peggy is elated. The blacks will eat well today.

We stay at Rail Yard three days. When the scooping finishes, we load up and head back to the station.

* * *

Rod is not satisfied with the track Frank Bridge found over the range onto the Fitzroy River. It is too rough and will cripple our cattle. I ride out with him while he looks for another way — he says to stay close. I am petrified. I am now thankful for the ponies we learnt to ride on at Julia Creek. Almost straight up, over great rocks and boulders. Rod's horse sure-footed and strong, Toddler plodding along. I do not try to guide him; he is better off without any help from me. We reach the top of the range and go straight down the other side, both horses sliding a lot but never losing their footing. As always, when afraid or in trouble, I pray. Thank the dear Lord, we are at the bottom at last!

Rod loosens the girths, takes the bits out of their mouths and then, wrapping the bridle reins loosely round their necks, leaves the horses to feed round. Taking his quart pot from where he has tied it to his saddle, he scoops water from a rock hole in the river. Building a fire, he puts the quart pot on to boil. He carries tea leaves and sugar in two Log Cabin tobacco tins in his saddle pouch. We sit under a lovely old gum tree and eat the corned beef sandwiches I had made.

What a glorious day and what a heavenly spot; late August, clear blue sky, birds chirping and singing in the trees, a kangaroo and two little wallabies drinking at the rock hole, the air so pure and fresh. Not a sign of another human being — utter and complete peace. This is nature at its most beautiful. Thank you, Rod, for bringing me here. I would like to leave a mark, a sign, to say that I have been here; but I do not.

* * *

The winter is over and beautiful September spring is here. How I hate the winter.

Men come and go. Some ride in, have a meal and move on, others come, riding one horse and leading a pack. They throw their swags down near the old bough-shed and stay for a few days. They all carry rifles. Rod makes them all welcome. We have little to offer, but they expect no more than we can give. Sometimes I see lubras travelling with them. The lubras stay in the blacks' camp, never coming near me or the men during the day. Hat in hand, the men come to thank me for letting them stay and to say goodbye. I cannot remember ever seeing any of them again.

* * *

I always considered myself healthy and strong; I had only been in hospital once for an appendix operation. Now I have started to feel nauseated and miserable every morning. The lubras become very protective of me. We still swim but underwater games are out and they deny me certain bush tucker. Because of this, I am sure it is the bush tucker that is upsetting me. Sitting one day with Peggy and Maggie, our feet splashing in the cool spring water, Maggie says, "'Im piccaninny gum muzer dime." ("The piccaninny will come at mustering time.") I look around, expecting to see some of the piccaninnies from the camp. Peggy and Maggie laugh. I laugh with them, but do not understand. Maggie puts her hand on my stomach, "'Im piccaninny 'ere." Slowly I begin to wonder, could they be right? Could it really be true? Yes! They know! I am pregnant.

I wait impatiently for night so that I can tell Rod. He is so excited. It is a boy, it has to be a boy. We talk about names but with our excitement and joy, we both know it means a separation. Rod decides that I will go back to Queensland for the birth. I think Wyndham or Derby but Rod is adamant — it has to be Queensland.

I am nearly three months pregnant before I can let my parents know. Rod had to leave for the Northern Territory soon after I told him. With no mail service while he is away, I am reluctant to send a telegram over the Flying Doctor Base. After the first uncomfortable weeks my health improves and I have never felt better.

* * *

November comes, hot and dry. The men talk of early storms before the monsoons. Whirly winds swirl and stir up the dust. Frank Bridge says it is not a good sign for rain. Dry storms and lightning strikes start bushfires. What a magnificent sight they are as they burn along the range. I watch them at night and wonder at their power. Bushfires at this time are not a problem for us; we have no fences or yards that can be burnt down.

I go for one more walk with the lubras before I leave for Queensland. I am feeling very well. We see an emu and the young lubras chase it; the old lubras stay with me. The emu, with great long strides, is off like a shot. The girls, laughing and winded, come back and we set about looking for eggs. The girls find one. Poking a hole in the end, they suck out the yolk. They tell me they used to make brownies with emu eggs before Frank and Sally brought fowls to *Lansdowne*. I did not know it then, but this was to be my last long walk with the lubras for nearly eight years.

* * *

Christmas is here. My first Christmas away from home. No Midnight Mass, presents, decorations, celebrations or the delicious food I used to know. Christmas Eve we all climb onto the old Maple Leaf and Rod drives us to Baker's Waterhole. He has scooped there and cattle are coming in for water, but we are not interested so much in cattle this day — we are after turkeys for our Christmas dinner. The boys, with their spears and boomerangs, catch four, being careful not to bruise them too much. One for the whites and half-castes and three for the blacks. The lubras pluck and gut them. We soak ours in vinegar and water overnight. Scrub turkey is rather tough and rank.

Christmas morning. Friends calling up on the Flying Doctor wireless to send their greetings. Everybody relaxed and happy, especially the men. The women busy with the Christmas dinner.

Tom Swift, a dogger, arrived Christmas Eve. A strange man, he hides his loneliness under a lot of silly, know-all chatter. He drifts from station to station, stays until the women can no longer put up with him, and then moves on. Rod makes him welcome. Tom has two bottles of OP rum. He will spend several days with us.

There is always an abundance of fresh vegetables. In season, we seem to be able to handle the supply and demand, however, our English potatoes produce huge crops. Although they are part of our every meal, except breakfast, we always have a surplus. We cannot throw them away. Rod has sand carted from the creek and dumped close to the old bough shed. He says to bury the potatoes in the sand. They will keep fresh and can be used all the year round. We keep the sand slightly moist and dig out the potatoes as we need them.

Our bread oven is outside, near the bough shed. It has a solid crushed ant bed rectangular base, sealed on the outside with a mixture of ant bed and water — which sets like cement. The outside of the oven is dome-shaped, moulded with ant bed and reinforced with chicken wire. A small chimney rises through the corrugated-iron roof that protects the oven from the rain. The lubras start a fire inside the firebox to completely heat up the oven. After the fire burns down, they rake out the ashes and the bread tins are slid in on steel racks. About three hours later, the bread is ready to come out. The insulation quality of the ant bed keeps the heat in and creates an excellent oven.

With spring onions from the garden and dry bread crumbs, I stuff our turkey. Sally Malay puts it in the bread oven to cook. I prepare the sweet potatoes and English potatoes, turnips, carrots, swedes and pumpkin, and put them in the camp oven to bake. Cabbage is boiled on the open fire. Sally is a big help. I would like to think he is my offsider but it is the other way round.

At *Springvale*, Olive had given me a recipe for a boiled custard; flour, sugar, eggs and milk. I pour half a bottle of rum into it. I could see trouble looming with too much free rum. Rod makes four plum puddings and cooks them in treacle tins, the lids sealed with solder. With an abundance of lemons, I make a bucket of lemon juice and so we have our Christmas dinner.

With their turkeys, wrapped in bark and cooked in a hole in the ground, and goannas cooked on the coals, Maggie tells me the blacks have had "proper good tuck-in". I give them an extra ration of stick tobacco — the 'nicky-nicky' they like so much to chew — and also all the sugar they need for their lemons. They have no liking for vegetables except for sweet potato. When Rod first went to the Kimberleys, blacks were issued with saccharin as a sweetener. It was much easier to pack a bottle of saccharin tablets than bags of sugar when mustering. By the early 50s, the blacks were banned from receiving saccharin.

I eat the vegetables but find the turkey is too tough. I also enjoy Rod's plum puddings, but do not have the custard. The smell of rum is very strong. Rod and the men toast absent loved ones and wish us all a Happy Christmas. I sit up late; I cannot sleep. The men talk and drink. On an old gramophone they play the only records they have, "Silent Night" and "Red River Valley". Happy and content, the blacks corroboree until their campfires burn down to embers. I hear the deep throb of the didgeridoo, the stomping of feet as they dance their tribal dances, and voices raised in song.

A hot moonless night, stars so bright and so close, thunder and lightning over the range, I wonder again why I am in this wild primitive land, expecting my first baby, with not another white woman within a day's drive of me, the nearest doctor over 300 miles (500 km) away. The blacks are kind and gentle, whites and half-castes considerate. I badly want to go home. This life is not for me, this is not my country… but it is, and I have to accept the fact I am not the only lonely white woman in the Kimberleys. They are scattered all round, our only contact via the Traeger wireless. We swap recipes, talk about our children, and build a picture to fit the voice, but we never meet. It is truly a man's world, a land of campfires, swags and distant friends.

* * *

Lansdowne kitchen and main building, with 'Diamond' Dixon and me next to Rod's Chev utility.

From left: (unidentified), Dave Fogarty, Yvonne Holland, Cec Watts, me, Dawn Johnson, John Gordon and Lloyd Fogarty at Wyndham Races, 2 August 1952.

Lansdowne, showing the house and kitchen, with the Maple Leaf truck in the foreground, King Leopold Range in background.

CHAPTER FIVE

Our family grows

A child is born
Motherhood dawns,
A parent's love
And faith in God above.

Matthew Quilty

My parents met me in Darwin and I travelled back to Queensland with them. Our daughter, Imelda Mary, 7 lb 7 oz (3.337 kg), was born in Brisbane, on 18 April, 1953. It was not an easy birth, which surprised me. But I was healthy and strong, and Meldie was a healthy baby. My sister, Dadie, and her baby, Michael, came to Brisbane to be with me.

Travelling back from Brisbane to Derby, W.A., where Rod met me, was a nightmare. Meldie was a bottle baby. Overnight stops, plane connections — bottles and nappies built up. Rod had gone to Derby to pick up some loading. He arranged his time to fit in with my arrival. I was so pleased to see him and he could not hide his joy in his baby daughter.

We had lunch with Charles and Mrs Stanwell, good and kind friends. Charles at that time was managing Goldsbrough Mort, Derby. Mrs Stanwell filled my flask with hot water and we were on our way. With Meldie on my lap, I relaxed on the front seat of Rod's Chev utility for the first time since leaving Brisbane. Derby Council had placed 44-gal-lon drums of water for travellers every few miles along the dirt road from Derby to Fitzroy Crossing. Dead wallabies littered the road; they had been hit by vehicles.

The road from Fitzroy Crossing to Halls Creek was not so pleasant. We had to carry water and the road was very dusty. We passed through Halls Creek late at night. The little town dark and silent. We went on and camped at the Palms, a popular camping spot for travellers. Fresh water and soft, green grass made a comfortable overnight stop. Early the next morning we called into *Springvale*. We had a cup of tea with Olive and Grandfather Quilty then went on to *Bedford* for lunch. We did not stay long. I was anxious to get to *Lansdowne* to get Meldie settled into a routine; I was also very tired.

Changes were made at *Lansdowne* while I was away. Rod had made a gauzed-in cot for Meldie, most welcome and appreciated. The cot had a strong angle iron frame with a hinged lid all covered in fly wire; the lubras had gathered bush cotton from the wild kapok trees to make a mattress. Proudly, the cot stood in the corner. To my surprise, I saw the mattress covered with flour bags, washed clean and sewn together by those faithful old lubras. No proper sheets or pillow slips but I knew my baby would sleep as healthy and happily as I ever did in our old family cot.

I could now call *Lansdowne* home, but I was still living in two worlds — the comfortable luxury I left behind and the harsh no-comfort existence I have at *Lansdowne*. I know that I must accept, settle down, and forget.

The piccaninnies come up and shyly indicate that they want to see the baby. I take them to where Meldie is lying in her cot. They gently touch her, and eyes dancing and white teeth flashing, they laugh and gabble in their own language.

The lubras start to look to me for orders. They are no longer just going their own way. They want me to tell them what to do and when to do it. Gone are the lazy, idle days. With a new baby, I am totally and hopelessly disorganised, struggling to cope. Rod is patient though, and with the help of the lubras, things slowly fall into place.

The lubras try to teach me to carry Meldie in a coolum. I try but it is no good. The coolum either up-ends or slips off my hip. Frank and Sally cut a kerosene box down, smooth it off, put it on wheels and attach two shafts. Just the thing. Safely tucked up with blankets and wild cotton-stuffed pillows, Meldie goes everywhere I go.

* * *

The months slip by, slow and easy. Rod and the men are away a lot. They discuss where they will set up the mustering camps, where to build yards, and where to fence — all this in the future and I am not really very interested; it is men's work. My whole life is centred round my baby daughter, but things must change. Rod needs to talk to someone other than the men and I have got to become involved in the running of *Lansdowne*.

While waiting my turn to receive or send traffic through the Flying Doctor Base, I listen to stations as far away as the Northern Territory, around Fitzroy Crossing and close by, sending telegrams or requesting skeds with other stations. Fred Ryle, the Flying Doctor Base operator, calls "MV" (Mike Victor), the *Lansdowne* call sign. I reply, and receive a telegram from the Broome Meatworks, wanting to know if we have any cattle for them. I acknowledge the telegram and sign off. Rod says no cattle this year — perhaps next season.

Rod talks and I listen. A horrifying picture gradually forms. We have no money, and we need so much to get *Lansdowne* started. Wages to be paid, stores and equipment must be bought for the station — and now there is another baby on the way!

I tell Rod I will ask his father to make good his promise to compensate us for what we lost in the fire.

"You will be wasting your time," Rod replies, "My father will give us nothing. He blames me for the fire."

"How could he possibly blame you?" I ask, "It was the miserable *Springvale* batteries that caused the fire. Even the men at the Julia Creek garage tried to persuade you to load them on flat, not fully charged, as your father wanted."

I approach Rod's father. He tells me he will think about it. He has been thinking about it for nearly two years now, so I know Rod is right, he will not pay us anything. However, he does tell me that there is £2000 ($4000) in the Arizona Account that must be paid to Olive and Basil, Rod's half-brother. Old Mr Underwood, living at *Bedford*, is doing all the station bookwork. *Lansdowne* is known as the Arizona Account.

Rod and I are certainly in a mess. We will have no money until we can turn off some bullocks, and we cannot turn off anything until we have money. I write to my father. He agrees to lend us £30,000 ($60,000). Overjoyed, I tell Rod. But Rod will have no part of it. He is determined we will make it on our own. Am I up to this huge task? I have never known what it means to be without money. It frightens me.

I arrange for Mr. Underwood to hand over the Arizona books to me. So neat and such beautiful writing. A policeman came from Halls Creek on a routine visit. He arranges for us to close the Arizona Account and open the Lansdowne Pastoral Account; he also arranges for the ⊢ Q2 brand to be transferred into Rod's name. Up until this time the ⊢ Q2 brand was in several names.

My parents and sister, Coral, came out on a visit and, while they are at *Lansdowne*, I fly to Perth. Calling on the Lands Department, Burns Philp, and the Bank of New South Wales (now Westpac); forms are signed, signatures witnessed — and I have the papers to say Rod is the sole owner of *Lansdowne*. The account will be known as the Lansdowne Pastoral Account, not the Arizona Account. I draw the £2000 from the Arizona Account and close it. Opening the Lansdowne Pastoral Account, I arrange with the bank to place £1000 to a working account and the other £1000 to be set aside as a sort of nest egg. Shortly after I arrive home, my parents and sister return to Queensland.

Now we wait for the wrath of Grandfather Quilty. It comes as we expect, right on top of Rod's head: I am not to be given any authority, nothing is to be put in my name, I must never be allowed to sign anything, especially cheques, and the books have to go back to Mr. Underwood. Nothing is ever said to me. Rod bears the brunt of everything, but we have what we want and there is no way I will hand those books over. My years as book-keeper and secretary for Australian Estates at Julia Creek have trained me well. I am fully qualified to do *Lansdowne*'s books.

* * *

Our son, Roderick Eckford (Tom), was born in Townsville on 4 June, 1954. Another healthy 7 lb 7 oz baby but again a difficult time for me. Travelling back to the Kimberleys with a new-born baby and our little thirteen-month-old daughter was fraught with problems. My parents, now living in Townsville, put me on the plane for Julia Creek, where my sister Dadie met us. Planes were ill-equipped to cope with a woman travelling with a three-week-old bottle baby and a thirteen-month-old child at foot. I dreaded the Julia Creek–Kimberley section of my journey.

We talked about chartering a plane to make the trip in the one day, but that was not possible. We discussed other options, finally deciding on a mothercraft nurse from Brisbane to help me. My parents would cover her expenses. Nurse Sally Thomas arrived within a few days. She was young, highly recommended, and very excited.

We left Julia Creek late one afternoon by train, arriving Mt Isa, where we would have an overnight and a day stopover, waiting for a connection to

Darwin. Water was restricted at Mt Isa. Nurse Sally was a little flustered. Out of her element, she did not seem to be able to improvise. City-bred, she was completely lost once she left that area, and the further we went the more frightened she became. She was a complete wreck by the time we reached *Lansdowne* and so was I. I did not keep her long. She was happy to leave.

The lubras set to, to spoil both Meldie and Tommy. Rosie, Big Mick's wife, sets herself up as nurse girl and boss of "dem piccaninnies". Rosie is a rogue. She dodges on the other girls; she always has "biggest headache" when there is work to be done. With no children of her own, she dotes on my babies.

* * *

My sister Coral has given me a good second-hand typewriter. I am now typing all our mail and keeping our books. This is a big load off Rod's shoulders. He is free to concentrate on the outside work.

We are still carting water from the garden well to fill the ship's tank outside the house for our domestic use. Bluey O'Malley, part owner of *Elgie Cliffs*, a station between *Bedford* and *Lansdowne*, has come from *Elgie Cliffs* to help deepen the well. We are using more water than the well is making. We borrow cement from *Bedford* and Rod and Bluey cement our bedroom floor.

Tom Dooley, an old man travelling round with Lucy, his young mission-reared tribal wife, comes to us early in the New Year. Tom thinks he has taken her far from the temptations of the towns — Lucy has a roving eye. Mission life has given her a certain contempt for old tribal laws. If she can shake Tom Dooley for a younger man, she will.

There is unease in the blacks' camp. I can feel the tension. Zachady creeps up one night as I am putting the babies to bed. In the dark he whispers, "Ar bin mak yoo noo Stormy and Tom Dooley bin fit (fight) ober dat nuisance woman Lucy." Stormy has been with us for three years. A big strong man, possibly in his early forties, easy going, a good stockman, and well liked by all the blacks, but without a wife. Lucy has set her cap for him and the two men have fallen out.

Lucy is unpopular, especially with the lubras. They blame her for the trouble. She is a no good nuisance woman. They will deal with the trouble in their own way. One night, Tom Dooley and Lucy walk away. I never saw them again.

* * *

Rod and the boys are mustering horses. There are foals to be branded — the males are to be cut as well. Mares are to be put with the stallion; filly foals and geldings are to be paddocked separately. I note all this in my diary and horse book. Two of Rod's horses, "Montie" and "Jock" are missing. Rod and two of the boys, Paddy and Demon, ride back to look for them. They find tracks of a shod horse and follow them. The tracks are on top of two sets of unshod hooves. They know they are on to the missing horses. The tracks lead over the range towards *Tableland*. They ride back to the station and Rod arranges a sked, through the Flying Doctor Base, with Ned De Lour, manager of *Tableland*. Ned confirms that a white stockman, Don Tait, had turned up there with two horses branded ⊢ ℚ2. Tait said he had bought them. Don Tait had worked for us for a few weeks. He had admired Montie, saying he would make a good racehorse. Rod sent Paddy and Demon to *Tableland* to bring the two horses back.

Some years later, a Don Tait was caught, in the far north, flying drugs into Australia. He was forced down in the Katherine (N.T.) area, arrested, and jailed. It was suggested that this was the man who had worked for us and stolen our horses. I am sure they were two different men.

Rosie and Demon want to leave. They are really Dunham River blacks — they have friends at *Lansdowne* but all their relations are on the Dunham. We ask them to stay until walkabout time. They agree. It is not good to try and hold blacks once they make up their minds they want to leave. They simply slip away in the early night, and are long gone before morning.

Rammie is also restless. Lulu, his promised wife, is a young lubra at *Bedford*. For reasons beyond his control, he cannot get her to leave *Bedford* and go with him. She is involved with a white man. Rammie wants us to help him. Paddy tells us that if we cannot get Lulu for Rammie, he and his family will leave. This would be a big blow to Rod. Rammie is a very good stockman. He has three cousins who are also very good stockmen. To lose five good men would weaken our stock camp considerably. I write to Rod's father. As he is paying Lulu's wages, I think he might arrange for her to go to *Lansdowne*. Feathers in the breeze; he isn't going to interfere. He does nothing, and we lose Rammie and his family.

Shorthanded now, Rod has to look to the Missions for help. What he gets are mostly desert blacks who are troublesome, the Mission staff pleased to get rid of them. Unable to adjust to the mountains and ranges on *Lansdowne*, they are unsettled and hard to handle. After several

50

unsuccessful attempts, he finally picks up four stockmen and one lubra. A motley crew — two grown men and two boys, one of the boys a sixteen-year-old king. The lubra, Lucy, 6–7 months pregnant, is the wife of one of the men.

They are all myalls, very much under the thumb of their young king. With his head of tight white curls (not uncommon among some desert Aboriginals), he deeply resents white man's authority and makes it impossible for Rod to work with any of them. Lucy never works. She stays in the camp but does not mix with our blacks. I check daily with the girls to see that she is well. Everything seems so. I think there is plenty of time to get the medical plane out to fly her to Wyndham or Derby for the birth, but I am wrong.

One morning about three o'clock, Alice, a half-caste, comes yelling up to the house, "'Im come, Yumman — 'im come." I panic. It has to be the baby and I have no idea what to do. Calling Peggy up, I get her to put a match to the fire and to put a bucket of water on to boil. With the hurricane lamp, a torch, sheets and a towel I start for the camp with Alice. She wants to know if I have scissors. Good grief, why scissors? I rush back to get them.

Lucy is on a blanket on the ground in a lot of pain. I go to her head and tell Alice to get on with it and to remember that I am watching her. Grumbling, she does what she is told. Taboo prevents our blacks from touching Lucy. I try to put a damp cloth on her forehead but she is biting and scratching so I do not get too close.

The sun is rising when Alice yells, "'Im come. 'Im proper good 'un." I relax, thank goodness, but it isn't over yet. Alice yelling again, "Gut. Gutem." What in the name of heavens is she yelling about now, cut what? Peggy there with a bucket of water said, "Gutem string, Yumman." The cord, of course, but where to cut, the middle, the end, where? Oh! Dear God! Don't put me through this again. Among their own tribe, the midwife would bite through the cord.

Dipping the scissors in hot water, I give them to Alice and tell her to finish the job. Once Lucy is free of the baby, she lashes out with both feet and kicks it. The poor little thing rolls down the creek bank and lands in the sand. I send Alice after it. A little girl covered in dirt. Wrapping her in a towel I take her up to the house, clean her up and then take her back to Lucy. Lucy puts her in a coolum and never lets her out of her sight after that.

* * *

51

Rod has taught me the cuts of meat, the rib and flap roasts, the steaks, and the first and second cuts of the briskets; he has also taught me how to make bread. I could not cook when I married. I find it very hard to cook on the open fire and in the camp oven. My bread is a hopeless mess, burnt to a cinder on the outside and raw dough on the inside, there is more ash than tea leaves in my tea, and the camp oven is forever upending, tipping vegetables and meat on to the ground. I get to hate station cooking more and more. I positively loathe it. Sixteen double loaves of bread, day in day out — great buckets of corned beef, five or six roasts, and huge pieces of fresh meat to be cooked the day after the weekly kill. I am eternally grateful to those faithful black women who stood by me and bore the bulk of the heavy work. They were my friends and my only companions in those early years.

Early storms and Rod is worried he will not get to Wyndham to pick up our loading before the rains. He arranges for Bert Sharpe, a carrier, to get it to *Bedford*. None of the carriers will take on the *Bedford–Lansdowne* track.

Frank Bridge and Sally Malay will leave us after Christmas. Frank is to manage Mornington Station and Sally goes with him. Sally is tribal married to a lubra. They have a big family. One daughter, Jossie, a very pretty little girl, died tragically in Halls Creek.

We have the usual drifters for Christmas. They all move on except one. Will Hobbs, who came riding a beautiful chestnut mare, is looking for work. Shorthanded, Rod puts him on. He is a quiet man, well spoken and very polite. With his long blond hair tied back with a pink ribbon, he is not popular with our white male staff but he is a good worker and keeps to himself.

Early March and the blacks are back from walkabout, the stockboys first, with the old men and lubras dribbling in later.

Preparations start to get the camp out early, but we are short of stockmen. We hear there are men available at a Northern Territory mission. Rod drives there and returns with two men, Toby and Bruno. He has been warned they are "bad blacks" and will bear watching. In fact, they are bad by any standard or colour, having been in Darwin's Fanny Bay Gaol several times for rape, murder and drunkenness. Our blacks are afraid of them.

Toby, a big black, possibly 35 to 38 years old, seems to be the leader. He uses all sorts of excuses to leave the yard where Rod and the boys are shoeing, to come to the house. I do not like him. Although they have been issued with boots and clothes, neither of them wear boots. I can never hear Toby coming.

At last the camp is ready to go. Before he leaves, Rod gives me his revolver. I am surprised. He always carries his revolver when mustering. A horse with a broken leg or badly gored by a bull would have to be shot; he needs his revolver. Safe at the station with the lubras and the old men, I surely do not. However, he insists, saying to keep it close to me at all times.

After a quiet day with little to do, we all have an early night. The lubras finish work and wander off to their camp. I settle the babies down in their cot, check that the revolver is under my pillow, and the torch handy; I turn the kerosene hurricane lamp out and go to bed.

I do not know how long I have been asleep when something wakes me. The blacks' dogs are barking fiercely. I know someone is close although I cannot see anything. The black-fellow smell is very strong. As I try to sit up, I feel rough hands on my head and face. I scream in fright and grab the revolver, pointing it in the direction of the hands. I pull the trigger. A man cries out in pain. Something sprays over me. I can hear him stumbling around until he gets outside. The sound of talking — two male voices, so there are more than one. Instinct tells me it must be Toby and Bruno. Gradually the voices fade — they must be moving away — the dogs have stopped barking. Petrified, I sit there holding the revolver, not knowing if I could use it again if they came back. The sheet is damp and sticky. There is no sound from my babies; I must go to them. Shining the torch, I see great patches of blood on the sheet and my nightdress. There is also blood on the floor. I have stepped in some. Both my babies are safe and sound asleep. I would like to pick them up but I am shaking too much and it would only disturb them. I go back and sit on the side of the bed, trying not to touch the sheet. My night dress is sticking to me. I want to change, but not yet, I need a little more time to get myself under control. I start to pray. Tomorrow, I will pack our few things, and when Rod returns, I will tell him we must leave this place.

Whispering and soft footsteps outside. I almost scream again and point the gun but it drops out of my hand. While I am down on the floor looking for it, Maggie, Peggy and Rosie slide into the room, their eyes flashing with fear. They are ready to run should the dogs start to bark again. Rosie heads straight for the cot. She feels the babies and croons to them. Peggy and Maggie confirm it was Toby and Bruno. Peggy gets a clean night dress out of the suitcase and I sponge myself with water she

53

has poured into the tin dish, before I change. By now the smell of blood is strong.

Taking the soiled sheet off, we sit on the bed in the dark, afraid to sleep. I look at my watch. It is almost three o'clock. Just then, the dogs start to bark again. Rosie bolts but Maggie pulls her back. We can hear horses coming very fast, then I hear Rod's voice. I feel weak with relief. It is a terrible thing to know such fear. I want to cry but can't. Lighting the lamp, Rod and I sit on the side of the bed but it is some time before the trembling stops and I am able to tell him what has happened. Sending the lubras to stoke up the fire and put the billy on, he goes out to see Will Hobbs, who has ridden in with him. I hear him tell Will to put the horses in the yard, to water them but leave the saddles on, then to come in for a cup of tea. Rod tells me that he did not know Toby and Bruno were missing until it was time for them to go on night watch — camped away from our blacks, they had slipped away in the dark without being seen.

After a quick cup of tea, Rod sends Will for the horses. It is just on daybreak. Thinking they were returning to the stock camp, I beg Rod not to go. I am terrified Toby and Bruno could be close and will come back. Rod takes the revolver, saying they will not be long and that they will be back. I know then they are going after Toby and Bruno.

We spend a miserable morning. Nervous and jittery, the girls stay close to me. Peggy says all the blacks in the camp have gone bush and will not return until they know they are safe. Maggie says, "Doby and Bruno bad puggers (bad buggers). Da bin steelum shin (They've been stealing gins) and killum people." Rosie gathers the babies to her and keeps them close.

About one o'clock Maggie says, "'Orses come." Rod and Will ride up, tired and dusty, their horses a lather of sweat. There is blood on Rod's horse. I ask what has happened. He says his horse had fallen and cut his shoulder on rocks. I want to know about the two blacks. Would they be coming back? Or were they long gone, probably on their way back to the Northern Territory? Rod says they are far gone and would not be coming back. I am to put the whole horrible nightmare out of my mind and never think or speak of it again. I ask why he had chosen Will Hobbs to ride with him and not one of our blacks. He said, "Because I trust him."

* * *

Will tells me his family had a property in Victoria. An only son, he had been educated first by tutors then attended boarding school in Melbourne. He also says Hobbs is not his name but that he would be obliged if we would accept that. He tells Rod far more than he tells me. We do not pry into his life. When he wants to talk, we listen. He is a very lonely man. He leaves us at the end of the bullock muster. He is not a 'gin man' — a white man who has sexual relations with black women — and does not fit in with the other white men. They give him a hard time. A gin man is accepted but a homosexual is not. We are sorry to see him go. He is a good stockman and loyal to Rod.

Rod and the boys take our small mob, 250 head, to Wyndham. We have a date in late August to deliver to the meatworks. Some of the boys have been left at the station to break-in and shoe horses. I am to supervise and give them what they need. Rod will be on the road three weeks before he delivers. I am not looking forward to being left alone for three to four weeks, especially as I am to keep an eye on the boys shoeing. I know nothing about it. However, Meldie and Tommy are both healthy and well, the lubras are good and the boys know their job, so I do not anticipate any trouble.

The boys come to me and ask for horseshoes, "Number 1s or number 3s or whatever." I pretend to know as I pull the bundles out, but thank goodness, they recognise the size they need. They also want extra breaking-in gear. Again, they know what they want and take what they need.

Five days after Rod left, trouble does strike. Bruce, a shy young black stockman, has been kicked by a horse. They bring him to me with the bone of his left arm, between the elbow and the wrist, broken through the skin and badly splintered. I nearly faint. I have never seen a broken bone before. Bruce is in terrible pain. He makes no sound but the pain shows in his eyes. Sending some of the boys to cut or find some straight, flat boards, I rush to the medical chest for a sling and bandages, wondering all the time if I should wash the bone. I wait for the session and I call the Flying Doctor Base at Wyndham. Trying not to panic I explain what has happened and ask for instructions. Fred Ryle contacts the doctor. Between them, they tell me I must give Bruce an injection for the pain, bandage the splint to his arm and put his arm in a sling. Trying not to cause any more pain, I get the bandage and splint on and his arm in the sling but I cannot give the injection. I simply freeze and cannot get the needle in. Bruce must have this injection now. I send one of the boys to get Lofty Stemble, a white man working on a well about a mile from the station. Lofty gives the injection.

Fred Ryle tells me the medical plane will pick Bruce up to fly him to the hospital but we do not have a landing strip. It is arranged that we drive him to the nearest station where there is a strip, we have a choice of *Fossil Downs* or *Bedford.* Lofty says *Fossil* is closer to a hospital. They will send a vehicle to meet us. Lofty checks Rod's Chev utility for fuel and water; he also checks the tyres. Making Bruce as comfortable as possible on a mattress in the back, I send two boys with Lofty. After they leave, I hug my babies and pray God will keep them safe. Bruce is in hospital for six weeks.

Things settle down, but Bruce's accident has shaken me. I feel I am not up to what this great, primitive land expects of me. I do no know what I would do if anything happened to Rod or to either of my babies. I wander down to the yard, where the boys are back shoeing and break-ing-in. I wonder at the courage of the boys even being in the same yard as those wild horses.

* * *

With three good seasons and winter rain this year, the country looks beautiful. We could have done without the winter rain though. Everything is so wet and cold. A lot of stockboys have "cold sick" and cannot go into the stock camp. The blacks can suffer almost unbearable pain without a murmur, but they seem to give up when they get what they call "cold sick". I sometimes wonder if it is pneumonia. It is all I can do to force them to eat and try to help themselves. Peggy and I make great buckets of rich beef soup. Every day we take it to the camp and almost force feed them. They spit and bring up horrible mucus. The hospitals are busy with evacuations. Like leprosy, the "cold sick" lays them low.

The men have made me a charcoal cooler, its four legs sit in treacle tins full of water to keep the ants away. I can at least keep food a little longer now. I have learnt to be grateful for small mercies. The men spent days burning to get the charcoal, and then ramming it between the layers of wire mesh. I take turns with the lubras, gently pouring water from buck-ets onto the charcoal to keep it cool. My parents find it hard to believe that things are so primitive here. We are almost uncivilised. I tend to agree.

The storms are late coming this year but the wet has set in now. This is always the best time of the year for me. With the rains, we cannot get out and nobody can get in.

The blacks go early on walkabout. How excited they always are at this time. The men, riding their donkeys or walking in the lead. Carrying their spears and stripped down to nargas, they walk and ride proud.

The lubras follow on foot, carrying swags, billy cans and all the gear they will need for the weeks they will be away. Dogs barking and running everywhere. They will camp on a waterhole and meet up with the blacks from other stations. There will be lots of hunting and always the initiation ceremony when the young teenage boys are made men.

* * *

Four months pregnant with our third baby and I miscarry — what a terrible shock. I don't want to believe it has happened. I can no longer accept this place. It takes everything and gives nothing. We must go back to Queensland before anything else happens.

Rod and the boys are mustering. I have no idea where they are but the girls look for the smoke as it rises from the fires Rod lights to burn off. They can tell me in what direction the camp is moving. Rod has bought a left-hand drive Willy jeep and covered the back with strong mesh wire. It is like a cage but safe for Meldie and Tommy. I take them for short drives. They are happy but I am falling into a deep depression again.

Concerned for me, Rod leaves the stock camp and rides in to the station. I know he is upset by my discontent. We talk and decide I will go out with him to the camp. I will drive the jeep, take Meldie and Tommy, and Peggy will also go.

It was the best thing that could have happened; it was also the beginning of the long years I was to spend in the stock camp with Rod.

* * *

Rod riding Toddler.

57

Meldie Mary (7 months) with me beside house.

Holding mob of cattle.

CHAPTER SIX

Tackling the Kimberleys

A harsh land
Of red blood sand,
Made up of beauty, splendour, serenity and bliss,
Which, without a doubt,
Is what the Kimberleys are about.

Matthew Quilty

There are no roads where we are going but Rod says to stay about a mile behind the cattle and to follow the mob. With Peggy on the seat beside me and the children in the back, I watch as a wonderful new world opens up to me. With cattle in hand, the musterers move off and we follow. Dust, galloping horsemen, cattle dodging and running for freedom, men shouting and cursing, the country broken and rough, great sandstone ranges and open valleys. Breakaway country — creeks, gullies and rivers — nothing stops riders and cattle. I could never have imagined anything like this. I have come into my own.

We pull into dinner camp. The men are already here, the fire lit and the billies on. Two boys out with the cattle, the rest catching fresh horses. Rod cutting dinner for the blacks; the whites and half-castes cut their own meat and bread. Half-castes are accepted by the whites. They eat in the white man's kitchen and drink beside him in the local bars. Many have been sired by some of our most prominent and respected citizens.

Proud of their white blood and their chocolate brown skins, they revel in the privileges their mixed blood allows them. They distance themselves from the full-blood black. No problem for the full-blood. He has little time for the half-castes, called "yella fellas" more often by the full-blood black than by the full-blood white.

It is harder for a half-caste girl or woman. They are not accepted as equals by white women. Often prey to unscrupulous white men who treat them like prostitutes, they end up that way. Paid off with cheap drink, they become hopeless alcoholics. Full-blood blacks are not yet allowed intoxicating drink by law. Hotels and bars are out of bounds for them.

I will never forget this, my first time in the stock camp. We are out a week before returning to the station. Tired, dirty and happy, my whole life has changed. There are still hard times ahead, but no more whinge-ing or wanting to leave when things go wrong. In July, drover Darkie Green takes delivery of 500 bullocks for Wyndham. Darkie, a good dependable man, never seems to be out of work.

After a few days at the station, Rod is ready for a cow and calf muster to send a small mob to Glenroy Meatworks. The meatworks, started by the Blyth brothers to try to recoup their flagging fortune after a disastrous deal with Sidney Kidman, the cattle king, was good for all of us. The Blyths own Mt House and Glenroy Stations. Set on the north-west side of the King Leopold Range, the meatworks caters for stations who have trouble getting their cattle to either Broome or Wyndham. We have three markets for our cattle, Wyndham, Broome and Glenroy.

Killed at Glenroy, the meat is flown to the Wyndham abattoir by MMA. The plane, called 'Air Beef', is back loaded with supplies for the stations. Captain Horrie Miller, husband of Mary Durack, was co-founder of the airlines with Sir MacPherson Robertson, the Melbourne chocolate millionaire.

* * *

Daisy came to me this morning to say Dolly is in the camp and "'Im nearly bin finis." As far as I know, Dolly is not one of our blacks but I do know "nearly bin finis" means they think she is dying.

Checking that Rosie is with Meldie and Tommy, I hurry to the camp with Daisy. Dolly, old and very fat, lying in her swag, is in a bad way. I tell the girls I will have to call the doctor. They are upset and beg me not to. Something is wrong here, but I cannot wait to hear the story; I must help Dolly. I lift her old grey head and hold water to her mouth. Gradually she starts to sip, and opens her eyes. I sponge her down with a wet cloth and she seems more relaxed. Her old feet, tough as leather, are badly cut about. Getting the girls to warm some water, we bathe her feet, then I get some ointment from the Flying Doctor medicine chest and soothe it on.

I am curious to know where she came from and why she is here. From the state of her feet, I know she has walked a long way, but the story will have to wait a little longer — she needs food. I have a junket in the charcoal cooler and there is always a big pot of rich beef soup near the fire. She drinks the soup and eats the junket. I tell the girls to keep giving her water to drink, and to keep her cool and in the shade. I will come back later. How I wish I knew more about nursing.

Time now for the story. Dolly had walked over the King Leopold Range from Mornington Station. She and her much younger husband, Kicker, had a pack of dogs who were chasing cattle and heeling horses there. Frank Bridge and Sally Malay had left *Mornington* and were living in Halls Creek. The new manager had threatened to shoot Dolly and Kicker's dogs. Rather than have this happen, they decided they would leave and head for *Lansdowne*.

Dolly left after work one night, carrying her swag and a few billy cans. Kicker was to leave later that night, with the dogs and the rest of their things. He was to catch up with Dolly. Dolly said she was "five sleeps" (five nights) on the way but did not see Kicker, thinking she had missed him and that he was already at *Lansdowne*. She told the girls she had heard a shot after she left *Mornington*. That seemed to be the end of the story. Days passed, Dolly improved, and I heard no more until Paddy came one night to tell me they were all worried about Kicker and the shot Dolly had heard. I thought that Dolly, old and probably a little deaf, could have been mistaken about the gunshot, and it was possible that Kicker had headed in another direction, looking for a younger wife.

Paddy became very agitated. "Kicker could not leave Dolly, she was his tribal wife, he would have followed her to *Lansdowne*. Besides, Kicker was the man-maker at their next walkabout. He had all the ceremonial gear. It was against black-man law for him to take that."

Paddy wants the police to find Kicker. However, before we can do anything, the police have been notified by another source.

About a week later, two detectives arrive from Perth. This is a shock to us. The detectives want to interview the blacks. They hint they suspect Dolly of doing away with Kicker. How ridiculous; Dolly, old, fat, and feeble could not possibly have killed Kicker. We ask, "What makes you think Kicker is dead?"

"That is what the blacks will tell us," they reply.

I explain to Peggy that these are two policemen from the big city who want to talk to them. She says only Paddy, Big Jack and Old Ben will talk to the policemen. We set the detectives up under the lean-to front verandah, and offer to help with the interviews, but they do not want us anywhere near when they are talking to the blacks. They move out under the gum tree. Dolly, helped by Daisy and Molly, waddles up and sits on the ground in front of the detectives. They wave Daisy and Molly away. This upsets Dolly. We cannot hear what is being said, but, from the look of Dolly, she does not understand them, and they are not going to get anything from her.

Paddy comes next, dressed in hat, boots, clean shirt and trousers. He shakes his head and points in every direction except *Mornington*. He understands but pretends that he does not. Big Jack and Old Ben follow, all dressed as Paddy is. The detectives get nothing from them. They come in for lunch, hot and annoyed. We again offer to help but again they refuse; they want to see some other blacks. I tell Peggy.

Settled under the tree, they wait for more blacks to come. To my surprise, I see Paddy walking up again, this time without hat, boots or shirt. Big Jack and Old Ben also come a second time. They have changed their shirts but both have come without hats or boots. They give their native blackfellow names. When they first came up, they all stood. Now, as they follow each other, they sit on the ground in front of the detectives.

Before the detectives leave, they tell us they have interviewed six male blacks and one female. They had no trouble with their whitefellow names but had trouble trying to spell their native names. They are convinced the *Lansdowne* blacks know nothing. They will have to look elsewhere. Little did they know they had only seen three male blacks. They had not recognised or were aware of the double-up. Although they wanted Kicker found, the blacks were not prepared to talk to two strange policemen. Kicker was never found.

* * *

With more men around *Lansdowne* now, there is need for a new staff toilet. The old one has deteriorated. The pit has caved in and the hessian flaps in the wind. A new pit must be dug. Everybody takes a turn at digging so many feet per day. They are close to the bottom.

Ringer Gibson, a stockman — the only one, so far, who has not done any digging — is put to work to dig. Ringer only spends a few hours down the pit before he yells to be pulled up. He tells Rod he is a stockman, not a gravedigger. The men think Ringer should pull his weight and do his share of the digging. One of them has a small nugget of Croydon gold. They decide to bury the nugget in the pit and lightly cover it with earth where Ringer is sure to find it.

Loudly protesting, Ringer is lowered down the hole and starts to dig. In no time, the nugget shows up on his shovel. Ringer jumps for joy — he has struck a rich gold reef, perhaps the Mother Lode. He digs madly. For two days, he stops anyone else from going down the hole. He will finish the digging.

As the men had hoped, Ringer digs until Rod is satisfied the hole is deep enough. Ringer would like to go deeper — there has to be more gold down there somewhere!

He took the joke well, but vowed, as he returned the nugget to its rightful owner, that he would never be caught again.

* * *

Rod said I would have to make soap for the station. The girls would show me how. Caustic soda, rosin, fat and water, boiled in a half 44-gallon drum until it thickened, left to cool, then cut into squares. I was to make thousands and thousands of squares while on *Lansdowne*. It was our toilet soap as well as our work soap. On killing night, I cut and rendered down the kidney fat for cooking, the rest of the fat was rendered down and poured into a 44-gallon drum for soap-making.

I finally have water piped from the garden well to the house. A big improvement on the ship's tank. Glory be! How we splashed under the running water!

* * *

The meatworks is slow to pay. It is three weeks after our bullocks are killed before the first of four or five payments is lodged in our Perth bank. Burns Philp Ltd and Southern Cross Ltd, our main suppliers, are very understanding. We need stores and equipment. They agree to supply and will wait until we are in a position to pay. We can hardly believe our good luck, however, as soon as we know the money is in the bank we settle our accounts with them. We worked on this principle for years.

With a few good seasons, our brandings improve, and cattle numbers increase. We are gradually clearing our debts, but it is hard work and we still have to do without a lot of things. There is so much I would like:

a kitchen with a stove, a bathroom, electricity, a fridge, doors and windows in my home. All these things came later, but I struggled for years with the Potts irons, watering dirt floors, rushing round with the girls in storms, trying to place sheets of iron over the openings where the doors and windows should have been. The carbide light took over from the hurricane lamp, then came the Tilly, a lamp I was afraid of, and finally we had a 32-volt lighting plant, which gave me an electric iron and electric lights. The charcoal cooler made way for a kerosene fridge, a temperamental thing that went with the wind, and from cooking on an open fire, I moved into a kitchen that Rod and Bluey O'Malley had built. Rough, bush-made, bush timber, but to me such comfort. With my wood stove, I could ask for little more — the rest would come years later. My cooking improved but I was never a good cook.

* * *

The usual hustle and bustle of getting the stock camp ready, but with a difference this year — I am to go full-time, taking Meldie and Tommy, Peggy and Maggie. I will drive the jeep but I also have my own horse, a quiet strawberry roan I call Troy. Peggy will have a horse too. We will ride when necessary, to help the musterers. We are still shorthanded. Maggie will stay with the children.

Rosie, upset that she is not going with Meldie and Tommy, fights with Maggie. The men are at the yard, packing the mules and saddling up. I go down to the blacks' camp. Rosie and Maggie standing toe to toe, each with a great waddy in her hand. Rosie is bleeding from a gash in her head. She raises her waddy and lands a heavy blow on Maggie's head. Blood runs down Maggie's face. She does not try to defend herself. Maggie in turn hits Rosie and splits her ear. Both receive the blows without trying to protect themselves. This must stop. Maggie will be in no condition to go with us and Rosie will need stitches.

I tell the other lubras to break the fight up, but they won't interfere. Daisy taps me on the shoulder and points to a bucket of water — just the thing. I tell her to throw it over them but she indicates that I must do it. I throw the water and the bucket. It stops the fight. I check both Maggie and Rosie, blood still seeping from their head wounds. What to do now? Old Biddy tells me not to worry, she will "fixem proper good." I can't do any more for them so I return to the house, convinced the stock camp will have to go out without Maggie and that I will have to call the doctor on the wireless to find out how I am to handle their wounds. Peggy comes in to help me get ready. I ask her about her swag. She says her husband, Big Johnnie, has all her things. While we are sorting out what I must take, Maggie and Rosie walk in. Both have their heads bandaged in some sort of grey rag with what looks like mud dripping down from the bandage. Considering the fight they had, they both look remarkably well. Any one of those blows would have finished a white person. Proof positive of the stories about the black man's hard head. It must be harder than the white man's. They tell me, "Fite finish. Old Biddy bin fixem proper good. Good friends now."

We would have taken Rosie, but as well as caring for the children, Maggie will help with the work in the camp. Rosie would not.

I will share Rod's swag. Blankets and small kapok-filled pillows for Meldie and Tommy go in the jeep, as well as extra clothes for all of us. I take several packets of arrowroot biscuits and two large tins of powdered milk for the children. Meldie has the comfort of her dummy. Tommy never took to the dummy.

Rod comes to check that we are ready. He loads his swag into the jeep. Maggie settles in the cage with the children, Peggy sits beside me and we are ready. Rod says to stay a reasonable distance behind the cattle but to keep them in sight at all times. My horse, Troy, and Peggy's horse, saddled and with bridles tied loosely round their necks, will go with the spare horses and pack mules.

This is the start of our bullock muster. We have booked 700 head at the Wyndham meatworks for a date in early August. I hope the bullocks turn up on time.

Rod and his head stockman each have four or five seasoned horses and two colts for the muster. They are going into rough country, putting in long days of mustering for about two to three weeks. The stockboys have three seasoned horses and one colt apiece. They do not like riding their colts. Some of them are skittish and hard-mouthed, depending on who broke them in. They are the cause of lost time and lost cattle on the musters, but they must be ridden.

We muster the bottom end or the south-east end of the run first. I watch as Rod and the boys quietly gather up the coachers and any calves, settle them down, and, leaving Bunchemup with them, they ride off to start the muster. Rod has stopped the white stockmen from yelling at the cattle. Paddy says, "Only white yahoo yell at cattle, not good black stockmen." How right he is. Rod does not like using the whip on fresh cattle either. He says horsemanship must do the work.

Cattle start running into the coachers. The mob is getting too big for one man to hold on his own. Rod cuts out Troy and Peggy's horse and leads them over to the jeep. Peggy and I are to help Bunchemup. Little Hand, who is with the spare horses, has to box them up with the cattle and help too.

I will never know how I make it through this day. Even with four of us trying to hold them, we still lose some. The boys bring the cattle right up to the coachers before riding off again. Some of the fresh cattle rush clean through the coachers and out the other side. I am terrified of the bulls. To see a great horned bull rushing towards me, not sure if I should let him go or try to block him, petrifies me. The tips of their horns are poisonous. What aged bulls we do hold are cut out later and shot. There is no money in bull meat at this time.

I decide it will be best for me to stay with the coachers rather than go after anything that breaks out. Not so with Peggy. I see her flat out after a beast, her mouth open, her dress flapping round her waist. Thank goodness she is wearing a pair of Big Johnnie's trousers. I don't know how she keeps her bare feet in the stirrup irons. I will have to get her some boots.

The mob is getting bigger and harder to hold. I want the muster to stop. I've had enough. Will it never end? Bunchemup stays close to me when he can, but that does not help much. I certainly do not want to do this again. I am covered in dust, my eyes are watering, I can't see properly and I am aching all over. I would like to ride away now but I know I cannot do that.

At last Rod and the boys ride up and, thank goodness, it is over for me. Rod decides we will have dinner here. It will give the cattle time to settle down. Bother the cattle! He says, "You did a good job. I'm proud of you. Do you want to bring the jeep up?"

"No! I don't want to bring the jeep up. I can't sit down, and I can't walk. I will have to eat my dinner standing up." He laughs and sends a boy to drive the jeep up to the camp. The boys let their tired horses go and wait to catch fresh ones after they have been cut out from the cattle.

Dinner over, stockboys and cattle move off. Peggy and I join Maggie and our two little darlings in the jeep and follow. The muster goes on all afternoon. Safe and comfortable in the jeep, I am enjoying myself again. The country is so beautiful. Great rugged ranges to the right and to the left as I follow the cattle down the valleys. Creeks, gullies, and break-aways, huge shady trees and ant beds higher than a man.

There are places where I cannot cross. Rod rides back, gives his horse to Peggy and gets me over the bad spots. I know Peggy would like to be with the musterers. Perhaps tomorrow. Maggie tells me she has the "cold sick". She does not look well. Thinking her head might be causing her trouble I ask if she has "head ache". She says, "No! Only cold sick." This is bad. I give her an aspirin and tell her we will take her back to the station tonight.

We get to night camp about five o'clock. Rod and the boys stay with the cattle, letting them feed about on a small plain until they settle down. Then, leaving two boys with them, he and the others ride into where we are making camp on the bank of a small creek with clear, running water.

The boys unsaddle their horses and hobble them out. All horses are hobbled for the night, to prevent them straying too far. Two night horses are caught, saddled and tied up close to the camp in case the cattle rush. Peggy has the fire going and the billies on. She is very capable but I must help her as Maggie is too ill. Rod sets the watch, two men on a one-hour watch. Leaving his head stockman in charge, we make Maggie comfortable in the jeep and, with Meldie and Tommy, head back to the station. Arriving about midnight, we do not stay long. I leave some aspirin with Maggie, telling her to take one every tucker time. She understands. Taking Rosie with us, we return to the camp. I have been able to doze in the jeep but Rod has had no sleep. He calls the camp at four o'clock and a new day begins.

Leaving Rosie asleep in the jeep with the children, I go to help Peggy with breakfast. She has the billies on and is cutting bread and meat for the blacks. I set out bread and meat for the whites and half-castes then prepare arrowroot biscuits softened and mashed with warm milk for the children. Two boys have brought the horses up, some still in hobbles, which annoys Rod. The boys hurriedly finish breakfast and, with their bridles, move in to catch their horses. They are to ride their colts this morning. There is a lot of commotion, or so it seems to me as I sit in the jeep with Meldie and Tommy and watch. The children are so excited. They are loving all this. As the boys catch their horses, they lead them out and saddle up. Some of the colts are hard to catch. They dodge and weave and it sometimes takes two or three boys to block them up before they are caught.

Some of the boys are with Rod, packing the mules. This is quite an art. Packs have to be well balanced. Bags of flour, sugar, heavy water canteens and beef boxes have to be evenly placed on the mules' backs. Some mules are rogues. Tuckerbox, Blue Tail and Spare Mule are hard to catch and hard to pack. Cubba Duck, a mule Rod brought from *Coolibah*, in the Northern Territory, stands quietly by.

It is hard to keep our mule numbers up. Mules do not breed and people are reluctant to sell any they have. Strong mules are valued. Good to pack and good for broncoing. We have bronco horses as well as bronco mules. Bronco horses and bronco mules are strong animals, used to pull cattle up to a bronco panel to be branded and so on.

At last, swags are rolled, mules packed and boys mounted; we are ready to move. Peggy goes with the musterers. Rosie in the cage with the children, I slowly follow. Hour after exciting hour, I watch the muster, marvelling at the primitive beauty of this land. About ten o'clock, Rod rides back to check that all is well with us. He says, "There's a creek about a mile up, it's in flood. Don't follow the cattle across, it's too deep. Go about fifty yards up the creek and cross there." No time to tell me more. No time to tell him I do not know how far fifty yards is. He is gone. I'll just have to follow the creek up and hope to find a good crossing.

Slush and mud — and getting worse. I'm going to bog. I've either gone the wrong way or not far enough but I will bog if I go any further. The jeep spins and comes close to slipping into the creek as I try to turn back. I'm going to cross where the cattle did, but I've got to get there first. Rosie is starting to whimper. Not a sound from the children but, looking back, I see their frightened little faces. Oh! Dear God get me out of this! All I can do is push the accelerator flat to the boards and keep a strong grip on the steering wheel. God will have to do the rest.

At last we are out on higher, drier ground and heading back the way we came. I do not like the look of the place where the cattle crossed. I'll be able to get down this bank but the opposite bank is steep and slippery, made worse by the cattle. Telling Rosie to hold the children, I move into the creek. As soon as we hit the water I know I have made a terrible mistake.

The jeep starts to float and Rosie starts to blubber, "We bin finis Yumman, we bin finis."

"Shut up Rosie!"

"Ahhh! Yumman, we bin finis."

"Will you shut up, Rosie?"

There is nothing I can do but pray. The water is lapping our feet, but does not get any deeper and we are facing the opposite bank, which is a small help. I don't know how far we float before we hit a rocky bar and I follow it across. Rosie is still blubbering.

"Shut up, Rosie, or I'll whack you!"

We are out at last. Thank you, God! Meldie and Tommy climb into the front and I hold them close.

I dry out the engine as best I can, say another prayer and turn the key. The engine kicks over and we are on our way. I will never try to cross a flooded creek again. I have completely lost the mob and will have to depend on Rosie to head me in the right direction. She does so, and soon I see dust and hear the cattle.

We pass Barney Springs and on to Galway Valley, our night camp. We will be here for several days. Good permanent running water and a lot of cattle. This was to become my favourite camp. We have a big mob of cattle in hand. Wild and restless, they are hard to hold. There is an old yard here, built years ago by Barney O'Leary. White ant eaten, the posts lie on the ground like empty shells; wire, twisted and rusted, lying round. Rod arranges with his head stockman to stay with the cattle, sending two boys in to hobble the horses; he and I then leave with Meldie and Tommy for the station, to pick up shovels, picks, crowbars and wire to repair the yard.

It is a wild, fast drive. Thank goodness Meldie and Tommy sleep most of the way. All is well at the station — Maggie much improved and no one else sick. While Rod gathers what he wants, I pack several packets of aspirin, eye drops, and bandages from the medical chest. I also take extra aspaxadrene for Rod. We get back to the camp about 2.30 a.m. The cattle are still restless but the boys are alert and on watch. Peggy has heard us coming and has made fresh tea. The billies are always on in the stock camp, tea sometimes stewing close to the fire, but always welcome by the stockmen. We off-load the fencing gear and I settle down with the children. Rod goes out to the cattle.

I would like to sleep longer this morning, but I can hear Peggy rattling billies and trying to get Rosie up to help her with breakfast. Rosie is whingeing, she has "biggest 'ead ache," her usual complaint, the rogue. It is still dark but the fire has been built up and is burning brightly. I wash in the clear stream and go to help Peggy. The early morning is quite chilly.

The boys gradually drift in for breakfast. All look so tired, but are cheerful and proud that they held the cattle all night. Rod is pleased, but they have a hard day ahead. Breakfast over, horses caught and saddled, they ride out to the cattle. Rod cuts out aged bulls. These will be shot later.

69

Meatworks bullocks, cows, mickies and calves are cut out and held until the bullocks can be taken into the station. Cleanskin cows, calves and mickies will be branded in the yard later.

The bulls are driven away and shot. They will later be burnt. With three boys tailing, the rest ride back to the camp to work on the yard. Posts and rails are cut and post holes dug. I watch as crowbar and picks strike rock and sparks fly. Shirts off, the boys labour all day, breaking only for smoko and dinner. Some are boring holes in the posts with a brace and bit. It is hard work but the yard must be finished in time to yard the cattle this afternoon. I take Meldie and Tommy down to the stream to let them paddle and splash in the clear water.

Frank Bridge had told me about the two old men who had blocks here, Barney O'Leary and Sandy McAndoo, a wild Irishman and a fiery Scotsman. Sandy built his little mud hut on a small rise; Barney camped closer to the stream. They hated each other. With less than two miles separating them, they hurled insults across the tree tops. Far away from their own countries, they lived their lonely, hard lives. The blacks told me there are still signs of where they lived. I would like to see their old places, but now is not the time.

The yard is finished, a strong bronco panel inside, and the boys are having a blow before yarding up. This is a lovely spot, well timbered, with unlimited water coming from a spring. The cattle are tailed out on a plain, the yard closer to the stream. They must be watered before they are yarded. Too far away to see them being watered, I sit with the children and watch the yarding, Rosie close by.

It takes all the skill and horsemanship of the stockmen to get the cattle into the yard, about 300–400 head. Rod cuts them into smaller mobs and brings them up. They have never been yarded before. They keep breaking and will not follow Paddy, who is riding in the lead, into the yard. Without any yards, all our branding has been done ' open broncoing'.

The boys work hard, and, with the exception of three cows, everything is yarded. They do not worry about the cows. With their calves in the yard, they will hang round. Tomorrow, the bullocks will be let out and tailed, cleanskin cows and calves will be branded and let go. Even with the cattle in the yard, Rod puts the boys on watch. He tells me this is a bad place for rushes.

Bobby and Pompy have the "cold sick". This is bad. Rod can ill afford to have any of his stockmen sick. I give them aspirin and tell them to stay in their swags and not to get up for work tomorrow. Rod is upset but knows how badly this sickness affects them. Branding tomorrow, he can manage without them, but will be hard pressed for the musters he plans around here in the next few days.

The cattle move restlessly round the yard all night. Nobody sleeps well. Anything can cause a rush, but the cattle are less likely to go when awake and moving about. It is when they are quiet, lying down or sleeping, that they are more likely to rush. Then they will take the yard and all before them. The boys sing on watch and hope that is the only sound the cattle hear.

Don, a white stockman, comes to me with a bad eye. Galloping yesterday, a branch hit him in the face. His eye is bloodshot, bruised and swollen. I put drops in and tell him to keep out of the branding yard. The dust will make it worse. I know he is not listening to me. He goes with the others to let the cattle out and works in the yard while they are branding.

Rod, riding Cubba Duck, lassoes and drags calves, cleanskin cows, and mickies up to the panel, using a greenhide rope — one of several he made over the wet. The ⊢ Q2 brands are in the fire that has burnt down to red-hot coals.

Calves are branded and earmarked. Any cleanskin cows are also branded and earmarked and, in some cases, dehorned. Mickies are branded, earmarked, dehorned and most of them are cut. Little dark-red, nobby mickies are not cut; they are kept for breeding, and so we lay the foundation for our herd. All earmarks (pieces) cut from the cattle are put in a bag and given to me to count. Two marks or pieces from each beast. This keeps a record of our brandings. The blacks carefully put the testicles, cut from the mickies, in a bag, to be cooked tonight. They consider them a rare delicacy.

Don's eye is worse. More eye drops — he will have to be careful. Bobby and Pompy are no worse but they are very sick. The boys will have a day off tomorrow and Rod will kill. It will be good to have fresh meat again. We have been living on corned beef and damper for days. Even the vegetables are withered and dry; only the pumpkins and onions seem fresh. The corned beef has to be washed and soaked for hours before it is cooked. It is so tough and stringy.

A day off and fresh meat puts new life into the boys. Peggy makes soup for Bobby, Pompy and Don. They will have to stay in the camp tomorrow while the rest muster. Rod is fidgety; I know he wants to tell me

71

something, but I have no idea what is bothering him. At last he says, "I'll need you on the muster tomorrow".

Oh! Good grief! I still clearly remember my last great effort. Being with the coachers was bad enough but mustering would be completely impossible for me.

"I can't do it, Rod."

"Yes, you can. You can ride Jock or Montie."

"What? Those are your horses. They're too fast for me; besides, they might buck. If I go, I'll ride Troy."

"No! Troy is too slow; he won't be able to keep up. Ride Montie. I broke him in, he is well trained, he won't buck, but he is fast."

"Oh dear! Are you sure you need me?"

"Yes! With three boys off, I will be very shorthanded. I could do with Peggy too but she will have to stay in the camp to look after the sick boys. Rosie won't, but Rosie will take good care of the children."

"Rod, I'm frightened."

"Don't be frightened. You can ride, and you will be close to me all the time."

Close to *you* all the time, I think, the fastest man in the camp — I'll be lucky if I see your dust!

I get up when I hear Rod come off watch and call the camp. Hustle and bustle; horses brought up, caught and saddled. Rod catches Jock and Montie, saddles them and ties them close to the jeep. How docile they look. Breakfast over, I check to see how Don's eye is. There might be a chance he can ride and I will not have to go with the musterers. His eye is much worse; it is bunged up. He can't see out of it at all. I will just have to go.

No need to tell Peggy what to do, but I must tell Rosie she is not to let the children out of her sight at any time. I know she will keep them safe. Rod is waiting for me near the horses. All the boys are mounted. Montie is a big horse, 16 hands. It is all I can do to get my foot in the stirrup iron. No longer docile, Montie prances round like a corn-fed racehorse. Even with Rod holding the rein close to the bit he still prances and I hop with him, trying to get up enough spring to land me in the saddle. Rod has tied a knot in the reins, thank goodness, so I cannot drop and lose them. At last I am in the saddle and Rod adjusts the stirrup irons to suit my length. He mounts Jock and we move to let the cattle out of the yard. They will be tailed out while we muster. Two boys tailing.

Rod and I ride in the lead, white and half-caste stockmen behind us, then the blacks. We round up cows and calves for coachers and, leaving two boys there, we ride off in twos and threes to muster. I go with Rod and Hilton. So far so good. I have a tight rein on Montie but Rod says to give him his head. This suits Montie but makes me very nervous.

We ride at a quick walk for about five minutes, then, without warning, Rod and Hilton are off and Montie goes with them! The sudden move from a quick walk to flat out gallop nearly snaps my head off my shoulders and almost unseats me. I wasn't prepared, but now I understand why I need a fast horse. Montie keeps up with Rod and Hilton — not because of any help from me. I hold the reins in one hand and cling desperately to the pommel of the saddle with the other. I haven't seen anything to cause this sudden move, but Rod and Hilton have seen cattle and want to get downwind of them before the cattle smell them.

Rod and Hilton split up, Hilton riding far out to the left. Rod signals to me to follow him to the right. By sheer good luck, Montie follows Rod. I am not enjoying this. I am so frightened. Galloping behind him, I see a bull dart out from behind an ant bed in front of Rod's horse. Jock stumbles and goes down, throwing Rod over his head. Rod lays still and the bull turns on him. I don't know what to do. I'm yelling, "Shoo, shoo bull. Get away, get away," but the bull continues to pummel Rod on the ground. I wonder if I should try to force Montie closer — but even if I can, I do not know what to do. I start to pray, but I am still yelling at the bull.

I hear a galloping horse and, thank goodness, Hilton is here. He has seen the accident and galloped over. He jumps from his horse and grabs the bull by the tail, trying to throw him — but the tail slips through his hands and the bull turns on him. Hilton runs for the nearest tree and climbs. Rod tries to get up but the bull is too quick; he charges Rod again.

Rod calls for me to back Montie onto the bull. I almost scream, "I can't. I can't," — but Rod could be killed. Terrified, I back Montie up and, as soon as he is close to the bull, he lashes out with both hind hooves. They land with a thud on the bull. Montie keeps this up until Rod is clear and Hilton is back to grab the bull by the tail again. He could not throw him but the bull has had enough; it trots away. Rod and Hilton catch their horses and mount. Rod is gravel-rashed and shaken but not hurt. He had trained Montie to back onto bulls and kick out at them.

I wonder at all the frights I have had, if I will ever be afraid again. What a muster! No time for a dinner break; no time to change horses. We muster all day. Losing some, but holding most. Cows, calves, bulls and wild little mickies. I do what I do, always close to Rod. Montie, true to Rod's prediction, keeps up. I give him his head and the intelligent old horse does the rest. So afraid at times, I just close my eyes, pray, and hang on. As long as I live I will remember this day. Into breakaways, up and over ridges and ranges, across creeks, over rough, stony plains and down the valleys — where the cattle go, we follow. Sometimes I catch a quick glimpse of the other musterers and the coachers as we bring cattle in.

I want to pull out, but that is impossible. Cattle everywhere and where there are cattle, we go. I desperately want the muster to stop, but I am part of it and will have to stay until the end. I trust my horse and keep Rod in sight. I simply fill a gap, trying to block cattle from getting away, or follow Rod as he guides them into the coachers.

We must have over 300 head now. At three o'clock, Rod calls it a day. What we lost will be picked up another day. I am so tired. Rod puts me on the tail with Barney and Bunchemup. With Paddy in the lead, Rod rides on the 'live' wing, the direction the cattle are most likely to break, with Big Johnnie on the opposite wing, Bruce, Tiptoe, Tubby, and Half-caste Billy behind him down to the tail. Jim Roberts (a good white stockman), Hilton, John Curtain, and Phil Smith behind Rod, we move the cattle towards the camp. I had hoped to relax now but it is not to be. Cows and calves move slowly, bellowing and mooing — they get separated; mickies trying to break out, and bulls, asserting their masculine dominance over cows, keep us busy. Montie bites and rears at the bulls. We push on slowly, finally coming to the tailed cattle on the plain, close to the camp.

I ride into the camp with Rod. Four boys stay with the cattle, the rest catch fresh horses for themselves and for the tailers. I get off Montie and give the reins to Rod. Meldie and Tommy are so pleased to see us again. I think I am finished for the day, but when I see Rod catch and saddle Troy, I know otherwise. He wants me to help water the cattle. I can ride Troy. I want to object but I don't. I am so stiff and sore. The insides of my legs, from the knees to the ankles, are red raw. Blisters from the stirrup leathers have broken and rubbed raw; some stick to my jodhpurs. I will have trouble getting on Troy. Rod knows I am in pain. I see concern in his eyes. He has enough to worry about; I will not add to it.

I learn that nothing is easy when working stock. We move the cattle closer to the water and Rod cuts off about 100 head. With some boys, he takes them to the creek. I stay with the main mob — Paddy, Bunchemup and Tubby with me. How safe I feel with these old blacks now. Pushing the watered cattle across the creek, Rod leaves four boys with them, then he and the rest come back for another cut.

The cattle are stirred up no end. Some want to follow the mob on the way to water, others seeing a chance to break out and run for the bush, calves separated and looking for their mothers, have all got to be held. I seem to be everywhere at once and I don't know if I am doing any good.

After several cuts, we follow the last small mob to the water. It is nearly dark, and they still have to be yarded. I find Rod and tell him I will go back to the camp; I will only be in the way now. He says, "No, I will have to cut them again to yard, and I will need you." Now I am afraid again. So much dust, I can't see. Something breaks out close to me and I go after it. Clear of the dust, I see it is a half-grown calf. It dodges and weaves and I try to stay with it, right on its tail. I surely can handle a calf. It turns and ducks in front of Troy. Troy falls to his knees and I am almost thrown. No more of this for me. I hope Rod has not seen.

Paddy comes over to ask if I am all right, and to ride with me back to the yard. He indicates I am to stay well back and not to go after anything that breaks out. I have learnt my lesson. Dust swirls over everything. I wonder how anyone can see. I wish I did not have to do this.

Everything ends, just as this day finally does. Cattle yarded, night horses caught and tied up, the watch organised, we settle down for the night. My legs are in a bad way. Rod gets warm water, tosses a handful of coarse salt in and bathes my legs. I scream with pain as the salt water goes on the raw blisters. Rod says I will frighten the cattle; I must try to suffer the pain. "An old bushman's cure," he says. "It will take the soreness away."

"I am not tough enough for this life, Rod. You expect too much of me."

"I never want you to grow tough and hard," he replies. "I only ask what I think you are capable of, and only when I need you. I would spare you this if I could."

As we lie in the swag, we talk. I wish there was an easier way for us. At least I am healthy. Rod is cursed with asthma; even now he finds it hard to breathe.

He says, "I saw you go after a calf when we were yarding up. Calves are the hardest things to wheel. They can be dangerous. Smaller than a grown beast, they will dodge in front of a horse and bring him down as that calf did to Troy. Also, you do not ride up his tail. Go wide of a beast when trying to wheel him. Leave the breakouts to the boys."

Surprised, I say, "I had no idea you even knew where I was at that time."

"I know where you are at all times," he says. "And if I am not with you, the boys will keep an eye on you. Trust them, they will not let you come to any harm. I sent Paddy out to you this afternoon."

We spend five days at Galway Valley, later to be known as New Lansdowne, branding and mustering. Don's eye is no better, in fact I think it is worse. Bobby and Pompy seem to be over the worst of the "cold sick" but they are weak and dopey, not fit for work yet. We pack up and head back to the station. Bobby and Pompy will ride in the jeep with me, Rosie and the children. Peggy will go with the cattle. Rod wants Don to go in the jeep also but, disappointed that he has missed the musters, he wants to ride with the men.

If I could find my way back to the station I would leave now, but, without roads or tracks, I would be lost in no time. I have no alternative but to follow the cattle. Always the cattle.

* * *

Oh! the joy of being back at the station! The native boys head for their camp. Some of them give their dirty clothes to their lubras to wash, others, the single ones, will throw them away rather than wash them.

The bullocks have to be tailed out and watched day and night. We will be here for at least a week. Fresh horses have to be mustered and shod, stock camp gear checked and more clothes issued to the blacks. They are very hard on boots. To ease the pressure on their feet, blacks will cut long slits in their boots, to allow their toes more room. They are flat out making one pair of boots last a muster. They also cut up their bridle reins to make belts and hat bands. Rod is forever making bridle reins to keep up with them.

I call Fred Ryle, on the medical session, to arrange to speak to the doctor about Don's eye. The doctor says it is serious; he must get to a hospital as soon as possible. Halls Creek is our closest hospital, more than 180 miles (290 km) away, over rough, man-made station roads. Rod sends Phil Smith to drive Don in. Phil, possibly in his early thirties, is a good worker. Stock work is not his trade, but he is willing to learn. We suspect he has a drinking problem and that Smith is not his name. He is the only one who can drive, other than Rod and me. He should be able to make the trip into Halls Creek and back to *Lansdowne* in three days. Five days later, Phil has not returned. The A.I.M. sisters call us from the hospital to say Phil has been on a drinking bender, but they have sobered him up and started him back to *Lansdowne*. They say the jeep has not been damaged. Thank goodness for that.

Phil arrives back a total wreck. He also has a dozen bottles of cheap wine we do not know about. He continues to drink, and like a lot of friendly drunks, insists on sharing the wine with the blacks. We pay Phil off and let him go. Seven days later, the camp is ready to go out again, two men short. Don had to go to Perth for treatment. He lost the sight in his eye and did not return to the Kimberleys.

* * *

Mustering the top, or the north-east end of our run seems easier than the bottom end, but it really isn't. The country is still rough and hard on horses. Everyone has fresh horses except me. I have Montie and Troy. That suits me. I do not want to ride strange horses. Peggy and Maggie, now over her "cold sick", will go with me and the children.

We get our numbers and count them over to Drover Wilson — 700 head. Rod asks me to help with the count. I watch as the boys hold the cattle in a mob before running them through a tunnel of riders. Rod gives me his whip and tells me to tie a knot in it at the count of every hundred. I do everything wrong. Riding Troy, I should let him dodge ant beds and fallen logs and just keep my eyes on the cattle. Instead, trying to steer him clear, I miss almost everything as they rush through. I drop the whip and am too afraid to get off to get it. One of the boys picks it up for me.

Knots in the whip did not work for me. My father wrote, suggesting I try transferring small stones from one pocket to another. That was no good either. I dropped more stones than I got in my pocket.

It was not until my third bullock count that I was able to cope. With a hole punched in a small notebook and tied with string to a pencil and then to my wrist, I was able to make the stroke of one for 100 head of cattle without dropping anything. I gave Troy free rein and he dodged and stepped over logs.

With my whole attention on the cattle, I became quite accurate at counting. Rod was free to concentrate on keeping the cattle running, or to check that the boys on the tail did not push them too hard.

I used my notebook and pencil and Bob Skeen used broken matches. Our counts were always spot on. Bob Skeen, of mixed blood, was a good and dependable stockman, and a faithful friend. He sometimes called himself Bob Quilty. Sometimes the cattle came slow, one, two, three; at other times they rushed through the tunnel of men in fives and tens. Sometimes they broke out close to me, and were not above giving Troy a good bunt on the rump as they passed. Bob and I stayed with them and kept the count.

* * *

Driving to *Bedford* one afternoon with Rod and the children to pick up our mail, Red Robin (our truck) breaks down. Rod will have to walk to *Bedford* for help, a hike of approximately fifteen miles (24 km).

Taking his swag from the back of the truck, he rolls it out in the bed of a small sandy creek, then he sets about gathering pats of dry cow manure. Placing them in a ring round the swag, he gives me a box of matches and says, "As soon as it is dark, light and burn the manure until it smokes. The smoke will keep the mosquitoes away; they are bad here. It will be dark in about an hour."

I wasn't looking forward to being left alone with the two babies but we had food and water and would be far more comfortable than Rod, with a rough road ahead of him, and the night dark and hot. Kissing us good-bye, he picks up the torch and leaves.

The children play in the sand until the sun sets and twilight comes down. Time to get them into the swag and light the manure. I wasn't sure how we would handle the smell of burning manure so close to where we were going to sleep. To my surprise, the smoke has an earthy smell, not at all unpleasant. After feeding the children and having something to eat myself, we settle into the swag.

The children sleep. I lie awake, listening to the night sounds and looking at the stars. The evening star, the saucepan, the seven sisters, the glorious Southern Cross — the Kimberley sky is a mass of brilliant, twinkling light. Cattle moving close to us, owls hooting, and dingoes howling in packs far off. I have nothing to fear, but I am worried about Rod.

About one o'clock Tommy wakes, wanting a drink. I move outside the ring of manure to get the water. Mosquitoes come from everywhere. I quickly move back. I sleep and wake at first light, the old bushman's piccaninny dawn. No sound of a truck coming. The children wake and play in the sand until they become bored and want to move further off.

I am afraid of snakes. The king brown, vicious and deadly poisonous, is everywhere. Still no sign of Rod or a vehicle. I see dingo tracks where they had prowled round our truck before they moved off down the road.

At last, the faint sound of a vehicle a long way off. We set out at a slow walk to meet it. The children skip along for a while but soon tire. I find a shady tree and we sit there to wait, the sound of the vehicle getting closer and closer. Eventually, it arrives. The children run to meet Rod. I am grateful for the flask of tea that Peg Underwood has so thoughtfully sent out.

The men work on the truck while I read our mail. An hour or so later the truck is mobile and we are on our way home.

* * *

Mary and Stan Jones have invited us to spend Christmas with them at *Gordon Downs*, a Vestey property south-east of Halls Creek. Stan is the manager, and Mary and I are good friends. It will be good for Meldie and Tommy to meet the three Jones children, Jenny, Randal and Laurence; they are about the same age. We set out early this morning, leaving Ringer Gibson to look after *Lansdowne* for the week we will be away. Overnight at *Bedford*, lunch next day at *Springvale*, then on to Halls Creek where we will spend the night — a wild, stormy night. It really is not a good idea to be travelling by vehicle at this time of the year; none of the roads are sealed.

Leaving Halls Creek on Christmas Eve, we stop at *Flora Valley* for a brief visit, arriving at *Gordon Downs* about 2.30 p.m. After spending two very happy days at *Gordon* with the Jones family, we return home. It took us two and a half days to drive from *Lansdowne* to *Gordon Downs*, but it takes us five days to get back. Wild storms, flooded rivers and creeks, getting in and out of bogs, all hold us up. The children are enjoying every minute. Running round in the rain, gathering rocks and bushes to fill the bog holes, they are so happy, but Rod and I are pleased to finally see *Lansdowne* on New Year's Day.

* * *

Mick Quilty (Rod's brother) and Rod at *Lansdowne*. Mick was on the road with a mob of bullocks for Glenroy Meatworks.

Tommy, with Johnny Ray, watering their horses at the trough.

Tommy rides his first "colt" (a carpenters trestle).

Mundy, Lucy, Peggy and Stephen, with Tommy, Johnny Ray and Meldie on horse.

81

CHAPTER SEVEN

Danger and heartache

Great sandstone Ranges
With all their Dangers.

Matthew Quilty

It is on my first muster for 1958 that I have a bad fall. I have gained confidence and am a bit cocky — too confident. Riding Montie and following Rod, I see him start to follow cattle up a small hill. He signals to me not to follow him but to go round the hill. I misread his signal, or that is what I want to believe. I am afraid if I lose sight of him I will be lost. It looks a long way round the hill and I am not sure I will meet up with him on the other side. I follow him. Montie's long legs and brute strength get me onto the top of the hill, rough and dangerous. I know I am in trouble as soon as I start down the other side. Montie, head down, is stumbling. I try to keep his head up but I know we are going to fall. I see Half-caste Billy beside me. He tries to grab my bridle rein but it is too late, Montie falls and pitches me over his head, momentum keeps him tumbling down the hill. Something hard hits me on the back; there is terrible pain. I lose consciousness.

I wake up in the camp. Rod is there holding my head, the children close and crying, everybody fussing round. It seems Montie came over the top of me and the saddle hit me on the back. I am sure my back is broken. Rod asks, "Can you move your legs? your hands? your arms?"

"Yes, everything moves, but it hurts," I reply.

"Thank God," says Rod.

I swallow some aspirin, Rod tucks me securely in the jeep and, with the children, we drive back to the station. Jim Roberts is left in charge.

Rod, waiting for a session, calls the Wyndham Base for a medical. Doctor will send the plane out to pick me up. I tell Rod I will not go to the hospital. Without an airstrip, we would have to drive to *Bedford* or *Fossil*. I am too sore and in too much pain to move; besides, I will not leave the children. I will stay in bed. The fact that I can move my head, and everything else, is reassuring. On Doctor's orders, Rod gives me an injection to kill the pain.

Those old lubras are there for me day and night. They do everything for me. I will never be able to thank them enough. The swelling goes down but the bruising stays for a long time. Six months later, I have my second miscarriage.

I am full of remorse. Guilt nags at me. I desperately want a big family, not a lonely little boy and a lonely little girl. They need brothers and sisters. I should never have been riding in my early pregnancy — the accident with Montie could have been the cause. I blame that, but I'll never really know. The doctor says there are other complications. I had not been riding when I lost the first baby. He suggests we try again as soon as possible. I blame everything — the loneliness, the harsh living, the rough life — everything. Bitter and moody, I make things miserable for Rod. Patient and loving, he bears the burden of my sorrow and my guilt, waiting for me to get over my terrible loss. I finally realise what I am doing to him when I find him, late one night, crying quietly in bed beside me. Selfishly, I had hugged my grief to myself. It was my loss, my sorrow. I never considered how he might feel. Gradually, I pick up the pieces and take control of my home again.

* * *

Good early storms and Christmas with us again. Heavy, low clouds and steady soaking rain. It rains all Christmas Eve and on into the night; rain coming from the north and north-west in a steady downpour. The little creek at the back of the station is running a banker before we go to bed.

About 4 a.m. on Christmas morning, all hell breaks loose. The creek at the back of the house is in full flood, and a creek running out of the hills to the north is also in flood and has backed up, flooding the homestead. The blacks run in panic from their camp on the bank of the creek. Gathering piccaninnies, belongings and dogs, they head for high ground in front of the house.

Rod goes with the boys to try to save what they can. I wake Meldie and send her to the high ground with Rosie. It is dark and still raining; she goes without a murmur. I know she will stay with Rosie. Not sure that Tommy will stay with the girls, I do not wake him until later. I try to put things up above the rising water but there is little I can do. It is not until the flood water is lapping the bottom of the cot that I wake Tommy and carry him out. Water rushing round my legs nearly washes me off my feet. I have no idea where Rod and the boys are. The old men, lubras and piccaninnies are with me, the stockboys all with Rod.

We lose saddles and a lot of stock gear; 44-gallon drums of petrol are washed down the Fitzroy River — we never get them back. Stores and records are lost, and our personal belongings gone. We lost so much in the fire on the Murranji Track, now our losses again are heavy in this flash flood.

We are grateful to the Flying Doctor Service, and the medical team, under the supervision of Doctor Lawson Hollman, who arranged to have stores and clothes flown out and airdropped to help make our Christmas a little less miserable. The kind people of Derby had made generous donations.

* * *

The New Year brings many changes. Meldie and Tommy must start school. The School of the Air teacher at Derby sends me the necessary books and papers to get them started. They enrol at Derby and I will teach them. We cannot afford a governess. The flood has cost us dearly. We are depending on Burns Philp and Southern Cross to stand by us. Meldie tries hard, but Tommy, who has learnt to ride, is not interested. There are many interruptions. I am called away, leaving the children on their own. The boys have Tommy's horse saddled and they wait in the creek for him. He is off like a shot at every opportunity. We are still picking up and sending our mail from *Bedford*. This is a hit and miss affair. I am not always able to get their school papers from Derby or return them on time. It is not fair to the children. Rod and I decide we will get a governess and worry about paying her later.

Theo Calwell and Gill Hepburn, aerodrome inspectors, are here to peg out a site for an airstrip. They drive around for three days with Rod, looking for a suitable area. We would like it close to the homestead but that is not possible. Finally they agree that the only place is eleven and a half miles (18.5 km) away, on the eastern side of the Leopold River. It takes weeks of hard work, clearing trees and ant beds, filling in break-aways and leveling the ground off, but at last we have two strips — a main strip and a cross strip: a mile clearance for the length and one hundred yards wide, running east and west and north and south. Big enough to take MacRobertson Miller's DC3 and later, their Twin Otter, and the Flying Doctor's 'Dove' and 'Queenair'.

With the windsock flying and a small bough-shed built at the side of the main strip, we are ready for our first landing. Rod grades and maintains both strips constantly. They are our lifeline.

When aerial mustering took over, years later, Rod had 15 strips cleared and graded at our mustering camps for fixed-wing, and later, helicopter landings.

* * *

Tommy has two bad accidents that could affect his whole life. Playing with the piccaninnies, he falls heavily on his elbow. Although there is no bone protruding, we know there is something seriously wrong. Waiting for the session, we call Fred Ryle for an emergency medical. They will send the Flying Doctor's plane from Wyndham to pick him up. I go with him but I must leave my darling daughter with Rod. She will be safe, but I hate leaving her. Rod is very upset.

Tommy is in pain but he is also very frightened. The doctor puts him through several tests. He cannot move the fingers of his right hand. The doctor says it is serious and that he must go to Perth. Rod says, "No! He must go to Brisbane." Doctor Michael Gallagher, an old Nudgee College school friend, is a leading orthopaedic surgeon there. Meldie will go with Tommy and me.

Rod packs a suitcase for me and the children and he drives, with Meldie, to Wyndham. He phones his old friend who makes all the arrangements. We are met at Brisbane and Tommy admitted to hospital. X-rays show that a small disc-like bone on his elbow has been shattered. Michael will operate, re-place the shattered bone and secure it with a screw-like pin. However, Tommy will never have complete and free movement of his arm again. Always bent, he will never be able to straighten it. The operation is a success and we are free to go home. I ask Michael if it will interfere with Tommy's riding. "Yes," he replies, "A fall or sudden jerk could cause irreparable damage." My poor darling son.

On the way home, I stop off at Townsville to take Tommy to an old friend, Dr Kjelberg, who has "Beachview", a clinic at Millaa Millaa. Dr Kjelberg says, "He is young; encourage him to use his arm naturally, and let nature take its course." Meldie fusses over Tommy as we head for home.

Tommy's arm is healing well; there is no pain, and, although at first we think we are imagining it because we want it so, his arm is gradually moving more freely. By June, he has full use of his arm. Only the long scar from the operation stands out. He wants to ride but Rod is firm — no riding yet. He will have to have the pin removed first.

A governess, Roseanna, is teaching the children. I want to include Peggy's son, Johnny Ray, but Roseanna is not capable of handling all three. It is all I can do to keep her on the job. She reads a lot. Typing up the mail about two o'clock one afternoon early in September, I am surprised to hear Alphonse, a young half-caste boy, call me. He sounds frightened. I go out to see him holding Tommy in his arms. Tommy is unconscious. Oh! Dear God! What has happened? Tommy should have been in class with Roseanna.

Alphonse carries him in and gently lays him on the bed. Tommy is wearing spurs, so I know it has to be a riding accident. While Alphonse removes the spurs, I try to feel for broken bones. I check his right arm. "What happened, Alphonse, was Tommy riding?" Almost afraid to speak, Alphonse stammers, "Bompy (Tommy) bin ride dat pig mule. I say No! but Bompy catch 'im, put bridle on and tell me put saddle on quick smart. I put Bompy in saddle and 'e ride out of yard. Mule strong pugger. Bompy spur 'im and 'e go quick smart straight for rocks then 'e stop, rear up, go over back. Bompy fall on 'is 'ead. Not my fault, Missus, not my fault."

"It's all right, Alphonse. You can go." I feel round Tommy's head and find a huge bump behind his left ear, close to the crown of his head. He is still unconscious. I wet a towel and put it on the bump. Not for the first time do I wish I knew more about nursing. Calling Meldie to stay with Tommy, I wait for the session and call on the Traeger radio. Fred Ryle answers and gets the doctor. Doctor says to keep him quiet and in bed — the bump will go down, but he will have a headache when he regains consciousness.

Rod is out in the stock camp. Tommy, half conscious, half delirious, drifts in and out of sleep as night comes on. I am worried and afraid, much more so than when he broke his arm. During the night, he vomits and I think he now has a stomach upset. On the early morning session, I report Tommy's condition is unchanged, no better, no worse. As an afterthought, I mention he vomited several times during the night. Without hesitating, Doctor says he will send the medical plane out straight away. I wonder why there is such urgency now. I send Alphonse out to find Rod, then I pack a few things for Tommy and me. I will go with him but again it means leaving my darling daughter. Rod arrives before the plane does. I explain what has happened and that Tommy had vomited during the night. Rod says the vomiting is a sure sign of concussion. Oh! Dear God! How little I know.

We do not stay long in Wyndham. Arrangements are made for me to take him to Perth. We are met there and Tommy admitted to hospital. Doctor shows me the X-rays. A great crack down the back of his head. We are three weeks in Perth before I can take him home. For the next four months, Tommy must not run or do anything that will jar his head, and it is possible he will have frequent headaches. As my old friend Dr Kjelberg said, "He is young, let nature take its course."

Roseanna, the governess, was reading when she should have had the children in class. Immediately on my return from Perth, I pack her up and send her home.

Tommy is ready for the rough life long before the time is up, but Rod insists he stick rigidly to the four months recuperation period.

* * *

A nurse from the Derby hospital is on the mail plane today. She will give Meldie and Tommy a tetanus injection. I do not like injections but it will be good for them to have this one. I explain to them they will feel a small prick as the needle goes in; it will be quick, with a little pain but the pain will not last. Meldie listens and nods her little head; Tommy is not interested.

Margaret Doman is on the plane on her way to the family property, *Billiluna*. She stands by as the nurse sets up and gives Meldie the injection. Meldie screws up her eyes and a tear rolls down her little cheek but she makes no sound. Tommy next. He is not going to take it as placidly as Meldie. I hope the nurse will get it over quickly. The needle goes in, Tommy turns and bolts down the airstrip with the needle in his arm. Quick as a flash, Margaret is after him. She is fast and gains on him. At full speed, she catches up, snatches him up and tucks him under her arm as she heads back to the plane. Tommy, yelling blue murder, has the needle still dangling from his arm. The nurse takes over. Meldie, now concerned for Tommy, starts to cry. Margaret has barely raised a puff. She holds Tommy as the nurse does what has to be done. I cannot look. At last it is over. Nurse packs her medical kit and she and Margaret board the plane. The pilot checks that I have the *Lansdowne* mail bag and all freight, climbs into the cockpit and they take off, heading for *Tableland*, over the King Leopold Range.

* * *

88

For days we have been hearing about the eclipse of the moon. Tonight we will see it. I have explained to Meldie and Tommy and I've tried to explain to the blacks but they do not understand. Standing on the lawn, we watch as the dark shadow moves over the moon. Suddenly the quiet night is shattered by wailing and cries of fear, and dogs howling. The blacks rush up and gather round me. They are terrified as darkness closes in. I gather Meldie and Tommy and the little piccaninnies close to me. The piccaninnies are trembling with fear. The old ones wail, "Debbil-debbil, debbil-debbil, Yumman." (Evil spirits — the devil.)

I look with pity on these child-like people; the lubras who protected and cared for me in those early years. They taught me not to be afraid of the bush, how to find water and bush tucker, so that, if I were lost, I would survive. They nursed me through the loss of my babies when I might have died. They were the superior ones, the strong ones then; now, petrified with fear, they look to me. There are times when I feel so inadequate, so helpless. Gradually, the dark shadow moves across and the bright moon shines out. The blacks are not ashamed of their fear, but it is over. They gather their children to them and return to their camp.

* * *

All untrained, the governesses are not a success. One girl in particular, Gillian, is a hopeless failure. I will have to get rid of her fast. But how? One day, on the Flying Doctor session, I hear Kath Foster, at *Mabel Downs*, asking round for a governess. I immediately offer to send Gillian to her. Kath kept Gillian a week, then sacked her.

After three untrained girls, we decide it is not going to work. I go back to teaching. To keep Tommy's interest, I arrange for Peggy to send Johnny Ray along to join him and Meldie. He is their favourite playmate. We struggle through the year, but they are not learning much. Johnny Ray sometimes gets thumped and pushed off the form. There are long breaks when we are out in the stock camp — no school at all. Meldie, Tommy and Johnny Ray stay in the camp with Maggie, while Peggy and I are with the musterers. Meldie shows no interest in horses at this time, preferring to fuss round the campfire. Later, she learns to ride the hard way. There are no quiet horses. She rides what Rod considers are quieter horses than others. My father always said, "Make a horse stand while you mount." None of these horses stand. As soon as your foot is in the stirrup iron, they are off. I cannot count the times I land on my horse's rump before I bounce into the saddle.

May, and I know I am pregnant again. I am so happy. I keep in contact with my Wyndham doctor, as close as our limited and distant

89

communications allow. Fred Ryle says, "Go carefully, go carefully." Dear, kind Fred. I keep out of the stock camp, just potter round, type the mail, keep the books up-to-date, teach and play with the children, nothing strenuous. The girls come to me for orders and they do the work.

A good, healthy diet, I do everything right, but there are times when I do not feel well, days spent in bed; are these signs I might lose the baby? I go for short walks with the children, always two or three old lubras with me. They do not let me walk far. I am worried. I should be feeling better. Rod wants me to go back to Queensland. Fred Ryle and my doctor want me to go to the Wyndham hospital. I don't want to do either. I am not that sick; besides, I am afraid to travel. I wish I could speak to my mother. The old lubras are always close. I need to get away from the station.

Rod asks if I am well enough to tail bullocks at the bore. I would love to. I check with my doctor. "Yes, it might be good for you. No hard riding. Nothing more than a gentle canter, and not for long."

At least we have a bullock paddock now — with a turkey nest and trough, water pumped from a bore, equipped with an engine and windmill supplied by Southern Cross Ltd. Good, shallow water in a tea-tree area. Roy and Lou Norton, with their little son, Kevin, came out from Halls Creek to put the paddock up. Rod had known Lou's family when her parents were on *Savannah*, not far from his old home, *Euroka Springs*, in the Julia Creek district. Rod and the boys built the turkey nest, and Tom Webb put the bore down.

Tailing our meatworks bullocks with Tommy and Johnny Ray, Rod says, "Don't let them lie down. Keep them feeding round, and bring them in to water about 11 o'clock." I ride round and through those bullocks with the two little boys; pushing our horses onto any that are lying down, to get them on to their feet.

We are paid on a weight basis over the scales at Wyndham. We have to try to keep the condition on them. Bullocks start to lose weight from the time they are mustered. Tailing is slow and easy. Getting them into water certainly is not.

We have to cross a dry creek to get them to the trough. I hate and dread the creek crossings. Cattle will scatter and go in all directions. Some go up or down the creek bed, others will go after they come up the opposite bank. It is so hard for us to keep them together and headed for the trough. Tommy and Johnny Ray, reins tied in a knot, their little feet barely touching the stirrup clogs, going like the wind to bring back whatever might have broken out. I put Johnny Ray on the tail and Tommy in the lead, while I try to control the wings. We need help. Rod will have to give me another man. I am worried that Tommy or Johnny Ray could have an accident.

We get the cattle onto the trough and hold them there until Rod and the boys arrive with the morning muster. The bullocks are tailed out again, the cattle from the muster held on an open plain. They will be cut out this afternoon. I go in for dinner with Rod. Tommy and Johnny Ray follow with the boys. Two happy little stockmen.

Dinner over, fresh horses caught, we go out to the cattle. Rod riding Toddler, his smart cutting-out horse. I ride Angel, a quiet but stubborn little grey mule that Rod has broken in. Angel and I get on reasonably well. I am to keep tally, or count, as the bullocks are cut out and run over to the coachers. Rod has shown me how he wants them marked down for the count, the tally system of four vertical strokes with a diagonal slash that represents five head.

I find a shady tree close to the face of the camp, the way the cattle will run towards the coachers when cut out, and wait. Rod rides in among the cattle, finds a bullock and brings him out. A rider takes him from there and heads him in the direction of the coachers. I mark him down. A ring of riders try to keep the cattle together, but it is not easy, they move and the riders have to keep pushing them back. I must follow, always keeping the face of the camp in sight. Angel does not want to move. I kick and click but she is stubborn. I break a small switch off the tree and she moves.

Drover Darkie Green took our bullocks to Wyndham. He made a good delivery.

* * *

I try hard to bring the children up-to-date with their school work. They have lost so much time. The School of the Air teacher is annoyed. Rod and I decide we will send them to a boarding convent at Julia Creek next year. This decision has not been taken lightly. It will be very hard for us to part with them but their education is of paramount importance. We worry, they are so young. Will they fit in with white children? They only know how to play piccaninny games, and mostly they speak the broken pidgin blackfellow way. One consolation, they will have lots of cousins about their own age at Julia Creek. My sister Dadie has several children going to the convent as day scholars, and my brother Jim's children are boarders. Meldie and Tommy will board.

My health is up and down. I have good days and bad days. I am not doing any heavy work. The baby is due about January. I am trying to be careful but time drags. The stock camp is out mustering close to the station. Early one morning in November, I know I have lost our baby. Seven months and I have lost our third child. My mother used to say seven was her lucky number. Two of my pregnancies terminated at seven months and one at four months. In four years I have lost three babies. I am devastated. Why can't I have the children I want? Why?

Zachady leaves to walk to the camp to find Rod. Peggy and the old lubras know what has to be done. Gently and sorrowfully, they clean me up, change the sheets and settle me back in bed. Rosie takes the children off somewhere. Quietly, the older ones leave; only Dolly stays with me. Peggy makes tea and toast and brings it in. All day they take it in turns to be with me. Too bitter and resentful to cry for the loss of the other two babies, I cry now. Tears for three little souls. I never knew if they were sons or daughters. If the lubras knew, and I am sure they did, they never told me and I never asked. I thought, some day I will leave this place and never come back, but before I go I want to see where the lubras buried our babies.

Zachady, almost blind, finds the camp and Rod comes in. He wants to drive me to Wyndham to see the doctor, but the doctor can do nothing for me now. I cannot get better care than I am getting here. The old lubras care for their own confinements and miscarriages. They will care for me.

Mid-December, dodging storms and before the wet sets in, I drive, with Rod and the children, to Wyndham to pick up our loading. Peggy with me and two boys to help Rod. We travel in our old truck. Not a very comfortable drive, but I have an appointment with my doctor, so we kill two birds with one stone.

The doctor examines me and says I am well; the lubras have done an excellent job. However, there will be no more babies. I want to tell him he is wrong. I will get another opinion. I will not believe I cannot have any more babies. He gives me a tablet and water to wash it down. I calm down and he says it will be easier if I accept that I cannot have any more children.

I ask if there was anything I could have done, or anything I should not have done, that might have saved them. He says he cannot answer that as he had not examined me during my pregnancies. I say, "Rod will have to be told. Will you tell him?" Yes, he would.

Oh! The hidden health problems. I did not know what they were. I had not allowed for them. Something in my system has let me down. My false assumption of good health had not been good enough to save the babies I so desperately wanted.

Driving back home, I look at that lovely, cruel country. It is so demanding, but I will not let it beat me. I have a wonderful husband and two beautiful children, I will accept what I have lost and thank God for what I have.

* * *

The children at the old homestead, *Lansdowne*, 1958. From left: Clancy (on the path), Tommy, Meldie and Johnny Ray, with Barney the dog in the background.

From left: Tommy, Johnny Ray, Meldie and Clancy in front, with Peggy holding 'Pud the Jud' on Tiny, *Lansdowne*, 1958.

Me with some of the boys who were doing road work near *Lansdowne* airstrip.

Me with Meldie, Tommy and Johnny Ray at *Bedford Downs*.

CHAPTER EIGHT

The end of the 1950s

A decade ends,
A chapter closes,
New lessons taught,
And new battles fought.

Matthew Quilty

Meldie helps me wrap Christmas presents for the blacks, and Tommy goes with Rod and the boys to find a suitable Christmas tree. They stand it in a drum of sand on a small patch of lawn in front of the house. Although we have three markets for our cattle, prices are low. Most of our meat goes to the United Kingdom, but it is a finicky market.

The British housewife wanted to see marbled meat with grains of fat running through it plus a thick selvedge of fat, but she wanted the fat cut off before she bought. This did not make for high prices for our cattle. Very few stations bred top quality beef. America came in with a demand for lean hamburger meat in the 1960s. This suited us. Prices soared and cattle boomed. Numbers counted for more than quality.

Because of the low prices, we are still more or less on the breadline. There is little money for presents. Almost everything we earn goes to develop the run. Fencing, paddocks, bores and wells, as well as wages. I order coloured shirts and neck scarves for the boys, dresses and petticoats for the girls and toys for the piccaninnies. We hang them on the tree, each parcel named and tied with string. We have a few pigs and ducks that have found their way here or been left by some wandering blacks.

A pig is killed, cleaned and cut up, and several ducks killed. I make four junkets, and custard for Rod's little treacle tin plum puddings. I also make toffee, which is a mess but very sweet. The blacks love it.

Peggy, Maggie and I struggle all day with the cooking. Most of the pig is cooked in the bread oven, the ducks in the camp ovens. Vegetables from our garden are cooked on the stove. Rod killed this morning so there is plenty of fresh meat. The girls have gathered lots of sweet little konker-berries and bush passionfruit. They wash them, put them in their native dishes and place them on the trestle table near the Christmas tree.

Everybody goes off to bathe and clean up. Nobody dawdles. We must start our party before dark as we only have one light. Just on sundown, the food is placed on the table. The blacks come up, shining and clean, smelling of strong station-made soap. Rod reads the names, hands the parcels to Meldie, and she calls the blacks to come for their presents. She is so serious and important. Tommy is busy helping the piccaninnies unwrap their parcels. Presents all given out, it is now time to eat. The blacks approach the table. Rod and Jim Roberts, who said he was a Sydney butcher before he came to the Kimberleys, serve them.

Strangely, they all point or indicate they want beef or bones rather than pork or duck. Each has his or her own tin plate. The bones and steaks are hot and juicy, straight from the fire. They come back several times. Showing no interest in the junket or plum puddings, they eat lots of konkerberries and passionfruit. It suits the whites and half-castes to have the blacks go for the beef. The pork and duck are left for them.

Peggy and Daisy bring a bucket of tea round and everybody sits on the small lawn or the ground, talking and laughing. It has been a happy time. The piccanninies fall asleep and Tommy and Meldie want to go to bed. I take them in and help them hang up their stockings for Santa Claus' visit later tonight. Before everybody breaks up, Stormy organises a clean-up. Paper wrappings, bones and all rubbish are dumped in a 44-gallon drum. The girls help me put the leftover food in the charcoal cooler.

I am not sorry to see the last of the 1950s. Hard, sad, lonely years which — heavily in debt, often afraid, struggling to accept a totally unacceptable life, the loss of three babies I so desperately wanted — came close to breaking me. That is all now behind me. I have shed the melancholia that plagued me all through those years. I look forward to the new decade with hope and understanding.

* * *

Leprosy is rife here and I do not recognise it. I do not know that it is leprosy. I hear the word "yaws". Those poor black people come to me with their sores and the flesh eaten away to the bone. They say they "bin burnim" in their campfires, but I know it is something more serious than that. I am advised to dab the affected parts with gentian violet and told that the medical plane will pick the patients up. The blacks dread the treatment, and being confined to a hospital was sometimes a death sentence. A lot go bush when the medical plane is due.

I worry about our children with the leprosy but am told there is little danger. I am also told not to worry about blood poisoning with the blacks. That changed with the years, as did a lot of other things. I was told leprosy is contracted through a break in the skin. Meldie and Tommy, playing for so long with the piccaninnies, are always gravel-rashed or cut.

* * *

Cyclones hover along the west coast. We are too far inland for them to be a danger to us. We sympathise sincerely with people who bear the full force of their fury further down the coast, but we are always grateful for the beautiful rain dumped on our parched land.

Seventeen inches (432 mm) of rain for January and still raining. Between cyclones and monsoons, we manage to carry on from season to season.

* * *

Late in January, I leave to take the children, now aged 6 and 5, to school in Julia Creek. This saddens both Rod and me, but it has to be. I can no longer teach them to the standard they should be at, and governesses have not been a success. To my surprise, they settle down well at the convent. Their cousins are there to soften the blows and to explain what they mean when they say, "Where we two fella go" or "Da went dat a-way." I was dreading having to leave them, but I had to get back to Rod. I thought it best if I did not tell them I was going. I arranged with Mother Superior to let them have lunch with my mother, my sister Coral and me on the day I was leaving. After lunch, they went off happily with their Dawes cousins, back to the convent. I feel so sad and miserable, parting with our babies for the first time.

My plane left at 5 o'clock that afternoon to fly me to Mt Isa. The nuns told me afterwards that Meldie and Tommy were sitting quietly at a table when the plane flew over. Meldie said, "That's Mummy," and with that, they both bolted for the door. Fortunately, the nuns were alert. They formed a ring and spread their habits. Everywhere Meldie and Tommy went, they ran into habits and were blocked off — and then the tears came.

More heavy rain while I have been away and the Leopold River is in flood. I am held up for three days in Wyndham, waiting for a plane to *Lansdowne*. MMA gets a clearance and flies me to our strip. The strip, hard and firm, is not a problem, but the Leopold is in high flood, a raging torrent. Choosing a spot upriver, Rod crosses on a tractor, leaving three boys to wait on the west bank. Bringing one boy, Montie, with him, Rod has arrived at the strip to meet me, complete with tarpaulins to wrap my luggage and ropes to tie it all on. I change into shorts, shirt and sandshoes, and stand on the tractor's step while Rod ties me securely to the framework. He gets behind the wheel, and, with Montie on the other step, we set out to cross the river. I feel the water rushing round me. Wet to the waist, I close my eyes and pray. The tractor lurches and jerks, my arms are almost pulled from my shoulders. I can hear the roar of the water, and at times feel the blows as debris washes against me. I am afraid, but I have learnt to trust Rod. With God's help, he always makes it. More heavy rain falls, and our airstrip is closed the day after I arrive home.

* * *

Lent starts early this year. Our blacks start to dribble back. Some have heavy colds, most of the children have sore eyes. I know I am going to be busy nursing them. Biddy and I battle with them continually. Biddy has little patience; she scolds and rails at them to do more to help themselves. I do not remember the piccaninnies having such eye problems when I first came here. I am forever telling the children to "chase the flies." Flies crawl all over their eyes as they squint and shut them tight rather than brush them away. Day after day, they line up to have their eyes washed before I put the drops in. Gradually, we are beating the eye problem, but the "cold sick" is another, more serious problem altogether.

The girls bring Peggy to me with a badly cut hand. Washing Big Johnnie's clothes, she has sliced the entire cushion of her right thumb on a razor blade which was in the pocket of his shirt. She will need stitches. Rod will have to do it; I can't. The doctor says we will have to use an ordinary sewing needle and cotton. Wet from the water, Peggy's hand is slippery and the skin wrinkled. The needle won't go in. I turn away, I cannot look. She must suffer terrible pain as he tries to force the needle through. She makes no sound at all. After several attempts, Rod gives up. We bathe her hand in warm solution of Condy's crystals and bandage it firmly. I give her a couple of aspirin and she goes off to the camp. I am concerned that her hand will be too sore for her to go with us when we start muster. I was wrong. Five days after she cut her hand she is back. There is a nasty red scar round her thumb but the wound has healed. In time, I think the scar will fade.

We start our muster very shorthanded; Peggy and I have more to do. We are camp cooks, bullock tailers and musterers. It is a wonderful, free, exciting life. There is danger, and I am often afraid. Open range, the cattle are wild, the country very rough, and there are always the terrifying night rushes. After settling the cattle down for the night, Rod puts me on first watch. It is the easiest and the safest, but I am never at ease. Riding round and round the cattle, I sing my heart out, "When I Grow Too Old To Dream." In those days I never thought I could grow old. Rod takes the dog watch, 2 o'clock until 4 o'clock, then he calls the camp. He calls it the dog watch because it is the hardest. I lie awake in the swag, looking at the stars and listening to the watch change. The boys sing their favourite songs, some play the mouth organ. The music is lonely and sad but in keeping with the time. Rod's favourite is "The Dog Sat On The Tuckerbox." He only knows a few lines but he sings them over and over. Later, when our son was old enough to do the watch, he would soothe the cattle with "Old MacDonald Had a Farm." The blacks sing their corroboree songs or sometimes a white man's song in their own language. Singing soothed the cattle and also covered any sudden or unexpected noise that might frighten the cattle and cause them to rush.

As the years passed, we built yards and there were less night watches, but there was always the danger of a rush. It was a terrible feeling to hear them go. In the dark, I never knew which way they went. I prayed they would not come over the camp.

Rod and his head boy would take the night horses, always saddled and tied up close to the camp. The other stockboys, with their bridles, would catch any of the horses hobbled close by. Peggy and I would stoke up the fire and put the billies on. I would hear the boys calling to each other and yelling at the cattle. I prayed they would all come safely back. Instinct must have guided man and horse. They must have had very good night sight and excellent hearing to be able to stay with the cattle and wheel them. I looked for Rod and counted the boys as they came in.

Early one morning, in the hustle and bustle of getting ready for the day's muster, I notice that neither Peggy nor Maggie are with me. Zachady is not here either. Rod calls to know if I have seen Jimmy Roberts or Big

Johnnie. Something is wrong. I go to look for them. Not far from the camp, I find the little group. Peggy, propped up against a tree, has been bitten by a snake. Jimmy Roberts has quickly tied his belt round the calf of her leg and is rasping the puncture marks, near her ankle, with the rough, perforated striking surface on the bottom of his tin matchbox. Blood seeps through her lacerated skin.

Peggy's eyes are wide and glazed. She stares unblinkingly at something I cannot see. Big Johnnie stands quietly by. Maggie kneels beside her. I ask Zachady if it was a bad snake. "Yar, 'im proper cheeky one."

"Did you kill it?" I ask.

Before Zachady can answer, Jim Roberts says, "The silly buggers let it get away. I wanted to kill it."

I tell them they have been very stupid. Maggie gets up, comes round and puts her hand on my shoulder. "Be quiet, say no more." I stop talking. Maggie says something to Big Johnnie and he leaves. Jim Roberts says there is nothing more he can do, and he leaves as well. As he passes me, he says, "She's not going to make it."

I look at my faithful old friend, say a quick prayer for her, then rush to find Rod. I cannot go with the musterers today, I will stay with Peggy. Rod understands. He tells me not to leave her, to keep her as quiet as possible, leave her under the tree but stay with her. Maggie and I never leave her. I am so afraid she will die. A "proper cheeky snake" must surely be a king brown. Zachady potters round the camp, checks the billies are close to the fire, the corned beef on to cook and ready for the musterers when they come in. From time to time, he brings water for Maggie and me. Peggy never moves as Maggie packs some grey mixture on and round the wound. I keep checking her pulse and praying.

The day wears on, the sun moves round and still we sit with her. Rod and the boys return. Rod and Big Johnnie come over, stay a while then leave. Toward sundown, Maggie begins to rock back and forth, back and forth. I think, this is the end; Peggy is dying and Maggie knows. I feel her pulse, rapid and jerky, her skin clammy. I start to cry. As she puts her arm round Peggy, Maggie says something I do not understand. I am not even sure she has spoken. The sun has disappeared. I think Peggy moves towards Maggie. In the half-light, I can imagine things. I wait. Gradually, Peggy draws her legs up, leans forward and places her head on her knees. Maggie says, "You go now, Yumman. 'Im better, snake gone." The sudden change leaves me floundering. I want to ask what is happening, is she better? But Maggie is not going to tell me, she wants me gone. I have a feeling Peggy is over the snakebite; she is not going to die. I leave.

We take Peggy back to the station. She seems well enough. There are no after-effects. Had she been bitten by a "proper cheeky snake", the deadly king brown, as Zachady had indicated? I'll never know. They are strange people, with so much hidden from the white man.

* * *

I have had another bad fall and it has frightened me. Riding Toddler, I went with Rod to check the bullock paddock fences. Toddler is an ambler and a beautiful horse to ride, but he shies at everything. Relaxed and enjoying the fast canter, keeping up with Rod, I was not prepared when Toddler faulted and jerked sideways. I saw a snake slither round the rocks but I was out of the saddle by then. I hit the ground on my face. A cut above my eye was bleeding, and I thought I had knocked my teeth out. My mouth covered in dirt, bleeding and hurting. I wanted to cry. My front teeth gone! Rod picked me up and carried me over to a shady tree. Clearing the dirt and blood away, he said my teeth were all there but they looked cracked. He was right. A great crack across my two front teeth. No dentist. I will just have to be careful until I can have something done.

I cannot go on much longer with my teeth as they are. Any small thing could cause them to break. Mustering, with my hat blowing at the back of my head and my chin strap in my mouth, could snap them. They also ache. Rod says as soon as the bullocks go, he will send me to Sydney. He has 'been in touch' (via telegram over the Flying Doctor Base because there were still no telephones) with his cousin, Betty Rose McInerney, wife of Doctor Bob McInerney. Betty Rose has made an appointment with their family dentist, Dr. O'Brien.

In September, I flew to Sydney via Perth and Melbourne. I flew into a different world. All the glamour and excitement of Sydney society. Betty Rose, one of Sydney's ten best-dressed women and a leading Sydney hostess, took me shopping. While I watched the shillings and the pounds, she looked for style and fashion. She took me to balls, lunches and the races. I watched the wealthy and famous mingle. I met Lady Clarke and Lady Fairfax. Lady Fairfax at that time was married to a well-known Sydney barrister. I met Tommy and Mrs Smith. Tommy, a little man who laughs a lot, had one of Bob and Betty Rose's horses in training.

I met Rebecca and Isaac, a wealthy Jewish couple who were in the 'rag trade'. I wondered, but did not ask, what the rag trade was. I guessed it had something to do with drapery or clothes. Whatever, it gave them a most elaborate home. Gold taps, a gallery of priceless paintings, servants, and a magnificent view of our beautiful harbour, in one of the most exclusive and pretentious areas in Sydney.

Dr. O'Brien said he would cap my teeth. It takes from nine to ten days for the caps to be made so, in the meanwhile, he gave me temporary caps. The days went by in a blur, with very little time to sleep. There was always somewhere exciting to go, or something exciting to do. I was having a wonderful time, enjoying every minute — but I was tiring. It would be good to be home again and back to regular hours.

Still hoping, I arrange with Bob McInerney to give me a thorough health check. Bob, one of Sydney's leading gynaecologists, has the largest single practice in Sydney. He confirms what I have already been told. I am in good health but there will be no more children. Oh! Dear God! Why?

At last I have permanent caps. A perfect match. My two front teeth are secure. Three days before I am due to leave Sydney, the bad dreams start. Nightmares that wake me, trembling with fear. So many horrible things come to me in my dreams. Toby and Bruno are always there. I fly to Wyndham and Rod meets me. We drive home over the now familiar track. No more nightmares.

* * *

Grandfather Quilty with Meldie, Tommy and the *Springvale* stockboys at
Springvale.

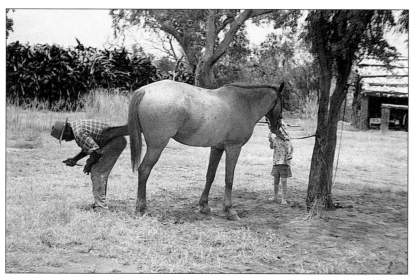

Bunchemup shoeing Troy, with Tommy looking on. Station woodheap
left background.

Tommy with the *Lansdowne* stockboys.

Meldie in front of ruins at Old Halls Creek.

From left: Theresa Eckford, Jan Eckford, Ronnie Eckford, Tommy and Meldie at
Isabel Downs, Julia Creek. Meldie and Tommy's first year at boarding school.
Holiday time.

Standing left to right: Tommy, Pat Dawes, Joey Dawes and Jim Dawes
Sitting left to right: Meldie, Rocky Gluyas, Mary Dawes, Mike Dawes. Meldie and
Tommy's first year at boarding school. Holiday time.

CHAPTER NINE

Land of life and death

A land of mystery,
And tainted history,
Of hidden secrets
And eternal regrets.

Matthew Quilty

The bullock muster is well underway, but we are again short of stock-men. Peggy and I are in the saddle long days. Rod, overworked and cranky, drives his men hard. I do not want him to worry about me, but I am cautious; with two bad falls, I do not want another. Riding close to Alfie, I see him jump off his horse and disappear behind an ant bed. Perhaps he needs to go to the toilet. We have about 20 head of mixed cattle, driving them towards the coachers. They start to scatter and I can't keep them together. I can see Rod coming and I know Alfie will be in trouble. I call to him and let him know Rod is coming. Alfie rides past me at a fast gallop, but not fast enough that I don't see the tail of a goanna sticking out of his shirt. He keeps well away from Rod. Between them, they get the cattle together. Rod wants to know where Alfie has been. I say, "Toilet." Rod leaves.

Meldie and Tommy are not happy boarding at the Julia Creek convent, and although it upsets us to know this, we cannot bring them home. We will have to leave them there until the end of the year. We are concerned that if we have them home for the mid-year holidays, we will not be able to get them back to board again.

Missing our babies so much, I become very fond of Mark, a little piccaninny — a dear little boy, six years old. He helps fill the aching longing I have for our children. Thin and frail, he comes up to the kitchen for morning smoko. Clean, his little face shining, and his hair slicked down with water, he stands beside me and puts his hand on my knee. I give what we have. He takes the offering and says, "Ar bin lebe yo noo." (I leave you now.) Then he slowly walks back to the camp before he starts to eat.

* * *

A message from Derby, over the Flying Doctor Base, to say the medical plane, doing a leprosy survey, will call this afternoon. A request for all blacks to be at the airstrip for checks. I load all the blacks on the truck except a few of the very elderly. Short Foot, very old and badly crippled, with both feet tied up with yards of dirty rag, will not go. A few of the old lubras, hands tied and covered with the same dirty rag will not go either. I do not force them.

A doctor, nurse and pilot are on the plane. There are also two blacks aboard who do not get off. Our blacks line up and bare their backs. There, the tell-tale signs stand out. Great grey spots. Not on all, but on some. The doctor says that leprosy lies dormant for a long time before the sores appear. Barney, Kitty and Nellie, who I have been treating with gentian violet, are far gone. Grey spots stand out on the backs of Helen, Dickie, and several others. Helen, mother of little Mark, has leprosy. She is also pregnant and has the "cold sick".

The nurse makes a list and gives me a copy. Barney, Kitty and Nellie must go on the plane back to Derby now. My faithful old Kitty clings to me. She does not want to go, neither do Barney or Nellie. They gather round me, begging me to keep them here. I cannot do anything to help them. They have a terrible disease, given to them by another race, at another time. Leprosy. God help them.

On the list are the names of all those with the grey spots showing. The plane will pick them up another day. They will also have to go to Derby for treatment. I am concerned about Helen, an attractive girl, barely out of her teens, and tribal married to Old Jacky, a very jealous old man. She is unhappy and I suspect that Jacky is not the father of her unborn baby. Benny, a young stockman could be the father.

It upsets me to see young lubras tribal married to such old men. I speak to the elders. They politely listen but do nothing. It is their law and they will not change. Helen is very sick. Mark spends more time with me. I

110

have a medical on Helen. The plane will pick her up tomorrow. I give her some hot soup, and two aspirin and tell her to stay in camp until the plane comes.

Helen died last night. I have cancelled the medical plane. There is such sadness in the camp and in my heart. Mark wants to stay with me. He is not close to Old Jacky, his father. I cannot take him from his people, but Biddy says, "Yo bin keep 'im yo-roan self." (You keep him yourself.) I think seriously about adopting him, but I must speak to Rod and I also want to discuss it with my good friend, Mother Damian, who is Matron of the Derby Hospital.

Rod does not commit himself but I know he does not approve. There are too many pitfalls that he knows about but I do not. I will not go against his wishes. Mother Damian is also against the adoption. She says it will be bad for both Mark and me. Mark would grow up in two worlds, belonging to neither. Best to leave him with his own people. I give up the idea but keep Mark with me as long as I can. One night, Old Jacky just walked off and took Mark with him. I never saw them again.

* * *

Rod has spent days trying to find where to put another well down, close to the house. Although he and Bluey O'Malley have deepened the garden well to increase the flow, it is not adequate to meet the demand now. He finally uses an old tried and true method that has stood him in good stead when picking other sites on *Lansdowne*. He uses a green, forked stick.

I had first seen him use this method successfully at Coral Spring some years ago. The forked stick unerringly pointed down to where he eventually found a good supply of water for the bore he put down there. Wanting to try my luck, I took the stick. It was dead wood in my hands. Meldie tried. It twisted down as it had in Rod's hands. Tommy tried next. No good. We all tried several times. It worked so well for Rod and Meldie but it was simply a piece of dead wood for Tommy and me.

With his green, forked stick, Rod wanders up and down beside the house. There is no response. I am beginning to have doubts. Someone suggests he use wire instead of the stick. Rod perseveres with the stick. I am close to him as we near the back fence. I see the stick start to bend towards the ground, Rod's knuckles going white with the strain. He has found the spot for his well. There must be an underground stream running east and west, in line with our garden wall.

111

The well goes down, to beautiful, sweet, clean water. With a 3000-gallon (13,650 litre) storage tank built high above the well, and our home-made hot water system, we are indeed fortunate. A 44-gallon drum — set in a strong steel frame, built over a fireplace, filled with water and connected to the overhead tank — gives us piping hot water when the fire is lit. There is always a plentiful supply of wood for the fire. We have a problem with a horrible green slime that forms on the top of the water in the tank. We have tried many ways to clear it but it is always there. However, it has never contaminated or caused the water to lose its sweet taste.

Peggy tells me that Albert and Sally are in the camp looking for work. I ask, "How did they get here?"

"Walked," says Peggy.

"Where did they come from?" I ask again.

She points with her mouth towards the south-west.

"Derby?"

A shake. No.

"Broome?"

A nod. Yes!

I tell her Rod will see them when he comes in.

"No!" she says. "They have a baby. They want to see you."

"All right, send them up," I reply.

Albert and Sally arrive, Albert carrying the baby. It looks very small. They are arguing. Albert says he is a good stockman and wants work. This brings a string of very bad language from Sally — and she can certainly swear. He wants her to take the baby; she refuses. I call Peggy to take the baby while I straighten things out with them.

It appears Sally, raised at Beagle Bay Mission but Albert's tribal wife, did not want to leave Broome. Involved with white men, drinking and gambling, she did not want to go with Albert. Albert is the father of the baby. *Lansdowne* is isolated and far off the beaten track. If she wants to drink and gamble, she will have a long walk to town.

I tell Albert that Rod will give him a job and that Sally can stay in the camp with the baby. I do not want her to work. She looks like trouble. True to his word, Albert is a good worker and a good stockman, but

Sally is a holy terror. She plays on the baby. If he stretches, she rushes up to the house, claiming, "He go stiff, must get plane out, take him hospital." If he relaxes in his sleep, she claims, "He nearly finish, get plane quick." For a while, she has me nearly out of my mind with worry, until Peggy tells me it is all a hoax to get back to town. There is nothing wrong with the baby, but Sally does neglect him. The old women have him most of the time.

One morning, early — Rod and Albert out for horses — Sally rushes up to the house carrying the baby and screaming. I take the little bundle. There is blood coming from his nose and ear. I know this is no hoax; he is badly hurt. I will have to call the doctor on the early morning session. Holding him close as I wait for the doctor, I feel his feeble little pulse, so faint I can barely detect it. I baptise him and wait. The Wyndham doctor comes on, loud and clear. As I am explaining the baby's condition to him, I feel a terrible stillness, a silence; nothing moves, no sound of the girls at work, absolutely nothing. It lasts barely a minute. I stop talking to the doctor and switch over to receive. I hear him ask if the baby is dead. Looking down at the tiny little black face, I know he is gone. "Yes, he is dead." I hope his little soul, pure and shining, is in heaven with the angels.

We buried him on the island in the middle of the creek, beside the remains of two old natives, Old Captain and Plum. It was a long time before I could ask Peggy what had happened. When Sally realised she was getting nowhere with her complaints, she took more drastic steps. Desperate to get away, the morning that Albert was out with Rod for the horses, she banged the baby's head twice on a huge rock. She must have crushed his little head and he would have been close to death when she brought him to me. She cried and screamed for days — either from remorse, which I doubt, or despair at not being able to get away. She was ostracised. None of the lubras went near her. They could not, and would not, condone what she had done. The old men spoke to Albert. He came to tell me he would take Sally away. Yes, that would be best. They left as they came.

Without help from the elders, I do not think Albert has any hope of holding her. My good friend, Mother Damian, told me that every Friday afternoon, lubras would start turning up at the hospital with their sick children. "You bin keepim till Monday, makim better." Nothing was wrong with the children; they were dumped there so their mothers were free to drink and gamble the weekend away. On Monday, they would turn up to collect them. The good nuns would feed and care for them and they always left in better condition than they arrived. I do not know of any white woman who might have asked for, or was granted, the same privilege.

* * *

With Meldie and Tommy away at boarding school, I start going walkabout with the girls again. On free days in the stock camp, I wander for miles with Peggy. She takes me to Sandy McAndoo and Barney O'Leary's old homes. So little left there now. The ant bed walls of Sandy's abode, on the hill, weathered away almost to the ground. The highest part still standing was about a foot (30 cm) high. I do not step over the remnant of wall, but move to where the door had been and go in there. In the corner stands a rusty old tin trunk, half full of rusty horseshoes. On the lid of the trunk, I can just make out the letters SCO. Could he have brought it from Scotland, kept and treasured it all the way, only to leave it here at this lonely place? His last link with his homeland. I try to rub it to see if there is a name but, worn thin with rust, the lid just collapses. Old iron from his roof, lying twisted and bent a few yards away.

Not much left of Barney's place either. Peggy tells me Sandy had burnt Barney's hut down one day when Barney was away. I can see the remains of the burnt stumps in the ground. Where Sandy's home had ant bed walls and ant bed floor, Barney had paved his floor with flat river stones, fitted smoothly and carefully together. Rough bush timber for his corner posts, and bush timber cut from trees close to the water for his walls. Nothing was left now. Barney had built the white-ant-eaten yard I had seen when I first came to Galway Valley. Sandy used no yard. While Barney yarded and branded his few head of cattle, Sandy open broncoed. Peggy says some blacks had worked for them but they did not like the place. Something in the hills frightened them. Although she freely told me the story of Barney and Sandy, she could not tell me the story of the hills.

At Melrod Yard, built by Rod and his stockboys, I go with Peggy and Maggie to where Tommy Mathews had lived in a little mud-walled hut, under the range and close to the water. A clear little stream ran close to the front of his hut. Like Peter Pianta, Sandy and Barney, and Ted Baker, Tommy Mathews had taken up blocks on *Lansdowne* years ago. Strong, hard-working men, they trusted no one. Apart from Barney O'Leary, they built no permanent yards, always on the move, they poddy-dodged each other's cattle and kept a sharp lookout for blacks. Blacks speared their cattle and were not above putting a spear into the men, either.

114

Although Pianta's Waterhole was named after Peter Pianta, I was never to see where he lived. The remains of Tommy Mathews' little one-room hut stood stark and forlorn, abandoned and forgotten. Three walls gone, just heaps of dirt and rocks lying on the ground. The remaining wall starting to crumble and break up, but still showing the narrow gun-slot openings where Tommy had shot at troublesome blacks. No windows, only a narrow opening for a door. Maggie says all the walls had slots for Tommy's guns.

A few spearheads and old horseshoes are lying around. The horseshoes are rusted and useless. The spearheads, bright and as hard as the day they flew from the hands of their black owners. The blacks could never get at Tommy in his hut and his faithful old dogs guarded his back out in the open, but Rod, who knew Tommy, says he had several narrow escapes.

There is so much history in this sparsely populated and forgotten place. Lonely men, unmarked graves, dead men, both white and black who did not die natural deaths. A white man's bullet or a black man's spear cut down lives swiftly and cruelly.

Scotty Saddler, an old local identity, died in Derby Hospital on 12 January, 1957, taking with him much history and, possibly, the answer to 'the Bowers mystery'. Scotty had owned Tableland Station at the time a man called Bowers disappeared. His body was never found. As the story was told to me, Bowers was working on *Tableland*. There was bad blood between Scotty and Bowers. One afternoon, with most of the blacks away and Scotty and Bowers the only white men left at the station, Bowers disappeared.

Police suspected he had been murdered. They searched the homestead and every possible place a body could be hidden. Looking for tracks or blood, they found nothing. Scotty swore he did not know where Bowers had gone or what might have happened to him, and he stuck to his story. Bowers could have wandered off, walked into quicksand or been taken by a crocodile. It was rumoured a policeman sat by Scotty's bed in the hospital, thinking that he might have rambled or, in his delirium, given a clue to the mystery. But if Scotty knew, he took the secret with him.

I had been at *Lansdowne* nearly two years when, one day before the early storms, Scotty arrived riding an old grey horse. He had come to visit, and would spend a week with us. He was an old man then. I sat with him for hours, listening to his thick Scottish accent while he told me stories of the early days — hard, lonely and dangerous. He told me how Tommy Mathews had raided stations around Fitzroy Crossing and stolen horses, then headed for *Lansdowne* with the police and trackers hot on his heels. Tommy was an outstanding bushman; not many could match him. He eluded the police at first, but deciding it was too risky to keep the horses, he drove them up a dead end and shot them.

Before he left, Scotty rode with Rod and me to show us Tommy Mathews' dead end. There in the sun, we saw the bleaching bones poking through the long grass. Our horses shied at the stark whiteness and did not want to go too close.

We spent days riding round with Scotty. He seemed to know *Lansdowne* as well as he knew *Tableland*. He showed us the ruins of Ted Baker's lonely old hut. We rode along the range and climbed to caves where blacks had buried their dead. We left them undisturbed.

Scotty, a good friend of Paddy Quilty, was at *Bedford* the day Paddy started a mob of bullocks for Wyndham Meatworks. Brown, a half-caste drover, was in charge with four *Bedford* blacks helping him. Brown had two of his own stockboys and his de facto wife, Mary, with him. Mary belonged to a tribe of blacks who were following the cattle. Paddy sent word to Brown to be on his guard, to keep a good watch on the cattle and to keep his revolver close. Brown was not unduly worried. He relied on Mary to warn him if there was trouble; besides, he had not seen any strange blacks. Unbeknown to Brown, Mary was finger-talking to her tribe — they planned to kill Brown and take Mary back. The *Bedford* boys were edgy; they knew what was going on. Charlie had ridden back to warn Paddy that they could be attacked. Paddy told him to keep a sharp lookout, and that he and Scotty would be there that afternoon.

On dinner camp that day, Brown casually propped his rifle against a tree, and with his revolver still in its holster, settled himself down to rest. Mary, building the fire and preparing the dinner, was nervous. Two *Bedford* boys unpacking the tucker mule noticed all this. Mounting their horses, they rode quickly out to where their friends were tailing the bullocks with Brown's boys. Whooping and screeching, blacks poured out of the hills. How many? Charlie couldn't count… "Biggest mob!"

Spears flew, bullocks and stockmen fell. Horses were clubbed with nulla nullas. Charlie, speared in the leg, crawled into a breakaway and hid. Peeping out, he saw the blacks rush Brown. With a spear in his chest, Brown desperately tried to get his revolver out. Charlie waited no longer, crawling towards a horse standing at the end of the breakaway, he mounted and headed for *Bedford* as fast as the horse could go.

Charlie galloped back to *Bedford*, his horse in a lather of sweat. Bleeding from his wound, with his eyes rolling and barely able to stand, he told of the massacre. Paddy asked, "Did you hear a shot, a gunshot?"

"Yar, boss," replied Charlie.

"How many shot?" Charlie held up one finger.

Scotty left to saddle their horses. After arranging for Polly to clean up Charlie's wound and give him something to eat and drink — and with strict instructions to keep him at the station until he returned — Paddy joined Scotty.

Although Mary and her tribe had gone, it was not hard to find the dinner camp.

Nine bullocks down, the rest scattered. They looked for the men. The three *Bedford* boys close together, mutilated, their kidneys gone. What was left of Brown lay close to the tree where he had rested. Blood, bone and sinew smashed to pulp. They had used their waddies on him until there was nothing left to break. His hat splashed with blood and brains, a great gaping hole where the bullet had passed through. Scotty said he and Paddy were sure Brown had managed to shoot himself before the blacks took to him.

All the rations were gone, pack bags ripped and thrown about, flour spilled, lying white and powdery on the ground. It took Scotty and Paddy a while to find Brown's two boys. They had been dragged further away from the camp and clubbed to death, mutilated like the *Bedford* boys.

Scotty had so many stories to tell. We wanted him to stay longer but he said he had to go. Paddy Quilty's death in 1948 had been a sad blow to him. They were great mates.

* * *

Frank Bridge's brother, Norman, is here repairing saddles. Last night, after the evening meal, sitting under the lean-to verandah with Rod, they heard a plane flying in the area. A dark night, the weather was very bad. Rain, and great claps of thunder and lightning, both flash and chain, ripped the skies. The plane was in trouble. Rod and Norman wondered what emergency warranted anyone flying on such a night. Rod tried to call the Flying Doctor Base but it was impossible to hear through the static.

This morning, Fred Ryle announced on our early morning session that the Flying Doctor plane from Derby is missing on a mercy flight from

117

Tableland to Derby with Jack Rudduck (the owner of *Tableland*), his sick baby, the pilot and a young nurse aboard.

The route, *Tableland* to Derby, does not pass over *Lansdowne*. The plane was off course when Rod and Norman heard it. The search was on but it was days before the wreck was found. It had gone nose-first into the soft mud, killing all on board. The search team found five bodies amongst the twisted wreckage. Another young girl, a friend of the nurse, was an unauthorised passenger on the fateful flight. It is a terrible loss and a sadness for the families of the pilot and the young girls. I feel so sorry for Joyce Rudduck, wife and mother, who lost her husband and baby daughter in this tragic accident. She and her sons have left *Tableland*. I do not think they will come back.

* * *

RFDS medical plane with its pilot on *Lansdowne* airstrip.

Chapter Ten

Celebrations

Astride a half ton of bone, muscle and ire,
Often tossed off ere you've even begun,
To be trampled face first in the muck and the mire,
And all in the cause of just having fun.

Every year during the off season, we set aside money and time to improve our home, but the run still has priority. Shutters have been put over the openings where the windows are; an office, and bedrooms for Meldie and Tommy, have been partitioned off; doors set in and all floors cemented. Gradually, we paint everything. It has taken several coats of paint to cover Toby's bloodstains on our bedroom floor. I am proud of my home.

Bill Glaster, a clever handyman, but an alcoholic, and Jack Liddell, also an alcoholic, are with us. Bill is responsible for the improvements. Jack had worked for the Quiltys in the Northern Territory and is now our cook. I am very fond of both of them. Kind-hearted, separated from their families and looking years older than their age, they cannot control their thirst for hard liquor.

Bill died in an accident returning from Halls Creek after several days drinking there, and Jack died at *Lansdowne* one year while Rod and I were away. I miss both of them so much.

Life is getting easier for Rod and me. Paddocks, fences and yards are going up. Gorey and Cole, and later Arthur Hughes, putting bores down. Things move slowly but surely.

119

Old Biddy came to me today to say they want me to go to their camp tonight to watch a corroboree. The blacks are happy when they corroboree. Often, as I lie in bed at night, I hear them singing and dancing to the tune of the didgeridoo, but I have never seen them. I go to sleep listening to the night sounds — the lonely night winds, the corroboree, the dingoes howling. Dingoes do not bark but their howls echo round the hills.

But this night, after the girls finish work, I go with them to the camp. Peggy places an old box for me to sit on. In the light of the campfires it is hard for me to recognise them. Faces painted, and bare to the waist, the lubras sit in a ring, slowly clapping. The men with their beating sticks, faces also painted, and stripped down to shorts, beat and stomp to the didgeridoo. Dust rises. I suspect, were I not there, the men would have worn nargas. Suddenly the tempo quickens. From out of the darkness, Stormy leaps into the light of the fire. Spear in his hand, he does a pantomime of hunting and spearing something. I watch as he prances round and through his friends. They continue to stomp and beat and clap. At last, with a mighty heave, he throws the spear. The stomping and beating and clapping stop. The blacks let out a long drawn out sound, "Ahhhhh". The corroboree ends.

Peggy tells me it was the Emu Dance. They would let me see that, but no white man could ever look upon their proper corroboree.

Their lives seem simple, but there is a mystery and depth to the blacks I will never fathom. They are a child-like people, but their Dreamtime and beliefs go so far back I cannot start to understand. I accept them as I know them. I wonder, do they accept me?

* * *

The children have been away for the school year; it is time now to get them home for the Christmas holidays. We have looked forward to this time for eleven long months. Their Uncle Peter Dawes will put them on Connellan's plane at Mt Isa for Alice Springs, where Rod and I will meet them. Before they leave Julia Creek, their cousin, Mary Dawes, decides to cut Tom's hair. She makes a terrible mess of it, so much so that Peter makes him wear his hat at all times — "Do not take your hat off."

Rod and I must drive over mostly desert country, south from Halls Creek, across the Great Sandy Desert, to Balgo Mission; then south-east until we cross the West Australia–Northern Territory border at the Tanami Desert, continuing south-east to Alice Springs. We stay one night with a dear friend, Father McGuire, at Balgo Mission, but all other nights we camp. Hot glary days and cold silent nights. These great deserts can be so dangerous.

Margaret Doman has put a string of bores down across the deserts to Alice Springs to get her cattle from *Billiluna* to southern markets. Some bores are brackish but the water is there and the cattle survive. We follow the bores over and back, but we carry our own water. Margaret spent a lot of time in the deserts, supervising the bores. She could be related to the Emanuels of Gogo and Christmas Creek Stations, but I'm not sure.

Oh! the joy of having Meldie and Tommy home with us. They have not been happy boarding away. We will not send them back next year; they are too young. We spend a happy Christmas and New Year. In January, I enrol them in the Derby School of the Air, and I will teach them. At this time, January 1961, Meldie is 7 and Tommy is 6. I will concentrate on their schooling, only going into the stock camp when they have school holidays. I know Rod will miss me but I cannot handle both the teaching and the camp.

I find teaching now is not the hard grind it had been in the past. School at Julia Creek has given Meldie and Tom a better understanding of what is expected of them. They can hold their own with the other children 'of the air', and, with our own airstrip, I am able to receive and return their papers on time. I also have a male cook. Things are running very smoothly at the station; I am not so sure about the stock camp.

It is Meldie's birthday, 18 April. She waits all day for birthday telegrams from her Queensland relations. We are giving her a little party on the front lawn tonight. I have held the telegrams back until then; she thinks her cousins have forgotten her. The stock camp is out, but Rod is in at the station. He will leave with Tommy, after the party, to drive to Fitzroy Crossing to pick up some barbed wire.

I make a cake. I am not sure my old bush cook can really make a fruit cake. Peggy says he cannot. The cake looks good and smells good when it comes out of the oven. Meldie cuts some coloured paper and wraps it round. I make coconut ice and my famous toffee. A table is set up on the lawn and we are ready for the party. The piccaninnies, clean and shining, come bearing their little gifts; something made from hair, an emu egg carved with fish and kangaroos, a spearhead, a boomerang. They place them gently in Meldie's hand and she carefully puts them on the table, so precious and rare. Rod reads her birthday telegrams. She is so happy and excited. The end of a perfect day for her.

A beautiful moonlit night. The children eat and play on the lawn until it is time for Rod and Tommy to leave. I feel such a sadness. I keep comparing life here with life at Julia Creek. I must be careful. I cannot afford to look back.

* * *

Great excitement. We are going to the Halls Creek Races and Sports Day. Everybody who wants to, will go. The long, rough trip will be too much for some of the old people and the little piccaninnies. They will not go. It will take three days to get to Halls Creek. We judge our travelling in days rather than miles. Our bullocks have delivered to Wyndham and we are free now until the cow and calf muster later in the year.

Rod sends a truck to drop off feed at Bridges' Yard. George Allen will be there tonight with our horses. He left early this morning. We have one racehorse, the fastest horse in our stock camp. He has been nominated as "Marmaduke" after an old friend from Julia Creek, Marmaduke Curr. Toddler, who will go in for the Walk, Trot and Gallop, and two other sports horses have been taken as well. George will camp at Bridges' Yard tonight, approximately halfway between *Lansdowne* and *Bedford*. It will take him four days to get to Halls Creek. Tomorrow night he will be at *Bedford*. A night there and then early next morning he will leave, with two *Bedford* boys and the *Bedford* horses, for *Springvale*. They will stay overnight there before boxing up with the *Springvale* horses on the fourth day for the last leg to Halls Creek. Three *Springvale* black stockmen will join the group.

All over the Kimberleys and across the Northern Territory border, small mobs of horses are carefully driven by two, sometimes three, black stockmen to Halls Creek for the most important event in our social year. Rod's father has sent a team of his stockboys to build stables on the outskirts of the town.

We leave the day after George Allen does. The children, excited and feeling important, toss their things in the jeep, and check to see that all the piccaninnies are accounted for. Rod would like me to drive his Chev utility, as it would be more comfortable than the jeep, but "No!" I would have trouble with his Chev. It is a low vehicle and the road, not much more than a track, would slow me up. I could rip the sump out on the rough roads.

I take the jeep with Meldie, Tommy, and George Allen's wife, Canny. George is of mixed blood, as is Canny. She has a lovely little dog she calls

Mr. Mitts. Meldie has become attached to Mr. Mitts and often plays with him. Afraid to leave her dog behind because of the dingoes, Canny wants to take him. Rod roars, "No dogs, no dogs." We smuggle Mr. Mitts into the jeep and hope Rod does not see him before we leave.

Rod drives his Chev with the stock gear, horse feed, etc. Harold Caporne, a white stockman, drives the truck carrying the blacks. It is the first time some of them have been to town.

We pull into Poison Camp for dinner. We killed yesterday, so there is plenty of fresh meat and bones. Fires lit and billies on, soon the clean fresh air is filled with the delicious aroma of steak and bones grilling on the coals. Rod has washed and greased his shovel. He cooks our meat and bones on it.

We get to *Bedford* about dark. The *Lansdowne* and *Bedford* blacks happily greet each other. Some are related, all are old friends. Tired, we are pleased to have an early night.

Next day, we get to *Springvale* late in the afternoon, too late to go on. We spend the night. It will be an early start in the morning. With three *Springvale* vehicles, two from *Bedford,* and our three, we now have a convoy of eight vehicles. I have no idea of how many blacks are on the *Bedford* and *Springvale* trucks.

The road, rough and dusty, twists and winds through the hills. We keep our distance from the truck in front. On the main highway, we meet the Lillys from *Bow River* and the McNamarras from *Mabel Downs.* They have their families and trucks loaded with blacks and stock gear. The blacks recognise and call to relations and friends. Harold McNamarra tells us that Nan and Ron Lanridge from Turkey Creek are ahead of them, and that Jimmy Kliene and Julia, from *Texas Downs,* are somewhere behind. We do not stay long. A message from Rod's father comes down the line to say we must get a move on.

Halls Creek at last. The *Springvale* and *Bedford* groups head for the stables. They will camp. Rod has booked me and the children into the hotel. He thinks I get enough camping out at *Lansdowne.* I agree, and love him for his thoughtfulness. He will camp at the stables.

In 1951, I came as a visitor. Confused, disappointed and critical, I left vowing never to return. Now a wife and mother, I am here and involved. I am part of it.

There are a few changes. Old forms under an old bough-shed serve as our grandstand. Leafy branches, cut from trees and tossed above us, keep most of the sun out — but not the dust. The women congregate here. Vestey managers' wives, in the majority, mix happily with the few owners' wives. This is mostly manager territory. In the Fitzroy Crossing area, more stations are privately owned and run.

The children, under the care of native nurse girls, are at the merry-go-round. About 70–100 yards away is the bar where the men are, and some of the women. Four long posts are set in the ground, with branches cut and tossed on top to form a roof. Long trestles form four square tables round the barmen. They are going like blue-tail flies, trying to keep the beer flowing. Shouted orders, money and drinks pass round and over the heads of those lucky enough to be close to the tables. The terrible sound of bottles being deliberately smashed. Because there was no way to return empties, they are smashed to make for easy disposal. The ground becomes a bog to the ankles. The shining boots and knife-creased trousers that the men began the day with are now covered and splashed with mud. Who cares? Certainly not the men — and the women cannot afford to let it bother them. They want to enjoy these few days.

Julia, from *Texas Downs*, at least three parts under the weather and finding her high-heel shoes too much for her tough old half-caste feet, takes them off and wanders around barefoot. She swings a shoe in each hand. The women have a soft spot for Julia. She is kind-hearted and, although they do not accept her as an equal, they are not unkind to her either. Not so with some of the men. They treat her as a joke and call out rude remarks as she passes. Julia gives as good as she gets. She lets fly with times and places where they have met her. Very few of the men are game enough to keep up the slanging match. The married ones cringe and cast a quick glance around to see if their wives are close before they disappear into the crowd.

On my first visit here, I was thoroughly disgusted with everything — the rough accommodation, living conditions and the people in general. Now, I am able to accept these things. This is my life, these are my people and this is my country. Although the Kimberleys came close to breaking me, I can now accept it.

After four days of hard drinking and late nights, the men start to sober up and gather their blacks together. It is time to go home. Sore heads and short tempers send the blacks scurrying in all directions. Some stations are returning with more than they took in, others with less. If a black does not want to be found, there is no way his white boss will find him. The blacks are loyal to each other. They will not inform on their own.

We are lucky; all our blacks are on the truck. It is the whites who are the problem. Either still too drunk or too sick, they want to stay another day. We have no driver for the truck. Rod, at this time, is not a heavy drinker. He drinks beer and has to stay reasonably sober to keep an eye on his father who is a heavy rum drinker. I will never get used to this drinking. How I hate it.

I am very annoyed with Rod and have no sympathy for him now, especially as I have to drive his Chev utility home while he drives the truck. We have to leave the jeep behind. Harold Caporne will drive it out later. After starting George Allen off with the horses, I leave and Rod follows in the truck.

Ten days after leaving *Lansdowne* for Halls Creek, we arrive back home — a long time to be away. Rod is very wheezy. His asthma is bad. There is little I can do for him. Drinking has certainly aggravated it. I know it is hard for him when his mates are drinking and his father keeps saying, "You are not a man if you cannot hold your liquor. Mine's a rum!" I could whack him.

No time to rest up. We must get ready for our next muster.

* * *

Native girls, Balgo Mission.

Halls Creek Races. From left: Maggie Lilly, Ken 'Apples' Dennis, Peg Underwood.

From left: Grandfather Quilty, Rob Moody, Lou McBeth, Rod Quilty and Beryl Moody in town for the Halls Creek Races.

Bore plant, rig, etc. at Wilson on *Lansdowne*.

CHAPTER ELEVEN

New faces at the station

Sometimes, when dust
Makes velvet shadows,
I think I hear them speak.

The stock camp went without me for the cow and calf muster. Rod was disappointed but there are so many things for me to do at the station — teaching the children my top priority. They are doing so well now, I cannot let them slip back. They will stay on the School of the Air for another year, then we will decide what is best for them.

The old blacks at night look for the 'walking star', their name for *Sputnik*, the Russian satellite. They try to get the children interested but it is hard for Meldie and Tommy and the piccaninnies to find it among so many brilliant stars. The old ones cry out excitedly as soon as they find it. They follow *Sputnik* as it moves round the sky. I watch with them. They are not afraid of it as they were of the eclipse. To them, the 'walking star' is friendly.

The good early rain ended too soon. The year is so dry. Hot winds blow and stir up the dust, waters dry back and cattle are in poor shape as they eat the fresh little spinifex shoots that spring up after Rod has burnt off the buck spinifex. Cattle follow the buck spinifex up and over the hills to get at the long tassels that sprout from this coarse, spiky plant. It keeps them alive. Rod's father comes with his dogs to help us move cattle from dried-out springs to the few water holes we have left. In the terrible heat, he loses all his dogs except one. A big loss to him, as he relies heavily on his dogs when mustering.

Cattle follow dry storms and we have to bring them back to the water before they perish. Riding with Rod and the boys almost every day, I am tired, sunburnt and depressed. Much as Rod dislikes shooting horses, brumbies have to be shot. We need the water for our cattle. I can at least be thankful that I have been able to spend so much time with the children. They are going to miss school for November and possibly the last school weeks in December, if it does not rain. I can only hope for early storms and a good wet season.

The blacks spend Christmas with us, then, on Boxing Day, they leave for their walkabout. Meldie and I wave to them as they move off, Tommy with Johnny Ray, trying to get the dogs moving. Little did we know then that Peggy, Maggie and their families would not come back. We are at a loss to know why. I will miss them, especially Peggy, and Meldie and Tommy have lost their special playmate. Paddy tells us, "Not you pusiness (business), 'nother blackman pusiness make 'em go." He will try to find new staff for us. He knows of blacks who want to come to *Lansdowne*. I hope he is right.

* * *

We have missed the early storms and receive very little rain for December. Cows and calves are dying, and there are some losses in our mares and foals. I go with Rod and the boys to muster our horses. They all have to be drenched. The mares are so weak, but we cannot afford to lose them to the dreaded worms.

Paul Gallagher, an English war orphan from Bindoon Orphanage, Perth, and Garth Edgar, a young teenager from the Derby area, come to us. Totally inexperienced, they have no idea what is ahead of them. Garth, whose mother has died, comes from a well-known Kimberley family. They are, in every sense of the word, "new chums". They are so young and eager, and Rod is such a hard boss. They must be utterly miserable and confused at times, as they struggle to saddle up, unsaddle, bridles on, bridles off, ride, keep up, get out of the way, block up there, shoe your horse, wash his back, grease your saddle. They eat on the run, always looking to see where Rod is, trying to please, and to keep out of his way. Hilton Gore would like to help them, but he has his own troubles. Dimpy, from Beagle Bay Mission, in her early thirties, and Hilton are too friendly. Hilton's wife, Molly, is very jealous. They have five or six children who spy on Dimpy and Hilton, and report back to Molly.

* * *

One morning, about a week before the stock camp went out, Paddy comes to tell us there are new blacks in the camp. He knows them, they are "'lations" (relations). One good stockman, some old ones, and two good house girls for me. Rod says, "Send them up." I expect to see a tired and tattered group, but they come clean and sprightly. We discover they have been in the camp for five days, Little Mick, his wife Liddy, and Mary, wife of Old Harry. Mary's mother, very old, does not come up. Harry is also very old. Little Mick will go with the stock camp, and I can do with Liddy and Mary's help. Liddy tells me Old Harry is a garden boy. That is good. He can potter round with Zachady and the other old blacks on the lawns and the house garden. Nora cares for the vegetable garden. She has green fingers. Dimpy will work and get on well with Mary and Liddy. She is clean and very easygoing, and I am very fond of her. Rosie is my laundress. She works when she feels like it, but she manages to get through the washing and ironing every day. Molly does not work for me. She is fully occupied with her little family. My old cook has gone. *Lansdowne* is a dry station. He said he could not live so far away from a hotel; so I am the station cook again. My time is divided between the kitchen and teaching. It is not good for the children, however, so we are on the lookout for another cook. Liddy and Mary fit in well with our blacks but Liddy is bossy. She bosses everybody, including me. Zachady and Old Harry dislike each other from the start. I keep them apart, one on the front lawns, one on the back. Old Harry has a bullet lodged in his leg. A long time ago, when he was a young man, he was shot as he ran away after being caught spearing cattle. He limps now but tells me it does not hurt. He seems rather proud of the scar he still carries.

Rod has bought three mares from Doug Davidson, of *Dunham River* — three beautiful thoroughbred mares, Call Girl, Terrylean, and Miss Thalia. The fastest horse in the stock camp is no longer good enough for our small town race meetings. We can afford this luxury now. We have also ordered several prefab huts and two-room buildings for the half-castes and blacks. They are married quarters only. Hilton, Molly and their family, Dick and Shirley Wilson, and Dimpy move in. With beds and wood stoves and a little furniture, the half-castes settle down happily. Single male half-castes will continue to camp wherever they throw their swags down. Dimpy is the only single female half-caste here. The blacks, like happy children, move all their belongings into their huts. They sleep there, but not for long; it is not in their nature to be locked away at night. They move their swags out, leaving their belongings inside, and the dogs take over the huts. There are lean-to verandahs on the huts, onto the roofs of which the blacks toss their bones and other food to keep it away from the dogs. They spend their free time under the verandahs.

Margo Blenton, a young cook, sent us by an employment agency in Perth, arrives by plane. She looks about eighteen or nineteen years old. I ask what experience she has had, as station cooking is not for the faint-hearted. She says she is a good cook with a lot of experience. I can only hope she is truthful. I show her to her room at the end of our building and tell her that she can start in the morning. She wants to know what time she has to get up. I tell her four o'clock. Ohhh! that's too early; she could not possibly be up at that hour. I tell her I will call her, and help her, the first morning; after that I will give her an alarm clock.

Although I call Margo at four o'clock, she does not come into the kitchen until eight, breakfast well and truly over. We are preparing smoko. Margo wants to know where she has her breakfast. Liddy tells her, "Doo lade, yo don' eat." (Too late, you don't eat). Margo, hands on her hips, turns to face Liddy. Margo's foolish mistake. Liddy moves towards her. Margo backs off and quickly steps behind me. She tells me that union hours are from eight o'clock in the morning until five o'clock in the afternoon. Oh! Good heavens! What have I got here?

Margo will have to go, but I will try to make things work for awhile; she might be a good cook. I tell her to watch as Liddy puts a bucket of corned beef on the stove to cook. She stands well back as Liddy heaves the bucket up. I ask if she can make bread, cook corned beef, make puddings? She tells me, "Any fool can cook beef, I don't expect to have to make bread, and no! I won't be making puddings; I don't like puddings." Things are going from bad to worse. I am beginning to wonder if she can cook at all. I leave her in the kitchen, standing over the corned beef. Every now and then she makes a stab at it. I ask her why she keeps poking it. She cannot understand my stupidity. "How in bloody hell am I to know when it is cooked if I don't keep poking it?" That's it, Margo, you are out of here as soon as I can find transport for you.

* * *

Kitty is back from the leprosarium. She comes on our medical plane wearing a white dress, black shining shoes and socks, making sure the lace on the bottom of her petticoat is seen by all, and that the piccaninnies do not get too close to put their hands on her dress. She is twisting and turning and slapping at their little hands. Nora tells me Montie and Kitty are husband and wife now. Montie, silent and brooding, and Kitty, a chatterbox, get on well together. Montie is Paddy's brother; a big man like Paddy, but totally different in nature. I don't think I ever saw Montie smile. He is very protective of me. He has a great round lump, on his back, that flaps round under his shirt. He says he has no pain but we do not let him go into the stock camp. He does lots of little jobs for me round the house.

Three days after Kitty arrives back, her shoes and socks have disappeared, and the dress, no longer white, has a few tears in it. She wants clothes from me. I take her to the storeroom and fit her out. She wants "bags longa milk." I look for the brassieres and give her two.

Rod has bought me a Holden stationwagon for my birthday. Don Sharpe, son of Bert, will take it off the ship at Wyndham and hold it until we can pick it up — a lovely green vehicle with dark green trim.

We struggled through 1962, but it was not a good year. As in 1961, good early rain ended too soon. We need good storms now, but they do not come. We have had such a turnover of staff. White men come, but few of them are stockmen, most are just handymen. They quarrel with each other and with the half-castes. They do not stay long and I am pleased to see them go.

Jack Brumby, a big, strong man of mixed blood, has been with us for twelve months. He is a good stockman but prefers fencing and yard building to stock work. We are in need of good strong yards and lots of fencing. Jack works alone for the most part but Rod gives him an off-sider when he can. He has a big drinking problem. I do not know how long he will stay with us, before his craving for drink gets the better of him. His cousin, Jack Gould, is also here. He will take our bullocks to Wyndham this year; in the meantime, he helps out in the stock camp. Jack says he comes from Cloncurry.

Early in January, we pick the Holden up and drive to Queensland for our first family holiday. After a short stay with relations at Julia Creek and Brisbane, we head for Sydney. We have promised the children we will take them to the famous Taronga Park Zoo. Sydney is big, fast, and overcrowded. The children enjoyed the zoo but nothing else in 'the big smoke' amused them. We returned to Queensland for the rest of our holiday. We arrived back at *Lansdowne* in March. The rush is now on to gather staff up and get the stock camp moving. We still need more rain, and I need to be free to teach the children.

Stan Coote is here looking for work. We snap him up. Stan, an Englishman, was a pastrycook on board a ship. He made his way out to the Kimberleys after jumping ship at Townsville. He has a lubra he calls

Narda with him. Our blacks call her Numagee, her blackfellow name, but they do not like her. Liddy says, "Dat Numagee no good woman. Send her 'way." Numagee, a big woman, stays with Stan. To all concerned, she is his wife. She does not work for me, but often helps Stan in the kitchen. He is very jealous of her. As far as I know there is no cause for his jealousy, but when he is in a bad mood, he stalks her with a long hunting knife, often catching and cutting her. Stan certainly is a good cook. He makes beautiful pastry, but although the blacks do not like him, they do nothing to help Numagee.

Tommy, Meldie and I go with Rod and the boys to muster the horses. Some are missing; Tommy's little mule, Fat-Fat and his favourite horse, Kevin, are dead. Old Montie and Jock are also missing. I think they are dead. While the boys are shoeing, Rod works on the old Bedford truck, with Bunchemup and me helping. Rod is doing up the brakes. He is under the truck, Bunchemup leaning near the front of the engine as I sit in the cabin, pumping the brake pedal. A stick holds the bonnet up. Bunchemup is very close to the stick. If he bumps it, the bonnet will come down on him. I lean out the door to wave to him to stand further back. He does not understand. His arm bumps the stick and the heavy bonnet comes down. It catches him across the forehead. A flap of skin comes down over his face. Rod scrambles from under the truck and goes to Bunchemup, telling me to go to the kitchen and get a packet of tea and some bandages. He sits Bunchemup down as I run off, wondering why he wants the tea. I soon find out.

Lifting the flap of skin, I hold it in place as Rod packs the dry tea leaves round the wound, then tightly bandages his head. Very little blood seeps through. We arrange for the medical plane to pick him up. Bunchemup suffered that terrible pain in silence. He did not return to *Lansdowne* after he left hospital — another of our good old stockmen gone.

* * *

Betty Rose and Bob McInerney come to visit. From Sydney to the bush, what a shock! Rough, dusty roads, flies, heat, and great ranges, rivers and creeks. Quilty country as far as the eye can see. City-bred, but of pioneer stock, Betty soon settles into the life, but it is not Bob's cup of tea. However, he admits it is an experience he would not have missed.

With the cooking in Stan's capable hands, I now find my time split between the children and the stock camp. This simply cannot go on. With young black stockboys drifting to the towns, we are always going to be shorthanded. I will finish this year with them, but Meldie and Tommy will have to go back to the convent at Julia Creek next year.

* * *

Rain on a tin roof is sweet music. Beautiful, drenching rain breaks the drought after three long years. The country responds quickly. Our springs come back to full force, creeks and lagoons fill, and rivers rush and roar down previously dry, sandy beds. The level of our wells rise to amazing heights. Natural and imported grasses sprout in the valleys and on the plains. The country looks beautiful. Bushfires are no longer a problem. I watch as lovely, long waterfalls gush out of the hills and ranges and flow majestically down to the rocky waterholes below — truly a gift from God. With reasonable seasons now, we will not have water problems for a long time. The waterfalls will dry up, and the grasses will brown off, but the waters will be there.

* * *

We have cleared our debts and are financially secure now, but staff is a big worry. We are always chasing good stockmen. It is an ongoing problem, and it will get worse. We still have five of our old black stockmen but they are no longer young. Whites and half-castes come and go; they do not stay long. Garth leaves us in May, 1965.

Meldie and Tommy have been at the Julia Creek convent for two years. We are well satisfied with the standard of education, but it gets harder and longer to get them there and home for the holidays each year. One year, my mother booked them from Julia Creek via Townsville, Brisbane, Sydney, Melbourne, Perth and then to Derby, where we met them. Little tags pinned to their clothes said "Meldie Quilty travelling to Derby W.A. to my parents" and "Tommy Quilty travelling to Derby W.A. to my parents". Air hostesses guided them on and off planes until they safely reached Derby. It was a long way for two small children to travel but quicker than had they been booked via Mt Isa and Darwin. Overnight at Mt Isa, two days at Darwin waiting for a connection to Wyndham or Derby, was something we could not ask of the children. Because they were going interstate, there was no financial help from the West Australian Government, however, that did not concern us as much as the travelling did. We decide we will send them to Perth next year, in 1966.

* * *

Stan Coote has been with us for two years, but I will have to let him go. Splendid cook that he is, his continual pursuit of Numagee with his hunting knife is getting on everyone's nerves. I will have to pay him off. Reluctantly, we put them on the station plane to Derby. Dick Wilson and Hilton Gore, with their families, left us in 1963, which was a big loss, however, they returned early in 1966. Molly's daughter, Barbara came with them. Barbara has a beautiful baby everyone calls Bull-Bull.

135

Molly says Barbara wants to work for me. Molly will care for Bull-Bull. I put Barbara to work making beds. Meldie and Barbara clash. Barbara's idea of making beds is to pull the sheets and covers up, smooth them out, and toss the pillows on. Meldie knows I have told Barbara, and shown her how, to strip the beds and air them before making them up. Meldie follows Barbara and pulls everything off the beds. Barbara comes to tell me, " Dat Muldie bin makem de beds narked (naked)." I have no idea what she means. I must go and check. Barbara must make the beds as I had shown her.

Rod's sister, Doreen, and her two sons come to visit. It is wonderful having her here. I have a lot of little pawpaw trees coming up. They are clustered together, and not all will be fruit-bearing trees. Some will be male trees which I do not want. I have one full-grown male tree now; I do not want any more. It is impossible for me to tell the male trees from the fruit-bearing trees; they all look alike. Doreen says she knows a way to separate them. Good! Find the fruit-bearing trees, Doreen. She takes her wedding ring off, ties it to a piece of string, and dangles it over the little shoots. The ring swings round and round, and from side to side. There definitely is a difference in the swing. This is really good. Now, which is which? Doreen looks confused; she has forgotten which swing indicates which tree! Bad luck, I will just have to take pot luck and hope I transplant the fruit-bearing trees and not waste my time on the males. I hope she and her sons, Peter and Paul, enjoy their stay as much as we enjoy having them.

* * *

Rod and I attend a wedding at Halls Creek, 17 April 1965.

Rod getting petrol on our way to Sydney for holidays.

Rod and Tommy, filling a waterbag at Charleville during holiday time.

Tommy saddling Tiny.

Dick and Shirley Wilson with baby Jenny.

The Holden Rod gave me for my birthday—broken down at Emu Point. Rod is in foreground with our portable radio.

139

CHAPTER TWELVE

God help us

Alone in the evening shadows,
I sit at the close of day,
And thank our Lord for the joys of life.

Tom Quilty

In mid-January 1966, Rod and I fly to Perth with Meldie and Tommy, to put them into boarding school. Meldie will go to Loreto Convent and Tommy to Aquinas College. They are not happy, and we are upset at leaving them, but they still have at least five school years ahead of them. Perth is closer to *Lansdowne* than Queensland, and they will be able to spend more of their holidays with us. Meldie knows Yarnie Laidlaw, a boarder at Loreto. Yarnie's parents manage Christmas Creek Station, south-east of Derby, for the Emanuel Group. Tommy does not know anyone at Aquinas but he will later meet Robert Davidson from Dunham River Station, east of Wyndham. Robert is a little older than Tom and has been a border at Aquinas for a year. Robert's parents, Doug and Shirley, are good family friends.

Peg Underwood is in Perth to put her youngest son, Reg, into his first year at Christ Church College. Her daughters, Marian and Anna, are boarders at St. Mary's College.

Peg and I buy school uniforms for our children and fit them out. The college suits are at least two sizes too big for Tommy and Reg. We hope that they will last them their school years, as the boys grow into them.

Great tucks in the sleeves and legs tell the story. It is to prove false economy, as the boys fast outgrow the tucks.

* * *

Visitors start to come to *Lansdowne*. Padre Ken Beckett and his wife, Beth, arrive, driving over rough roads, tracks and no roads at all. Based at Halls Creek, they will spend the night with us. They have newsreels and short films to show. With a makeshift screen set up on the lawn, and our 32-volt power supply, we have pictures. All staff gather round. It is a special night. Tomorrow, Ken and Beth will go on to *Fossil*, or wherever they can travel.

Major Peterson also flies in from time to time. He is of the Presbyterian Church. He borrows needle, cotton and an old sheet from me to patch the wing of his plane. God alone keeps it in the air.

Rod's drinking was not a problem in our hard years, but as our living conditions gradually improve and things get easier for us, he goes from beer to whisky — *Lansdowne* is no longer a dry station. I do not know why he has started to drink more heavily, possibly because he is more relaxed and has more free time, or perhaps it is just the country. There are no cafes, and very little in the way of soft drinks, in our small towns. All social life centres round the hotel bars and beer gardens. We quarrel often and bitterly. Every mail plane brings more whisky. More and more responsibility falls on my shoulders. The boys come to me for orders. I do not like this. Fortunately, we still have a few good black stockmen, and three good half-caste men, Dick Wilson and Hilton Gore, who have returned to *Lansdowne*, and Jimmy Johnson. I can work well with the blacks and with Dick and Hilton but, although Jimmy Johnson is a good man, he usually ignores me and goes his own way. He pretends he is deaf. I know he is not, but he knows his job and does it well, so I leave him alone. Dick's father boasts of "My three sons, Tom, Dick and Harry." All the Wilson boys are good stockmen.

I can never find where Rod hides the whisky. I put Liddy on to tail him, armed with her turkey-wing duster and konkerberry broom. She actually uses a turkey wing for a duster, and konkerberry bush bound together on the end of a stick for a broom. Both are effective. Liddy follows him round, dusting and sweeping, until she sees where he has hidden the bottles. As soon as she finds the plant, she holds her hand in the air and the piccaninnies rush to tell me. We take the bottles. Although Liddy annoys Rod, he has no idea of what she is up to. I start hiding the whisky in the woodheaps at our stock camp sites. Every stock camp woodheap is a cache of whisky. Rod suspects he is not getting the full quota, but he can't be sure.

I try to cover for him. I do not want the children to know he has such a bad drinking problem, but they know. The first question they ask as they return from school is, "Is Dad still drinking?" His drinking nearly breaks my heart. I beg him to give it up, however, he does not consider he has a problem. I open bottles, pour in Epsom salts, then carefully recork them. I dilute it with cold tea, but nothing I do or say will stop him. I write to the hotels, asking them to stop sending the whisky out. I should have known better — they do not think he drinks to excess, because his "grog" order is no bigger than any other station. I pray for him.

* * *

We go to all the races now. I have made many friends and look forward to meeting, among others, Jean Back, Dot Smith, Billy Dalzell and dear, kind old Ciccy Le Tong at Wyndham; Maxine McDonald and Lex Jones at Fitzroy Crossing; and so many women at Halls Creek. Peg Underwood is possibly my best friend, and I always look for Maggie Lilly and Hessie Schultz at the meetings. I sometimes meet Mary Durack at Wyndham and Derby. Mary has a passionate love for the Kimberleys. Years ago, when I was a boarder at St. Mary's Convent, Charters Towers, my best friend there was Winsome Costello. She often spoke of her relations, the Duracks of West Australia. There is not a woman I have met in the Kimberleys, and on into the Territory, that I did not like. I can talk to them, laugh with them, and be happy with them. We have so much in common. I do not think they will ever know how much their friendship means to me.

Rod always likes to kill a beast the day after we return from the races. It settles the staff down, and gets them into work mood again. On killing night, everybody cooks their own. The kihii (short ribs), the Smiths, and the McNamara bones, grilled on the coals, and eaten with a slab of bread are very sweet. I cook the brains and liver. Much of the fresh meat is left out overnight to cool, then cooked the next day. Fresh meat does not keep long. I cook as much as I can. Huge pieces of fresh meat — five or six roasts, and great buckets of corned briskets. We like to cook the briskets early. I never get out of the kitchen the day after the kill. The salt beef is left lying in brine overnight and hung out the next day.

Fred Ryle contacts us over the Flying Doctor Base to say there is a male cook in Wyndham, looking for work. Do we want him?

"Yes! We certainly do. Send him out on our next mail plane!" we reply. Rod meets the plane, picks the cook up and drives him back to the station. He says his name is John Smith. He looks to be in his mid- to late thirties. He is not a very big man . He admits that he has never done any station cooking. He has cooked for hotels and has been a shearers' cook. That's good enough for us, but I wonder what brings a man like this to such a remote and isolated place. Smith is a very common name in the Kimberleys; perhaps because it is easy to remember or easy to spell.

John starts well. He checks with me to know what I want cooked and when. We will go over the menu every day and I will show him where the garden is so that he can get whatever vegetables he needs. Something seems to be bothering him. I have to know what it is, so I ask him, "Is there anything else you want to discuss with me?"

He looks round carefully, then, seeing we are alone, he whispers, "Are these blacks cannibals?"

I am shocked. "No, they are not! Whatever gave you that idea?"

"Those two in the kitchen, not the fat one (Mary) but the other one (Liddy), looks dangerous. I don't think she likes me."

It is hard for me not to laugh. I tell him he has nothing to be afraid of, but not to cross Liddy. She won't eat him, but she will give him the rounds of the kitchen if he annoys her.

* * *

I miss Meldie and Tommy so much. This is the fourth year they have been away from us, and they still have several years to go before they will be home for good. There would be few families on the land whose children have not spent a lot of their growing up years away at boarding school. It is hard on the parents and hard on the little bush children. How we miss them and at what cost, emotionally and financially — a great sacrifice of blood, sweat and tears. I hear black children are being taken from their parents and out of the camps, to be sent to Mission schools to be educated and taught hygiene. How I sympathise with their parents, especially the mothers. I know how they feel, but these children are the lucky ones, the little privileged ones. In a fast-changing world, whether you like it or not, your children and grandchildren will have to move into the white man's world. There will be no magic jump from your primitive world into the sophisticated world of the white man. Teach your children all the mysteries of your Dreamtime or whatever, but do not begrudge them their white education — be thankful. So few of your children now are interested in your old tribal ways and laws. Not many are interested in any sort of education.

Schools and churches in the Kimberleys are accessible to both whites and blacks, with the advantage probably going to the blacks. The churches cater for black souls; they compete with each other to gather their flocks in. White school children are disadvantaged by being kept to the level of the black child, as the black child is slow to learn. Not always interested, they often wag school. Schooling is compulsory for the white child, but the black child is not forced to turn up every day. Schoolteachers must be at their wits' end.

* * *

John continues to do a good job in the kitchen. He wants Barbara to help him rather than Liddy. I know he is afraid of Liddy. I bring Liddy into the main house and put Barbara in the kitchen. For a week all goes well, then John starts to complain that Barbara does not always turn up for work. Perhaps Barbara wants to spend more time with Bull-Bull. Molly says Barbara does not want to work in the kitchen and would rather work in the house with me. I am puzzled by what is going on. Liddy does not want to go back to the kitchen because she does not like John. I leave Mary in the kitchen and keep Liddy and Barbara in the house. John comes to the house looking for Barbara. I can hear Liddy telling him, "Get out, get out. Yo bin 'um bug dat girl." She is flapping her old konkerberry broom in his face. John backs off. Now I know why Barbara does not want to work in the kitchen with him. Molly confirms that John has been annoying Barbara. I had no idea — they should have told me. John is barred from the house, confined to the kitchen and his quarters. He is to keep away from Barbara; she is only fifteen years old. John sulks for days but continues to work. However, I have a feeling he is not going to stay long.

The stock camp has been out for three weeks. We are mustering the bottom end, round Goads Yard, and we are low on stores. Rod and I drive back to the station for more. Rod starts to drink as soon as we get back. We load the jeep but he is too drunk to drive. I will have to wait until he is sober. John tells us he wants to pull out. Rod slept. I sat on the verandah and prayed during the dark, lonely night.

I will never know if I dreamt it or if I imagined it, but suddenly I saw a statue of the Blessed Virgin standing in a patch of clean, red ground, ringed in by bright green spinifex. Clear, ice-white marble, her hands by her sides, palms turned towards me. Praying for so many things, I thought, this is a sign that one of my prayers will be answered — but

145

which one? I also thought I would recognise the place when I saw it again. I looked at my watch — almost three o'clock. Rod woke and we drove back to the camp. Although I drove all over *Lansdowne* many times, I could never find the place of my dream.

I was sorry to see John go, but perhaps it was for the best. He could have a problem that we could not possibly handle on *Lansdowne*. How I hate being the station cook again.

We cannot get a drover for our bullocks this year; Rod and a station plant will have to take them. Like the good old stockmen, good drovers are gradually fading away. Rod wants me to go with him as he does not have many men. I can take Liddy. Oh, heavens! Now I am to be a drover.

Liddy agrees to go only because Little Mick is going. I am not looking forward to droving, especially as Liddy and I will have to do the cooking as well as helping with the bullocks. Oh! that life can be so cruel.

Things start well. We have our numbers, bullocks counted, and in hand; we slowly move off. I absolutely refuse to ride anything but Troy. Rod says I will need a second horse but I am simply afraid of horses now. I will take Angel. Rod puts me on the tail and tells me, "Don't push the bullocks; take them slow and easy. The country is very rough; we do not want to cripple them." Paddy will be with me. Liddy, riding a mule, stays with Joe and the horses.

Keeping in mind that the *Gibb River* mob rushed on the road to Wyndham, causing the Russ family to lose their entire income for the year, and the *Ruby Plains* bullocks turned back because of red water fever, Paddy and I, and the rest of the team, will carefully nurse our bullocks all the way to the meatworks.

Two days out and Liddy has had enough. She is not a drovers' cook; she is "head station girl". Amongst other things, she tells Rod what he can do with his mule and his bullocks. Her "pum" is so sore from riding that "pluddy mule" that she cannot sit down. She says she will go back to the station and I am to go with her.

"No, Liddy," I tell her, "I must stay with Rod. You go back. Take the mule; he is very quiet." Liddy nearly has a fit. She will not. She cannot ride. Rod can put the mule in his ear for all she cares. She will walk. We give her some rations and she leaves. She will be all right. She has enough food, and there is plenty of water along the way. She will take her own good time.

Rod and the boys share the extra work with me but I miss Liddy. With all her grumbling and grouching, we managed to do what had to be done. The boys gather wood and get the fires going and the billies on. They wash their plates, and carry their quart pots on their saddles. On the fourth day out, just as we are settling the bullocks down for the night, Zachady walks into the camp. Liddy had sent him to help me. Bless her dear old heart.

Light rain during the night was a nuisance, but the storm that seems to be working up today could be a real problem. Rod pushes the bullocks. He wants to get them out of the timber and breakaway country before the storm breaks. We do not stop for dinner. The clouds get heavier as the afternoon wears on. Five o'clock, and we are in a small clearing where we will camp.

Paddy, Joe, Little Mick and I stay with the cattle. Rod and the others quickly unpack tarpaulins, gather wood, and put it under the tarpaulins with our stores and stock gear. They hobble out the spare horses. The bullocks are restless. Claps of thunder and lightning cause them to jump and try to break. I am so afraid I could cry.

Paddy stays close to me but I tell him I am all right. He must watch the bullocks; I haven't a hope of blocking them if they come my way. We give them plenty of room as we ride round them. It has started to rain, great, heavy, stinging drops. Within minutes, I am soaked to the skin. My hat flops over my face, I slip it off, and let it hang round my neck. My blouse sticks to me. I can only see the cattle when the lightning flashes, and what I see only frightens me more. I stop riding round. I hear the boys trying to steady them. "Whoa! Whoa, bullocks." Some are singing. I chant, "Oh! dear God! Let Rod come, let Rod come." Little Mick comes close and tells me to go round to the other side so that I have the rain at my back. Troy stumbles and splashes water but it is better with the rain at my back. Troy is more settled with his rump to the rain also.

Someone yells; the bullocks have broken through somewhere. I scream for Rod. Someone is close to me; he grabs Troy's bridle rein. A flash of lightning and I see it is Rod. He says, "Zachady is here. He will take you back to the camp." As I huddle under the tarpaulin, shivering with cold and fear, I think of all the lightning stories I have heard — how lightning can strike. Oh! dear God! Keep Rod and the boys safe. I wonder could they possibly be as afraid as I am.

We spend a miserable night. The storm passes, but there is no let-up.

Rod and the boys stay with the cattle until daybreak. Zachady and I try to keep the fire going and the billies hot. The boys ride in one at a time, during the night, for a quick drink of lukewarm tea. No one sleeps. Dawn, and time to count our losses. We count the bullocks; we are down eight on our numbers. It could have been worse. No one is hurt. Our stores and stock gear are damp but not wet. We must get going; we have to keep our date at the meatworks.

This was my first droving trip. There were to be many more over the years, but none as frightening as this one. Rod sends Zachady and me back from our last camp before *Bedford*. He and the boys will take the bullocks on. I do not like leaving him, but I am pleased to go. I've had enough; I've really had enough. It will be a long ride but we will be home before dark. Riding with Zachady, I can still hear their voices as the boys called and sang to the cattle that terrible stormy night.

Just on dark, we ride in sight of the station. Liddy and the girls fuss round. All I want to do is have a warm bath and go to bed. Liddy will have none of it. She agrees to prepare the bath but I must eat. Tea and toast is the best she can do, but I am deeply grateful to that kind, bossy old woman. Rosie takes Zachady off to feed him.

The bullocks are on the road for a total of 22 days — five days *Lansdowne* to *Bedford* then 17 days *Bedford* to delivery at Wyndham Meatworks. I have no contact with Rod for 18 days. I hear from him as soon as he gets to Wyndham. Fred Ryle arranges for him to speak to me from the Flying Doctor Base. How good it is to hear from him. They have made a good delivery, with no further losses on the road. He will start the plant back, but he will stay until the bullock kill, then fly out on the station mail plane.

The girls are happy to have their husbands back. The boys take the shoes off the horses and let them go with the mules. I do not give them any jobs while Rod is away. They have earned a rest. Life is peaceful and quiet. The blacks corroboree every night. They are happy.

Rod arrives home with a bottle of whisky and a lovely gold wristwatch. He gives both the whisky and the watch to me. I love the watch, it is a perfect fit. Rod is so kind and thoughtful. He promises that he will ration himself to one drink before the evening meal, nothing more. I wonder if he can keep that promise? I know he will try. I leave the whisky out where he can see it, but Liddy watches him constantly. Should he sneak a nip, she will surely know.

* * *

My beloved father died in November. I knew he had been ill, but I was not prepared for his death. How sad for my mother, sisters and brother. I feel such a terrible loss and sadness that I will not see him again. I would like to have seen him just one more time.

Father Karney arrived this afternoon with Father Nicolas; they are two priests of the Palatine Order. Father Nicolas is based at Halls Creek. As far as I know, all the Palatine priests in the Kimberleys are Germans except one. It is a German missionary order. As their surnames are too hard to pronounce, the priests are known by their given names. Bishop Jobst lives at Broome. A tall, handsome man, he is a pilot who would like his own plane.

Father Nicolas makes frequent visits to *Lansdowne* but he is not a happy man; he feels he is not getting through to the blacks and the half-castes. They play one religion off against another. If they cannot get what they want from him, and it is usually money, they tell him they will go to someone else; there are other religions around. He came one day to say goodbye. He had requested and received a posting in South Africa. Some years later, we heard that he had died in a swimming accident.

Father Peile came next. The only non-German in the Order, that I know of, Father Peile is an authority on languages, and also a polio victim. A kind man, often misunderstood, he is to record the different dialects of the many Kimberley tribes. I often hear him talking to Meldie, trying to get the right pronunciation and spelling of the words. Meldie was quick to pick up the native language, which I could never speak — I was always too busy trying to teach them to speak like whites, a mistake I regret. I spoke one language, they spoke and understood two.

George Tancred, of the Tancred Meatworks family, comes to work for us. He really wants experience in judging cattle weights. I often ride with him as he teaches me about cattle. He points out the straight backs, the round fat rumps, the long legs and the short legs. I have never taken much notice of the shape of cattle but I want to learn as much as I can while George is with us. He says the Kimberley cattle need long legs for walking during the long droving trips, but the time will come when they will be transported by truck, then we should look to breed a short-legged beast. George is engaged to Pam, an attractive air hostess. He and Rod are good friends.

Rod and the boys have always done our breaking-in, but I think Rod should give it up. We can afford to pay a horse-breaker now. Joe Atkinson is looking for work; Rod picks him up in Halls Creek and brings him out. He is just the man for the job. Rod and I know Joe from our Julia Creek days. He used to travel round outback Queensland with a buckjumping show. There is very little Joe does not know about horses. I watch him breaking-in. His methods are similar to Rod's, with one exception. Before Joe gets on a horse, he always rubs his hands on the hard corn on the horse's front legs, near the knees. I ask him why he does this. He says, "A horse can smell fear in a man. It makes him hard to handle. By rubbing my hands on the corn, it takes away the human smell."

Joe stayed on after he finished breaking-in. A quiet little old man, he stayed with us for eighteen months. He repaired flood gates, cared for the vegetable garden and helped in so many ways. He was contented, if not happy. He never spoke of his family. I think he would have stayed longer, but one day he received a letter. There were many addresses crossed out and others written in as it followed him round the country until it finally reached him at *Lansdowne*. The letter upset him very much. It was a shock. His wife had divorced him. He could not understand; he had never given her cause. But Joe was behind the times, divorce laws had changed. If a married couple had not lived together for a certain period of time, that was cause enough. Heavens knows when Joe, the wanderer, had last seen his wife. He left us, saying he would have to go back. I will miss him.

* * *

I came in from the stock camp four days ago, to get our mail ready for the mail plane. Big Mick rode in this afternoon with a message from Rod. He will be at the Bullock Paddock bore tomorrow. He wants me to meet him there, to bring dinner for everybody and to come in Red Robin. Red Robin is a four-ton International truck that my father gave us. We have been mustering for Glenroy Meatworks. The final cut-out will be at the bore.

I am early; Rod and the boys are not here yet. Lying in the shade of the tea trees, I watch as crows croak and fly above me. Their raucous calls mingle with the screeches of the pale grey and pink corellas as they settle in the trees. Glossy black cockatoos have their own trees; there are not so many of them. I can see the bright red that shows under their tail feathers. Brilliant green, red and yellow parrots fly round looking for a place to settle. Like the cockatoos, they want their own trees. Most numerous of all are the white cockatoos. They land and leave and land again, always on the move. Numerous little birds twitter as they gather to drink from the overflow. The only man-made sound comes from the windmill as it turns and clangs in the wind. There is so much beauty in this land. There is cruelty, too. I doze off.

The sound of cattle bellowing wakes me. Hustle and bustle everywhere — tired horses let go and fresh ones caught, cattle tailed out, stockmen ready for their dinner — no time to waste. We eat, then go to cut out what Rod will take to Glenroy. I keep tally. Three hundred head will go. Rod has cut out a 'killer'. I ride back to the bore as Rod and the boys kill. They will have fresh meat tonight and take salt meat on the road. I will take the rest of the fresh meat back to the station. Sitting round the campfire, grilling bones and steak, someone sees that Red Robin has a flat tyre.

I have no idea what to do. I can't go with the drovers tomorrow, it is too far for me to walk back to the station, and I can't stay here. Do something, Rod! He does. He cuts the killer's hide, still wet and pliable, into strips and winds them tightly round the tyre. That got me safely back to the station, over eleven miles (18 km) of rough, stony track that I could hardly see in the dark.

After Rod delivered to Glenroy, he rode back home, then we drive to *Mt House* together. I will stay with Doug and Rita Blyth while Rod goes to Glenroy for the kill. Driving to *Mt House* and Glenroy, we pass *Elgie Cliffs*, now deserted, cross the head of the mighty Ord River, climb the Durack Range, pass through beautiful, dangerous Tarone's Gorge, and cross the Little Fitzroy, Traine, and Hann Rivers. We drive through *Tableland* country where Jack and Joyce Rudduck had lived. Only our jeep would have got us over this rugged, trackless land.

Rita is a charming hostess. A university graduate, she is a splendid cook, but, like most mothers, has no patience teaching her children. I meet the author, Jon Cleary, at *Mt House*. He is here gathering material for his novel, *Justin Bayard*.

* * *

There were no set award wages in the Kimberleys. Whites were paid more than blacks and struck a deal with owners to their mutual satisfaction, a sort of gentleman's agreement. I do not know how managers overcame the problem. Although blacks are paid less in money, they are kept in clothes and blankets, and all our staff's non-working relations are fed and supplied with clothes.

Clothes, especially stock clothes, along with blankets and swag covers, are expensive, and blacks are hard on them. Once the winter is over, blankets are thrown away or laid down for their dogs. Boots and hats barely last a season, and shirts and trousers are often thrown away after a muster, rather than be washed and worn again. Whites supply their own clothes and swags, and they have no non-working relations. Though, generally, things balance out for us, the time will come when there will have to be an award.

Our biggest worry is staff. I accept now that Rod needs me more than ever in the stock camp. I just have to be available, letting nothing interfere with my being there. Rod, overworked, hard drinking, with his health deteriorating, needs me to be a ringer and drover.

* * *

Late in January, we put the children into boarding school again and Rod and I fly to Sydney for our holidays, staying at the lovely old Wentworth Hotel. As usual, I have a wonderful time — races, lunches, dinner parties and shopping — but Rod is bored. He does not like the cities. At Lady Fairfax's beautiful home, *Fairwater*, for lunch one day, I meet Liberace, her house guest. As we are introduced, he gives me his hand. I am surprised to see how small it is. Heavy rings on all his fat little fingers, his hand is broad. Charming and effeminate in his white satin suit, I take his hand, but get the message, "Do not squeeze", so I gently let go. He plays for us and the sheer magic of his music makes me forget everything about him. His music is joy perfected. He is a wonderfully gifted man.

On our way home, we hear disturbing rumours of general unrest among the blacks. Stories whispered of white women raped by blacks in our little towns, policemen's wives waylaid and beaten by blacks who bear a grudge, white women abused by drunken lubras. Rumours or truth, it is the worst possible news. I cannot believe *our* blacks are involved, if it is true.

We pick up a new Toyota utility at Julia Creek and drive home. We come across a band of blacks spread over the road between Kununurra and Wyndham. We pull up; they do not move. We are too well known to be mistaken for tourists. Laughing and waving, they finally part and let us through. There was no menace. It was more a mischievous act, but it frightened me. It was so out of character for the blacks. In our little towns, we see blacks gathered with raised arms and clenched fists, as they demand, "Let our people go free." I do not recognise any of them. Half-castes boast, shamelessly, of their white fathers and then cry, "Black is beautiful".

* * *

Rod with Major Peterson at *Lansdowne*.

Father Nicolas and Father Karney on a visit to *Lansdowne*.

Wyndham Races. From left: Ken 'Apples' Dennis and Ivy Dennis, Peter Monger, Rod, Lloyd Fogarty and Harold Caporne. (unidentified) and Tommy in front.

CHAPTER THIRTEEN

Times change

Time is precious,
Time is on the wing.

Tom Quilty

It is good to be home again. All our blacks are here. I am sure they know of the changes among their people, but they are confused and do not want to speak about it. It seems to me that Paddy wants to cling to the old ways, the only way he knows. He is an old man, who has known and worked with Rod for a long time. The lubras are loyal to me, but we can no longer depend on that. There are strong influences working against the white man by other white men. To whose advantage? We hear that archaeologists, travelling round, show more interest in the present than the past. Rumours and more rumours, and the the old saying, "Where there is smoke…" comes to mind.

* * *

The stock camp has only been out two weeks and Little Mick has had a bad fall. His horse, with a broken leg, has been shot. There is no bone showing, but Little Mick's foot is twisted at an odd angle, and he is in pain. Rod says the bone is broken and we must get him to hospital. Rod and I ride with him back to the station. Using the whistle, we contact the Flying Doctor Base and are put through to the doctor. He says to give Little Mick an injection for the pain, and the medical plane, on its way from Balgo Mission to Derby, will detour to *Lansdowne* and pick him up. Liddy fusses round with clean clothes and advice, but she is upset. Rod leaves for Halls Creek to pick up two black stockmen. I ride back to the camp.

Rod returned three days later with Long Jimmy and Short Jimmy. Not long in from the desert, the Mission could not control them and turned them out. Long Jimmy and Short Jimmy, surly and hard to handle, keep to themselves. They are fearless riders, but not good stockmen. Hate seems to ooze from them, directed mainly at Rod. He will have to watch his back. They ignore me.

After a long morning mustering, we settle the cattle down on the plain, and I ride to the Bullock Paddock bore with Rod, Paddy and Long Jimmy, leaving Short Jimmy with the tailers. I sit under a shady tree while the men catch fresh horses. After dinner, we will cut out the meat-works bullocks. Loud, angry voices disturb me. Looking up, I see Rod and Long Jimmy locked in a fight. Long Jimmy has a tomahawk in his hand. Paddy is there, calling to me but doing nothing to stop the fight. Long Jimmy puts his leg behind Rod's knee and throws him to the ground, the tomahawk raised. I look round for a weapon. As I run towards them, I see a pile of old fencing wire. Grabbing a piece, I keep running. I get behind Long Jimmy and slip the wire round his neck, putting enough pressure on it to pull him down and give Rod time to get clear. There is blood on Rod's face. He gets up and tells me to catch my horse and go out to the cattle. Long Jimmy is still on the ground. As I come close to the cattle, I notice a riderless horse standing under a tree, bridle trailing on the ground. Instinct tells me it has to be Short Jimmy's horse. Bruce, close by, tells me Short Jimmy had ridden over to the tree, jumped off and headed for the hills on foot. He looked frightened.

Although Long Jimmy and Short Jimmy were hard to handle, and we knew they would not stay long with us, we did not consider them bad, not in the way we knew Toby and Bruno to be bad. They were dangerous, though, and I was always afraid for Rod. They did not recognise the white man's law. I am glad they are gone.

Little Mick was in hospital for six weeks. He returned to *Lansdowne* with one leg shorter than the other, and now always rides with one boot on and one foot bare.

The words "Citizen Rights" are being bandied about. We hear the breweries are very much in favour of giving the blacks equal rights with whites. We have no idea who started this rumour, or if there is any truth in it. However, the breweries would certainly benefit. Someone is working hard to put the blacks on an equal footing with the whites. For most blacks, the term Citizen Rights merely means drinking rights.

Citizen Rights really did not affect us until the day a strange black man came to the front gate. This surprised me, as our blacks never came to the front gate. I went to see what he wanted. In his pidgin English, he told me his name was Barney, and that he had walked over the range from *Tableland*. He wanted work, but he wanted to eat and sleep where the white men did. He pulled a tattered little folder from his shirt pocket and gave it to me, showing me a piece of paper to say he had Citizen Rights. I told him to go down to the camp, where he would probably meet friends or relations. "No!" He could not do that. He could not "box up with them myalls. I like white man now."

How sad, how very sad. He denied his own people for the sake of a small piece of paper that told him he was too good for them. Someone surely must answer for this.

* * *

One day, tailing our bullocks on the road to Wyndham, I watch as three dingoes try to separate a small calf from its mother. Every time they rush in, the old cow is ready for them and bunts them off. The dingoes change tactics; they prance round the calf in a playful fashion, gradually drawing it away from its mother. Before the old cow is aware of it, the dingoes have the calf. I've seen enough. I gallop over and scatter the dingoes. They are a cowardly breed, cunning enough to keep well away from humans.

How well I know the droving stages now, Black Flag, Cheese Tin, and all the others — a mob ahead of us, a mob behind, as we slowly wind our way through the hills to Wyndham. Like a lot of other things, I wonder how much longer I will be doing this.

On returning to *Lansdowne* after the bullocks have been delivered, all except the cook have a few days off. Not all come for meals, so I have a little free time. I have just prepared the vegetables for the evening meal when John Curtain brings his little baby to me. The lubras follow him, wailing and crying. The baby's eyes are turned back, and his little body is jerking and twitching. Oh! dear God! I don't know what to do. I ask, "How old is he?"

"Three years," John Curtain says. He looks much younger.

Something far back in my memory comes to me — immerse him in water, add mustard, or is it sulphur, and warm or cold water?

157

Whatever I do cannot be worse than just watching this little boy as violent spasms rip through his little body.

I send the girls for a bucket of warm water, and mustard from the pantry. I lower his body into the bucket. With help from his mother, we gently massage his body until the jerking stops and his eyes focus normally. I take him out of the water, wrap him in a towel, and tell his mother to dry him while I call the doctor. I hear her talking and crooning to him as he lies on our bed. Suddenly she is screaming. I rush to see what is wrong. The little boy is in another convulsion. More warm water and mustard. I keep him in the water longer this time, as we massage. There is no more mustard. For the second time I take him out of the bucket, and wrap him in a towel. Placing him on the bed, I tell his mother to stay with him while I again call the doctor. She begs me to stay with the baby. I gently dry him, and rub olive oil over his little black body. I continue to massage the frail little limbs until he sleeps. His father picks him up and they return to the camp. His mother puts her arms round me and, crying, tries to thank me. Her tears fall on my blouse. This upsets me, not because of her tears — I could have cried with her — but because I feel I should know for sure, not just wonder if I am doing the right thing, when they come to me for help. Did the warm water and mustard work, or did the convulsions simply run their course?

* * *

We hear of great road trains transporting cattle to the meatworks. Where have the drovers gone? I should think many of them are more than ready to hang up their whips and saddles. Old men now, whose sons are not interested in carrying on, they gladly bow out. I am prepared to make way for the road trains.

Award wages, when brought in, hit the stations hard. Young black stockmen, who have been drifting to the towns in increasing numbers ever since Citizen Rights, are no longer interested in "money longa finger". They now want "sid down money" in town. They do not have to work for 'sit down money'. The right to drink openly is also a big attraction. They hang round the hotels until they collect their cartons of beer or flagons of wine. Some take it back to their camps; others drink close to the hotels. The local police are kept busy. Race meetings and rodeos erupt into brawling fights, black against black and black against white.

Cooks come and go in a steady stream — the work is too hard, it is too lonely, the blacks are too lazy — whatever the excuse, they barely stay twelve months, and only that long because then their airfares are paid both ways.

Father Peile comes to visit. There will be Evening Mass, for everybody, on the front lawn tonight. The blacks come. There are not many of them now, but Liddy is determined they will all turn up. After mass, I go to organise the evening meal, leaving Father to talk to the blacks. I hear Liddy's voice raised in anger. I go back to see what the trouble is. Apparently Father asked them where the Infant Jesus was born. Liddy says, "'Ere at Lan-as-don."

Father says, "No! He was born in a manger in Bethlehem."

Liddy has never heard of a manger or Bethlehem. Her Jesus was born on *Lansdowne* and no one will convince her otherwise. I do not know where she got the idea, but I am not about to contradict her; I know my old Liddy. Father tries again. She looks at me and says, "Yumman, yo dell dis man Jesus bin born at Lan-as-don."

I nod, "Yes, Liddy, if you say so." Father gives up.

A Native Welfare Officer comes from Halls Creek to put all our blacks on pensions or child endowment. Their cheques will be sent to them care of *Lansdowne*, and made out to their white and native names. He tells me his department is now known as Community Welfare and that they have the interests of both blacks and whites at heart. I take this with a grain of salt. The pension and endowment payments are a big money-making scheme for someone.

Nora spends all her time in the vegetable garden. I help her pollinate the bright yellow pumpkin flowers and wait for the pumpkins to form. When full-grown, there is no knife strong enough to cut them, only an axe can slice through the ironbark-hard skins. But they are a beautifully-flavoured vegetable. Watermelon vines spring up all over the run. The blacks throw out the seeds every year, and gather in the sweet, ripe melons. Nora is proud of her garden; lovely fresh vegetables every day — rockmelons, custard apples, mangoes, pawpaws, grapes and passionfruit flourish under her hands.

* * *

Easter is nearly here. *Lansdowne* is completely meat-free on Good Friday. No one complains. The whites and blacks accept this day of abstinence, and there is plenty of fish. Yesterday, I made two hundred and three ginger nuts. Without scales or any other method of judging weights or volumes, I used the syrup tin. Over the years I was able to turn out batch after batch of tasty ginger nuts; the old syrup tin my faithful measure.

159

Ginger Nut Recipe

Ingredients:

two and a half to three syrup tins plain flour

1 tin golden syrup

1 syrup tin dripping

quarter syrup tin sugar

half syrup tin water

2 tablespoons ginger

2 tablespoons powdered milk (put in dry)

1 teaspoon baking soda

(a little spice or cinnamon if have any)

Method:

Put everything in mixing bowl, mix well.

Let stand overnight.

Next morning roll into balls about the size of a large marble.

Place on a greased slide and bake in a moderate oven until golden brown.

Mixture can be doubled.

Like the day after the weekly kill, ginger nut day is a day on its own. There is little time for anything else as tray after tray slides into the oven. Liddy, Mary and Rosie help. Liddy and Mary are good. Liddy keeps a steady eye on Rosie, who eats more than she puts into the oven. On Good Friday I make our hot cross buns. As I knead the sugar and sultanas into the dough, I wonder how much longer I will be doing this.

* * *

Rod takes me to see his Uncle Paddy's grave on one of our visits to Wyndham. The grave is well cared for. We have been told that Darl Smith, now living in Wyndham, cares for it. We appreciate this and are grateful to Darl. There are so many old, neglected graves in this sad little cemetery, set in "The Gully" between Wyndham town and the meatworks. Forgotten men — buried here, possibly, without their families even knowing of their passing. Some had left their real names behind them. Jack Liddell, dear, kind old Jack, lies buried somewhere here, in a pauper's grave. We will arrange to have a headstone put over his grave.

160

Wyndham now has a new big cemetery. There will be no more graves in "The Gully", but this is where history lies.

A friend, Jack Camp, wants to buy our bullocks this year. We agree to sell to him, but it is a disastrous sale. He takes delivery in early June, but because we do not want two incomes in the one financial year, we ask him not to make payment until the first week in July. We trusted him. The first week came and then the second, with no payment and no word from Jack. Rod flies to Derby, only to hear bad news. Jack is insolvent. He was flat broke when he took delivery of our cattle. There are at least three creditors ahead of us. They took his road train, others took his home. There is nothing left for us; we have to suffer a big loss. No income for this year.

Twelve months later, Jack and his wife, Betty, made a supreme effort to reimburse us for the cattle, but we never did receive the full amount we were owed.

* * *

We hear, via the gossip session, that the police are on a cat and dog shoot. Although I know our blacks have too many dogs, and Nora's cats are numerous and still breeding, I will have to warn them. These shoots are necessary, but they stir the blacks up no end. They depend on their dogs for hunting at walkabout. We could lose all of our blacks because of this. Two policemen arrive at noon and want to go to the camp immediately, before the blacks become suspicious and get their dogs away. I have warned the blacks; it is up to them now. Soon, I hear shots, so I know that some animals have been found. After about an hour, the police return to the house. They have shot nine dogs, but there were no cats. They hope they have not frightened the old lubras sitting in the bed of the creek. They do not stay long; they want to be at *Fossil* before dark, a long drive.

After they leave, Nora, Liddy and Rosie come up. I expect to see them upset at the loss of their dogs, and I can hardly wait to hear about the cats. Liddy said Zachady took all the good dogs to the One Mile before the police arrived, and only old pensioner dogs were shot. They want me to go to the camp so they can show me how they saved the cats. "Come quickly!" Not upset about the pensioner dogs, and well pleased with themselves at saving the cats, they lead me down to the creek. I am surprised to see Nellie and Polly still sitting in the sand, their dresses spread out around them. The girls slither down the bank onto the sand and I go with them. Laughing, they help Nellie and Polly up. I see the open ends of sugar bags just above the sand where they have been sitting. The girls clear the sand back, dig down and pull out two bags of squealing, scratching cats. I have to laugh. They had put the cats in the bags, dug holes in the sand, and put the bags in the holes, leaving the tops open, while Nellie and Polly sat there with their dresses spread over the bags. The cats, hissing and spitting, scatter as soon as the bags are open. I think, or hope, they will all go bush and stay there, but Nora is not worried; they will come back.

I decide I will give myself a 'Toni' (home perm). Kitty wants to help, says she knows all about it, "I bin watchem longa leprosarium." Although a little dubious, I agree; I could do with some help. However, Liddy, not to be outdone, will also help. I know there is going to be trouble; it will be best if I send them away now. I read the instructions. I will need Kitty, at least, but that means Liddy will stay too. I hope Kitty is as confident as she sounds and that Liddy will not interfere too much.

Kitty fills a dish with warm water, testing it with her hand to make sure that it is not too hot. She grabs my head and pushes me, face down, into the dish. I quickly close my eyes and mouth. With the bottle of shampoo, Kitty goes to work. Every time I bob up to tell her, "Only little bit shampoo," she pushes me down again. She empties the bottle over my head and starts to scrub. Liddy rants at her, and turns the hose on me — froth and shampoo bubbles everywhere.

Kitty is ready for the next move, but I need to gain control. She will have to do as I tell her. We get to the roller stage. I show her how to place the small piece of paper at the end of a section of my hair and roll it. OK! Kitty knows all about it. Liddy is to pass her the papers and rollers as she needs them. They snatch and grab and quarrel. We are too far into the perm for me to bush them now, but I should have known better than to accept their help in the first place. Rollers are on here, there and everywhere — some tightly rolled, others barely hanging on. I remove the top of the setting lotion and give it to Kitty. She starts to squeeze it onto my head; much of it runs down my face. As she grabs a towel to wipe it off, Liddy grabs the setting lotion. Kitty won't let go. Blows and language fly — as does the setting lotion. "That's it," I tell them, "Toni finish, you can go!" Kitty is not sure, but I am. If I ever do another Toni, it will be done inside and without their help. From the way this one turned out, I doubt I will ever try again.

* * *

Meldie and Tommy are home for the school holidays. Meldie has brought a friend, Sue, with her. It has been a dry year; cattle bog repeatedly at Mud Spring.

Princess Margaret and Lord Snowdon, staying at Gogo Station while visiting the Kimberleys, will lunch at *Fossil Downs* today. Maxine McDonald has invited us to attend. Rod and I will go, and we will take Meldie and Sue. Tommy will not go. Rod and I will be presented to Princess Margaret. However, before we leave, Rod and I drive out to check Mud Spring. Two old cows are bogged to the hilt; they are weak and distressed. We get one out, but nothing we do moves the other one. We push and pull and shove, but she remains firmly bogged. We give up, winded and covered in mud. Driving back to the station, I look at my hands, mud caked under my nails. Will I be able to clean them before we leave for *Fossil Downs*?

Meldie and Sue are dressed and ready. I hurry to bathe as Rod organises the boys and starts them off for Mud Spring. Tommy goes with them. As soon as Rod is bathed and dressed, we set off for *Fossil*. Maxine McDonald, as gracious as she is beautiful, meets us. Her daughters, Merralee Wells and Annette Henwood, are with her. Maxine, calm and relaxed, is used to entertaining. She has entertained heads of State and many other famous and important people at her lovely station home.

Princess Margaret and Lord Snowdon arrive about a half an hour after us. The Princess is tiny and slim. Hatless, not a hair out of place, and sporting a perfect suntan, she is not a striking-looking person, certainly not pretty. However, she has a lovely speaking voice and lots of charm. As I am presented to her, she holds out her hand. I take it and go down on one knee, in what I hope is a graceful bow. She asks about my life at *Lansdowne*, how many children I have, do I like the life and so on. She shakes hands with Rod; he merely bows from the waist. Rod has a very strong handshake. I hope he has been gentle with the Princess.

Lord Snowdon, slim and elegant in his jeans, dark-blue shirt, white shoes and ten-gallon hat is excited. Never has he seen anything like this. "I say, old chap! So many cows, so much space, so much land where nobody lives. By Gad! Can one person really own all this, old boy?" Princess Margaret, interested but less enthusiastic, would prefer to sit in the shade, I think. The heat and the dust must be very hard on her. Her lady-in-waiting sprained her ankle at *Gogo* last night and did not accompany her. The aide-de-camp carries her umbrella but never seems to be close when she needs it.

We go to the yards, where the stockboys will demonstrate getting a calf into a cradle and, after tipping it onto a tyre on the ground, branding it. Lord Snowdon stands close to the cradle. It is suggested that he should stand further back, but he does not move. It's difficult for the boys to get

163

the calf into the cradle with him so close but they manage it. They tip the cradle and it falls onto the tyre. The calf kicks up a mixture of manure and good earth into Lord Snowdon's face. The Royal pilot, standing next to me, says, "I hope he had his mouth closed."

* * *

One day, on the road to Wyndham with our bullocks, as I wait for the boys to come in for dinner, I turn over a pat of manure. White ants scurry in all directions. Red bull ants come out of an ant bed close by and attack them. I watch as the white ants are caught and killed. I had not known this to be possible. A little willy-wagtail hops round, picking up what the bull ants have left, his little tail constantly moving from side to side in quick, jerky movements. He is a cocky little bird. My old Uncle Joe calls him his lucky bird. The blacks call him debbil-debbil bird. Like my Uncle Joe, he is my lucky bird, too.

* * *

We are camped at Piantas with a mob of cattle when Major Springer and seven soldiers drive up in two jeeps. They are on their way to Fitzroy Crossing. We are surprised and pleased to see them. They say an old black at the station had given them directions. I am sure that would have been Zachady — he always considers himself "boss boy" when we are not there. The soldiers stay several hours, sharing their dinner rations with us.

Disappointed that they will not see any mustering, they are eager for the cutting-out and branding to start. They follow every move and ask a lot of questions, watching as the cattle are yarded, the fire built up and let burn down to red-hot coals before the brands are put in. Rod catches and saddles Cubba Duck, the bronco mule; he gathers the greenhide rope up and hooks it onto the bronco gear before he mounts, then he eases it out until he has the loop in his right hand, leaving his left hand free. Old Cubba Duck knows his job — he has been doing it for a long time. He responds to pressure from Rod's knees.

The boys gather round the bronco panel — leg ropes, horn saw, dehorners, ear pliers and sharp, very sharp, pocketknives ready. Rod drops the heavy lasso over the head of a half-grown micky. The soldiers are surprised that he does not twirl the rope several times over his head before catching the micky. They, no doubt, have seen pictures of American cowboys in action. A man would soon tire, twirling a heavy greenhide rope over his head every time he lassoed a beast.

Rod pulls the micky, bellowing and resisting, up to the panel. The boys wait until the rope slips down between the panels and the micky is close before they rush in with the leg ropes, one on the hind leg, one on the front leg. With the micky stomping, butting and bellowing, it is not always easy to get the leg ropes on, but the boys work frantically and the ropes are on. Quickly, they wind them round the panel posts, someone calls, "Head", the ropes are tightened and the micky falls to the ground, near side up. A stockman grabs the tail and pulls it between the micky's legs. The lasso is taken off and Rod rides out among the cattle again for another cleanskin.

The head stockman cuts the micky, then he firmly and unerringly places the brands on the micky's rump. Smoke rises and the smell of burnt hide drifts over us. While the head stockman is doing this, Paddy, with his foot on the micky's neck, neatly cuts two pieces out of the ear, and another stockman, with the horn saw, cuts the horns back to the butt. Leg ropes off, the micky trots back to the mob, a much-chastened beast. Paddy puts the ear pieces in the bag hanging on the panel post, then drops 'something else' in a bag hanging from the fence, not far from where we are standing. I explain to the soldiers, as best I can, what has been going on, but if they want to know what Paddy has put in the bag on the fence, they will have to ask someone else!

Watching the brandings today, my mind goes back to the days when Rod and the boys did open broncoing without benefit of a panel or yard. It was hard and dangerous. There were not as many cattle, but still, it was hard and I was terrified.

* * *

Father Crotty, Chaplain of Aquinas College, reads my letters to Tommy and they fire him with enthusiasm. He will go to the Kimberleys and build his church for both whites and blacks. It must be on a station. He approaches Rod and me to see if we are interested. I am, very much so, but Rod is more cautious. We discuss it with Bishop Jobst. He is very reluctant to become involved; Father Crotty does not belong to the Palatine Order and the Brothers of Aquinas could be annoyed at our interference. We back away from the idea, but Father Crotty perseveres. He gets permission from Aquinas College to leave, and Bishop Jobst clears the way with the Palatines. Now it is up to us. Rod agrees only because I am so keen.

Father Crotty travels by MMA from Perth to Derby, then catches the station plane to *Lansdowne*. He arrives in all his glory — vestments, chalice, candles, altar wines — I'll have to keep an eye on those — and a long-handled jaffle iron! I explain to him that, until we can have a church built, with a bedroom attached, he would have to stay in the men's quarters and we will have mass on the front verandah of our home. He is not dismayed. In true missionary tradition, the harder the conditions, the better it suits him. He has brought a supply of Holy Communion wafers, but when they are finished, I will have to help him make more. Sounds simple enough — flour and water, mixed to the right consistency and cooked, not burnt, in the jaffle iron.

There will be mass in the morning. Father Crotty interviews all the blacks. Mary's mother, very old and senile, gets special attention from him. If she can't come up to the house for mass, he will give her Holy Communion in the camp. Mary tells me her mother is frightened of the holy man, "Might be he gidarchie." (He might be a witch doctor.)

Morning Mass is not a success. It disrupts the entire station. No breakfast cooked, no horses in, and Rod is annoyed having to wait for the boys to start work. Father will have to have Evening Mass. Mary's mother has walked away during the night; everybody spends the day out looking for her. They find her body late this evening. I ask Father if he would read the burial service. No, he couldn't — Mary's mother was not a Christian. He had hoped to make her one. We are not getting off to a good start at all, Father. It is now too late for Evening Mass, and the blacks are not interested anyway.

Next morning, Father is out in the yard, ringing a bell. I am in the kitchen with the girls. Nobody turns up for mass. Father waits at the kitchen door with the chalice. As each stockboy passes, he gives him Holy Communion. I am beginning to have doubts. Rod tells me Father will have to go. I would still like to see it work. I want to give it at least a week — things can't get any worse. I blame myself for Mary's mother's death. I should never have let him near her.

The girls tell me the holy man is looking for me. I find him in the kitchen, collapsed on a chair. He has the jaffle iron with him. He has no more communion wafers left. I am not surprised. We will have to make some. Father Crotty tells me they will take about an hour. I think that will still give me time to make smoko and have lunch ready.

I mix the flour and water and pour it into the jaffle iron. Father holds the iron through the open stove door. The fire is too hot, and the handle burns his hands — he drops it — one batch of Communion bread ruined. We wait until the fire burns down, then we start again. I give

Father a towel to wrap round the handle. The next batch is too thick. It is tossed out. More water, less flour, and we try again. Too thin, out it goes. Father is losing patience with me, and I know I am going to be late with smoko. I tell him I will leave one of the girls to help him while I get the boys smoko. Liddy steps forward. Father grabs the jaffle iron and says, "NO!" Liddy will have to get smoko. Rod is not pleased.

After three or four failures I get the mixture right, but Father says his arms are tired. I will have to hold the iron in the fire. Now I am not pleased. It is lunchtime, and we will have to stop. Father wants to keep going but I have made up my mind. The few wafers we have made will be more than enough.

Rod puts a stop to the boys going to mass; the girls can go if they want to, but I must not let it interfere with their work. Like the boys, the girls are no longer interested. They do not go. The blacks have no idea what mass is all about, and Father does not understand them.

I rush to fit mass in every morning before I start work, but Father hardly ever has it at the same time — it ranges from six o'clock to nine o'clock. This is a strain. I will not be able to keep it up. I write to Bishop Jobst and explain that the arrangement is not working out well. Could he arrange to have Father Crotty recalled with the least possible fuss?

Father gathered his things and said goodbye. I do not know if he was pleased to go, but, like me, I think he regretted that things had not worked out as we had hoped. He left the jaffle iron. I gave it to Father Peile. *Lansdowne* settled back to normal.

* * *

Stockboys washing down horses.

Rod drafting horses at old yards, *Lansdowne*.

Chapter Fourteen

The end of the 1960s

I lived so long away from you,
In places that you never knew.

Rod and I had glorious, relaxed holidays. The children were at boarding school, money was no longer a worry, and — with flood gates, water, and fences checked — we headed for Sydney, staying at the Wentworth Hotel. We spent two weeks there — not as long as we used to stay, but Sydney did not have the attraction and excitement that it did in those early years, and the air was not good for Rod's asthma. Still, I loved the time we spent there. Shopping with Betty Rose, I bought beautiful clothes — without considering the cost. Rod bought me expensive jewellery. I spent a lot of time at Betty Rose and Bob's stunning Sortie Point home. I really enjoyed those two weeks, but I was ready to leave when Rod was.

We spent the next three or four weeks visiting relations, my family's and Rod's, then driving round Australia, most times well off the beaten track. We'd leave the bitumen behind and drive over rough country roads, through beautiful timbered country, fertile open plains, drought-stricken 'poor man's country', deserts, cold snow country, cattle country, sheep country, all and everywhere, heading for home about mid-March.

Driving back from one of these holidays, we got to Mt Isa about six o'clock and I wanted to go to Evening Mass. Rod said, "There is no time — I want to get through the hills before dark."

I pleaded; Rod gave in. Father Devereau, a priest we had known at Julia Creek, was parish priest at Mt Isa. The church was not crowded; I found a seat about halfway up; Rod sat at the back. After Communion I returned to my seat, said a brief prayer, then got up to leave. As I walked towards the door, I saw Rod waiting outside and I heard someone call, "Wait! Please wait." Surprised, I turned towards the altar. Father Devereau was calling me. I knew we could not stay; we had to go. I gave him a small wave, then joined Rod and we left. I never saw Father Devereau again. He wrote not long after we returned to *Lansdowne*, saying that he was not happy at Mt Isa and had been surprised and happy to see us, and had hoped to talk to us for a while after mass. He died not long after that. I will always regret that there was just no time.

In the early years when Rod and I travelled, we always camped. We carried a tuckerbox, swag, and jerry cans of petrol and water. We drove until we were tired, or until we found the right place to camp. Rod would toss out the swag beside the vehicle, then get a fire going and the billy on. We had tea, sugar, bread and lots of tinned food in the tuckerbox. While I cut the bread, Rod would open a tin of bully beef or sausages, or whatever we fancied, warm it on the fire, and we would eat. After, while I cleaned up, Rod would build up the fire and roll out the swag; it was big and bulky — a married man's swag. There was no fear, no sense of danger; only a relaxed feeling of peace and safeness.

Those nights and days are gone. We still travel, still carry our tuckerbox, swag and jerry cans of petrol and water, but it is more convenient, and safer, to pull in to one of the motels that dot our highways and byways now — although it may be more convenient and much safer, I miss those nights under the stars.

The Vietnam War put a big scare into families here, as it did throughout Australia. Sons born on certain dates, decided by lottery, were eligible for call-up. Families desperately needed their sons, but so did our country, we were told.

Do the men in smart tailor-made uniforms or fashionable suits, who sit behind city desks, ever go to war?

* * *

There is an old grave near Murphy Spring, on *Lansdowne*, and a story that goes with it. Frank Bridge told it to me and I will tell it as I heard it from Frank: Murphy, an old Irishman — no one ever knew him by any other name — camped alone at the Spring that bears his name. He was a dogger. Although his camp was close to the Spring, he never slept there. Every night, in the dark, he would steal away with his swag and sleep at a different place, and return cautiously to his camp in the early morning. The blacks knew his movements; they suspected he was a police spy, put there to report on the poddy dodgers. Frank believed this was true because of the poddy dodgers in the area. The blacks said police patrols supplied Murphy with tucker. Frank did not know if this was true, but Murphy was afraid of someone or something. Often in contact with the blacks, he showed no fear of them.

One day, the blacks came to Frank and told him, "Ol' man Muffy bin finish."

Frank knew what that meant. He asked them, "How did he die?"

They said, "Muffy bin lie under tree, 'e kick an' fight, then 'e bin finish."

Frank asked if they saw a fight.

"No, only ground where Muffy bin kick an' fight."

Whatever, or whoever, Murphy had been afraid of, had finally caught up with him. He was buried under the tree where he died. I wanted Frank to show me the grave but he couldn't; he never saw the grave himself. He thought that Clifton, from *Bedford*, would be the only one alive who would know where it was.

I asked Paddy where the grave was. Although he knew Murphy's story, he never saw the grave. Like Frank, he thought Clifton was the only one who could take me there. I would have to wait until Clifton came to *Lansdowne*. I would have liked Frank to have stayed with us longer, but he was getting old and his health was not good. He wanted to go to Mornington Station with Sally Malay and his family.

Doing a bore run with Rod one day, I found a strange little bundle in the fork of a tree — twigs, hair, bark, and it could have been gum. Rod said to put it back exactly as I found it because blacks sometimes left messages for each other in the forks of trees. This could have been a message. I put it back. I had at first thought it was a bird's nest, but this had been woven by human hand.

* * *

Mining companies come and prospect all over *Lansdowne*. They are polite and considerate, never interfering with our musters, or disturbing

171

cattle, but they are also very secretive. We never know what they are looking for. Men from the Bureau of Mineral Resources also come. They find traces of an ice age, millions of years ago.

Bill Laurie, on his way to *Bow River* with *Gogo* bulls, camps at Baker's Water Hole for three days. He drops off two bulls, which are lame, and leaves with the rest. *Gogo* cattle are prone to T.B.; we have always had a clean herd. We hope it remains clean. Dave Ledger, Sean Murphy and Jimmy Rowe, from the Department of Agriculture, come out to inoculate our cattle against brucellosis. Some stations have a problem with the 'three-day sickness', and we hear that foot-and-mouth disease is coming in from the Top End. We have enough trouble without these diseases depleting our herds.

Life at *Lansdowne* runs smoothly. Our musters go well, but the work is getting harder for Rod and me. Liddy and Mary help me with the camp cooking, but we have few stockmen. Our herd has increased; we no longer shoot scrub bulls — they are held, earmarked, sometimes dehorned, and sent to the meatworks for the American market where bull meat brings high prices. For me and, I think, for everybody else, it is easier to let them go than to hold them. I have always been afraid of them. They madly charge all and everything. In the yards, they roam round and round, stirring up all the cattle. As Rod ropes them to pull them up to the panel to be earmarked and dehorned, they bellow, thrash and gouge with their poisonous horns. I am afraid for Rod and for all the boys, but I make sure I am well behind the panel, hoping it will hold, or that I have my foot on the bottom rail, ready to go over the top if the bull breaks free.

Eddie Hackaman, who later became famous for sculpting bronze statues, arrived last night. This morning, he wants to go with us and help cut out the bullocks for the meatworks. Rod is not keen but he is polite; he just hopes Eddie will keep out of his way. But it is not to be — Eddie's idea of what a meatworks' bullock looks like is totally different from Rod's.

Eddie rides one of Little Mick's horses and goes after everything that moves. I see Rod's patience wearing thin. He rides over to where I am keeping tally and tells me to go with Tommy, who is home on school holidays, and try to persuade Eddie to take a break, have a spell, anything, as long as we get that "bloody jackaroo" out of the mob. Tommy and I do our best, but it is some time, and there are lots of unacceptable cattle in the cut, before we can get Eddie to give up.

Back at the station, Eddie admires Meldie's little Syd Hill saddle. She had learnt to ride in this saddle, but has outgrown it. Like all Syd Hill saddles, it is a beautiful piece of work. Eddie wants to buy it but Rod gives it to him. Rod swears by Syd Hill saddles, especially the Barcoo Poley model.

When in Brisbane, we always called on Len Hill and his brother at their workshop in Queen Street, and would often have lunch with Len and his wife, Mary, at their home. Uhl, another well-known supplier of stock saddles, also had his shop in Queen Street. The Hill brothers later moved to the industrial area of Brendale, north of Brisbane. They needed a bigger work space as they went into the lucrative racing pad business, supplying Australia and an overseas market.

* * *

Rod and I drive to Wave Hill Station, in the Northern Territory. Rod wants to see an old friend, Tom Fisher, before Tom retires. Tom is the manager of *Wave Hill* for the great English company, Vestey. Rod also wants to buy some spurs made by a man called Guthie who works at *Wave Hill*. Rod already has one pair of Guthie's spurs but wants two more. Guthie's *Wave Hill* spurs are the best ever made, according to Rod.

Rod and I go the Katherine bull sales. On the way over, we spend the night with Lloyd and Camille Fogarty at *Auvergne*, on the East Baines River. Lloyd is also going to the sales. Camille comes from a family of girls, I think; all very attractive. My father had known Mick Fogarty, Lloyd's father, in the Queensland Gulf country. At the sales, we meet an old friend, Tontie Garbutt, who is one of the auctioneers. Tontie is married to Jean McInness; two well-known Townsville families united.

We join up with Pat and Peg Underwood, and stay at a friend's home in Katherine. Pat and Peg now own *Inverway* in the Northern Territory. Pat's brother, Jim, and his wife, Billie, are on *Bedford*. We bought eight little nobby Granada bulls; they are a Shorthorn breed. There isn't a big demand for Shorthorns — the Santa Gertrudis is more popular and brings higher prices — but we are pleased with our choice. The Shorthorn is a go-getter, on the move all the time. Sometimes he is too active. Rod's father bought half-zebu bulls in 1954. He was the first to introduce zebus into the Kimberleys. He prefers zebus to Santa Gertrudis.

* * *

Rod's father has donated a grandstand to the Halls Creek Race Club. Our little club is moving with the times. We are grateful to Tom Quilty for this generous gesture as we proudly sit high up to view the events. Drunken blacks stagger back and forth below, most bombed out of their minds; this once proud race brought down by Citizen Rights.

173

Frank and Dolly McMahon move from the Northern Territory to *Alice Downs*, just north of Halls Creek. Frank's drinking upsets and embarrasses Dolly. We all know the feeling. It seems that drinking is the mens' prerogative. Dolly and I become very good friends. One day, while I was holidaying in Townsville, a woman phoned me to say that Dolly had died in an accident. Driving from Halls Creek to *Alice Downs*, the utility in which she was travelling had overturned; and my dear friend was dead. I will miss you Dolly. It was Dolly's cousin who had phoned me.

Rod gives me a little alsatian pup for my birthday. He gives me so many presents — for birthdays, anniversaries, Christmas — some for no reason at all. I love this little pup. Rod had her flown up from Perth. She has been sterilised, and is a bundle of fluff. I call her Silver. As I sit on our verandah, with Silver at my feet, I admire our front garden; cool green lawns from the verandah to the fence, colourful lilies in full bloom, pawpaws close to the verandah, tamarind trees and bright pink oleander all make a very pleasant picture. But the two huge ghost gums, standing on either side of the gate, dominate the scene. They cast their majestic shade as their branches gently sway in the breeze. They were planted here in 1954 for the births of Meldie and Tommy. Maggie had dug up the two little shoots from the creek bank near their camp and brought them to me in treacle tins. Rod had deep holes dug, filled in with rubbish, and I planted the little trees. They were so frail, I never expected them to grow. Montie watered and cared for them. He seemed to know they had special meaning for me. Zachady, who considers he is boss of the house garden, never dared interfere. There should have been five of these lovely old gums, but there never will be.

* * *

We sign up with Jack Martin to send our bullocks to Broome Meatworks. Rod and I drive there for the kill. I never cease to marvel at, and enjoy, the glorious blue of the ocean around Broome; it is like no other in Australia. Broome — "Port of Pearls" — with great cargo and passenger ships sitting in the mud at the wharf. High tide floats them off, low tide dumps them there. I have a necklace of Broome pearls, another gift from Rod. As I admire their beautiful lustre, I wonder how many divers might have died, bringing them up from the pearl beds. There are so many Japanese graves in the cemetery here; nearly all were pearl divers.

We stay at the Continental Hotel while we are in Broome. Jim Conlan, the proprietor, runs two dining rooms, first and second class. First class has spotless, white starched tablecloths and serviettes; polished silver that catches the eye, with crystal goblets and delicate china. Second class is far more ordinary, but acceptable to the clientele who eat there. I remember our mother telling us about class distinction in her young days, and we were aware of it, on a small scale, when we were growing up. Although I should not be, I am surprised to see it in this small, cosmopolitan town.

Our bullocks dress-out well, and we are pleased with them. We think we will probably send them to Broome again next year. It is when we see results like this, that we know all our hard work has been worthwhile. On our way home, we spend a night with Maxine McDonald at *Fossil*. The road to *Fossil* is in good to reasonable condition but from *Fossil* to *Lansdowne* it is a hazard. However, sober, Rod is a good driver. It is only after a few drinks that his driving becomes questionable. This is when my "Hail Marys" fly heavenward by the dozen.

Travelling, we hear rumours of benefits, big benefits, going to the blacks. Half-castes want a share of these benefits, and, with the help of fringe whites, they will get it. Half-castes no longer mention their white fathers, who ignore them. They start talking, oh so proudly, of their forgotten mothers, the gins in the black camps.

There are families with a coloured mother and a white father who live happily together and are well respected in the community. They have the same privileges as an all-white family. I cannot imagine that they are behind the unrest now.

We were not conscious of the colour bar when we were growing up. My brother Jim's best friend at school was Bobby Flores. I don't know what colour Bobby was; it didn't matter. Tommy and Meldie's only playmates, for some ten years at *Lansdowne*, were piccaninnies. They played and quarrelled the same as children without colour. The division crept in over the years and was upon us before we knew it, only because we chose to be blind.

* * *

Winter rain makes life in the stock camp very uncomfortable, in fact it can be quite miserable, riding behind slow-moving cattle, from camp to camp, water trickling down inside my windcheater and shirt, no matter how tightly I pull the collar. My vision is blurred. Troy moves too fast and bumps into cows and calves on the tail. Watch it, Troy; I am depending on you; I can't see.

Because we are all riding, Liddy and Mary are not with me. It is only when I have the jeep that they come out. However, Montie is here. He is always close. He catches and saddles my horse, checks that the girth is tight, the stirrup leathers the right length, and that I have a knot in my bridle reins. He waits until I am in the saddle before he mounts; Rod had told him his job is to look after me. This suits Montie; he has no heart for mustering.

Rod and the boys are wet and cold. I hope none of them get head colds from this. It seems that, like us, the cattle are too miserable to try and break out. We stop for the night camp. Mules are caught; swags, damp and smelly, are tossed onto the wet ground. Everything is off-loaded, and the mules hobbled-out with the horses. Rod covers our stores, along with the ropes and saddles, under a tarpaulin,. He rigs up another tarpaulin for the boys. I start to wonder where, in the name of heavens, we are going to find dry wood for the fire.

The boys gather round Big Mick. Curious, I join them. The boys hold their hats over a small bundle of dry leaves and twigs on the ground, where the wet topsoil has been scraped away, uncovering the dry earth beneath. Big Mick is rubbing two sticks together, close to the little bundle. Slowly, smoke starts rising and, as Big Mick blows on it, a tiny spark appears and the leaves ignite. Gently, he puts more leaves and twigs on and brings the flame up. Miraculously, wood appears, some of it quite dry, some a little damp but not soaking wet. The boys had begun to gather the leaves and twigs, and carried them in their pockets, as soon as the rain started — and they know where to look for dry wood. I have much to learn from my black brothers. I am so wet and cold. If I stand perfectly still, it is not too bad, but when I move, the wind blows through my clothes and I shiver. We all gather round the fire, by now burning brightly, as the boys put more wood on. We turn like toast, first the front, then the back, as we warm ourselves.

Rod wants to know if I will make a fried curry. It will have to be a big one — we all need a good hot meal tonight. Yes! I'll make the curry if he will make sure the fire burns high and bright all night.

The curry is big and hot. It warms all of us — which is more than I can say of the fire. Rod and I crawl under the tarpaulin and sleep among the saddles. The boys move in under the other tarpaulin.

July is always a cold, treacherous month. The rain is with us for three days and nights. Flooded creeks have to be crossed. As we slosh through pools and puddles, I ask Our Lord to let the sun shine, please. We sleep in the rain at night, and ride through it all day. There is no shelter, and, yes, everybody gets a head cold. I have no more Vicks® or aspirin so we do without. And then the sun comes out, weak and watery at first and then strong and brilliant. Steam rises from our clothes and from our horses. It will still be two days before we get back to the station.

* * *

The nuns at Beagle Bay Mission send me two teenage girls, Sarah and Suba. They have been trained as house girls. Suba, I think, is a full blood; Sarah is half- or quarter-caste. They have been trained well and seem to settle happily at *Lansdowne*. Ted Bolton, who has been with us for twelve months, takes a fancy to Suba, and Jimmy Johnson, who is still with us, is looking at Sarah. Ted, who has a white father and a full blood mother, has very poor eyesight. He is a victim of trachoma, an eye disease that strikes both black and white.

Father Flynn, a Catholic priest based in Darwin, is an eye specialist. He travelled round the stations and small towns treating the disease, sometimes with Dr. Ida Mann who is also an eye specialist,. Then Father Flynn was told he could not be both priest and doctor, that he must make a decision. To the detriment of trachoma victims, he chose to be a priest. It is his vocation.

* * *

New Year's Eve, 1969. I sit and ponder what has been, and what is yet to come, as I wait for the minutes of the old year to tick away. I look back on the 1960s as the beginning of our good years. 1968 had been a year of many changes, a lot of sadness. Deaths in our families, and sickness and deaths at *Lansdowne*. One of the old lubras, Ginny Yarlu, died in March. I miss seeing her and hearing her loud screeching as she called her dogs to order. My dear mother came to visit in March and was sick all the time she was here. Evacuated first to Wyndham Hospital, then later to Derby Hospital, I was so afraid for her. My sister, Coral, came out and took her home. Meldie, sick with asthma, spent a week of her May holidays in Derby Hospital. Tommy returned to school alone. Meldie did not go back until the first of June.

* * *

Breaking-in and handling a horse, *Lansdowne*.

Aerial shot of *Lansdowne*, 1969.

178

CHAPTER FIFTEEN

Faith in staff

And pain has walked and talked with him,
And pain has shared his bed.

Helicopters and charter planes land and off-load men and equipment for the mining companies. BHP, International Oil, Plantas, Minox, Rio Tinto, Planett, Inspiration Drillers — they are all here somewhere. We supply them with meat. They come into the station for various reasons — to pick up meat and mail or to repair broken equipment. The station is very busy. It is good to see them and they are always welcome — they don't bother us. Our musters go on, although Rod is not well. We have thirteen men in stock camp, including Tommy, when he is home on holidays.

Major Peterson flies in from time to time. Duncan Ord of Demco Meats calls in, and other meat buyers also come by. George Applebee, Halls Creek Shire Clerk, drives out to discuss the *Lansdowne–Bedford* road. It is not much more than a track, and it has to be improved to allow the road trains to move over it. George says he will send council equipment out to upgrade it. About two weeks later, the grader driver, Sam Calwin, and his crew are on the job. The Calwins, Rivers, Butters, and Wilson families — all of mixed blood — are highly respected in the community. Jack Armstrong and John MacMicking arrive. They want to discuss blood-testing on our herd. So many visitors, so much movement at the station.

There are also big improvements round the station homestead. All floors are cemented, huge paving stones cover the verandah floor, blue glass louvres line the verandah, and I have amber louvres in my kitchen. I have a gas stove. We tried a combustion stove in the big kitchen but it did not work; we could not get the right coke for it, so I went back to the reliable old wood stove for heavy cooking. Rod has also installed a big freezer room. To me, that is one of the best improvements of all. The great pit toilets have gone, and are no more. How good, how very good, it is to be rid of them. We now have septic. I am happy.

When I married Rod, I went from a life of middle-class comfort and comparative luxury to a life of raw harshness, very little comfort and certainly no luxury. Pampered daughter of loving, indulgent parents, I cannot compare these two lives. There is no comparison.

Now I have moved back to the good life again. It is good, and will continue to be so, but it will not always be trouble-free. We will have droughts and dry seasons, cattle prices will fluctuate, and the ongoing problem of adequate, capable staff will only get worse. There are so many reasons why trouble will always be just round the corner. However, we have good permanent waters now, bores and wells that will see us through the droughts. They will dry back, but never dry up, we hope. We have planted out good protein grasses, built yards and fenced paddocks. Rod has increased our herd, from branding 45 to branding 3,000 per year. Hard slogging work. We are both tired, and Rod's health is not good. He is never free of the cursed asthma. Meldie and Tommy have two more years at school. When they leave, they will share in the running of *Lansdowne*.

Leo Wills and Bob Wainright, of East Kimberley Transport (E.K.T.), call in to discuss road transport for our cattle. Ronnie is with them. Ronnie and I are good friends. I thoroughly enjoy her company for the short time they are here.

In the early morning of Tuesday, 19 August, we truck the first of our meatworks' bullocks to Wyndham. The E.K.T. road trains arrive very late at night. We have the cattle in the yard and load eighty head. It is not easy. Frightened cattle bump and bruise themselves as they baulk and refuse to go up the race and onto the trailers. The drivers, experienced at loading, are a great help. They are a special breed of men. It would have taken them all day and half the night to get to *Lansdowne*, yet they help with the loading, then they get back into their trucks and drive for long hours, back to the meatworks.

* * *

Rod's health does not improve; it gets worse. On 14 November, I fly with him to Perth. Father McGuire is also on the plane, ill and Perth-bound. An ambulance meets us at the airport and both Father McGuire and Rod are taken to the St. John of God Hospital. I lose touch with Father McGuire. I do not see him in hospital. Rod takes up all of my time. He is so very ill. There are times when I think he is not going to get well. Meldie is sitting for an exam. It does not help, knowing her father is so sick. He is in hospital for two weeks. Discharged on 29 November, but not well enough to go home, we make daily visits to the doctor's surgery for another five days. I did not think that we would be away so long. I can only hope Dick Wilson and Jim Ruck, a good white handyman, can handle things until we get back. They have a lot of responsibility. On 5 December, we leave Perth, with the children, to fly home.

Dick and Jim have had a bad time while we were away. Although we had left them in charge, and had advised the staff of this, it did not work. Everybody wanted to be boss. Dick, placid and easygoing, did what he had to do; Jim fizzed and tried to keep things under control. We let our blacks go off early on walkabout, and settled down to enjoy a quiet Christmas.

I put on another cook, Kevin Brady. None of the cooks I have had were what they seemed to be. They could all cook, some much better than others, but they all had secrets they guarded closely. Kevin is a bitter man; a returned World War II veteran, he has a very strong dislike of a certain race of people. He has no sympathy for displaced persons, and every now and then he gives the good priests and nuns the sharp edge of his tongue. A Catholic himself, he had worked as a handyman for a Catholic order of priests in Melbourne and he has no good, or kind words for them. They worked him like a heathen, and made him pray like a Christian. You are a hard man to understand, Kevin, but as long as you do your work, and do not interfere with the lubras, I am not interested in your private life.

Jim Ruck is not a heavy drinker but he likes a nip of rum to start and end his day. We have some pretty heavy drinkers working for us so we cannot let Jim have his rum and deny the others; they can smell rum a mile away. We agree to buy the rum and dole out the nips. I do not think it is a good idea. A heavy drinker will not be satisfied with one nip a day, but it is the best we can do. Rod does not like rum; he is a whisky drinker. We decide it will be best if I am barman. They all have different ideas of what a nip is. Kevin's nip is a full glass; Jim Ruck's, half a glass; Jimmy Johnson's, a quarter of a glass, and so on. I need to keep a special book to know how to charge them.

181

The mail plane brings boxes of dung beetles, sent out from Canberra in an attempt to restrict the breeding of buffalo flies. It is an unpleasant and messy job, putting the beetles out round the run, but if they can really control the buffalo fly, it will be worth it.

I do a general clean-up round the station buildings. The white ants are bad. I am liberal with the dieldrin®; it makes me feel quite sick. Rod continues to have asthma attacks. I wonder how long his heart can take the strain. He strains and gasps for breath, day and night. We are not getting much sleep.

Kevin tells me he has gallstones — maybe! I have a medical on him and they send the medical plane out to fly him to Derby Hospital. Once again I am the station cook, but not for long. Kevin does come back.

Rod complains of chest pains. He is on so much medication: Lasix®, Ventolin, Anginine®, Brondecon®, Tryptanol®, and Valium®. He does not want to go to hospital. The doctor has to try and guess what is best for his asthma and chest pains, but nothing seems to work.

We have definitely missed the wet season, and we are late getting the stock camp out. The boys are getting restless. Knowing this does not help Rod. I think worry is the cause of a lot of his asthma. I know that if he is no better in a week's time, the boys will have to go without him, and I will have to go with them.

Taking Liddy and Mary, I drive round to all our stock camp sites and gather up the hidden whisky. If I am to be in the camp, alone with the boys, I do not want them finding the caches.

Graham Corbett, from Wyndham Meatworks, flew in early this morning. He tells us Wyndham is paying 20 cents per pound (44 cents per kilogram). He leaves after lunch.

I have to send Montie out to keep the fuel up to the engine while we are pumping at the Bullock Paddock bore. He does not want to go. He says his job is to look after me — he has to be wherever I am.

"No, Montie," I tell him, "I have no choice; you must keep the engine going at the bore. I will be all right."

For the fourth time, I break out in a rash that looks like measles. It comes every time I hand out the leprosy tablets. The medical plane comes and I drive Rod to the airstrip to see the doctor. Doctor says Rod is a very sick man and will have to take care. He can only keep him on the tablets he is already taking, and hope some will work. I find out that my rash is caused by the leprosy tablets; I am allergic to them. Migraine headaches also slow me up; they are so severe. I take lots of Bex® powders. I know they are not good for me, and they have little effect, but it is all I can do. The pain is so excruciating that at times I can hardly see. I wish, many times, that Tommy and Meldie were here to take on some of the responsibility. If I go with the camp, I have to leave Rod at the station and that will not be good. Thank goodness, Kevin Brady is back, and Jim Ruck is also here to keep an eye on Rod.

* * *

The clouds build up, but there is little rain. We cannot wait any longer, the camp has to go out; we have delivery dates with Wyndham and Broome. Rod gives me a list of where to muster, the number of cattle to expect in different areas, how long to stay at each camp, and so on — everything I need to know. I have done this before, but I feel more confident with the list. He also gives Dick a list. I tell Zachady that he must help look after Rod.

We have been out a week and all is going well. Dick and I work well together, even Jimmy Johnson comes round; he is not so deaf. He gives me a friendly, cheeky grin whenever he sees me. I think, perhaps, that the daily nip of rum has something to do with it. Everybody is making a special effort for Rod's sake.

On dinner camp one day, Little Mick says, "Jeep come." I can't hear it, but if Little Mick says it is coming, he will not be mistaken. I wait with a terrible feeling that it will be bad news about Rod. Jim Ruck drives up. He does not look worried. I ask, "Is Rod all right?" Yes! Rod is much the same as when I had left him, but he wants me to go back with Jim. On the drive back, all Jim can, or will, tell me is that two men have arrived at the station this morning, and are talking to Rod. Once back at the station, I am not left long in doubt. Peterson Brothers, builders from Bundaberg, Queensland, are here to discuss the new home Rod had long promised me. It was to be a surprise. Bless my darling old Rod.

We pore over sketches, and the books that they brought with them, full of wonderful ideas. We discuss plans. Rod leaves it entirely to me to decide what I want. I finally choose a three bedroom, split-level home with verandahs, but there is one hitch. Petersons have several orders for the type of houses they build, but most of them are in the Northern Territory, where they can link up, moving from one job to the next, with the owners covering travel expenses one way. We are the only order in the Kimberleys at this time, and the cost of carpenters' air fares from

Bundaberg to *Lansdowne* return, plus freight on building material, adds considerably to the cost. We have no one to share these expenses with. Rod is prepared to pay the extra, but I just can't.

We try to find ways over and round the problem, finally agreeing that Petersons will supply all the materials, we will pay the freight, and we will find our carpenters locally.

I can only stay long enough to check that Rod is resting and taking his tablets, and that, at least if he is no better, he is no worse. Jim drives me back to the camp. I think of my darling Rod. There are times I could whack him one, for his drinking, but he is so considerate and loving that I can never be angry with him for long. We have been through so much together. There is this nagging thought with me, all the time, that he is not going to get better, and that terrifies me. He has been ill for so long.

Dick has the camp ready to move the next day. Up bright and early, we get on with the muster. For the next two weeks, we muster round Mt. Laptz, Bend Yard, Galway Valley, then back up north again. We have dinner at Lolly Water Flat, we fill our water canteens at Drafting Yard, then go on to Collas for night camp. We will cut out our meatworks' bullocks here, and the boys will take them on to *Tableland*, where they will be trucked to Broome. I return to the station.

* * *

Rod sends Skipper, Wallace and Johnny Ah Won to Crocodile Gorge, to attend a muster with the *Tableland* stock camp. Some of our blacks are sick. Liddy is on penicillin, Rosie is on potassium citrate and Furadantin®, and Stephen must have eye drops three times a day. Rod has a temperature of 102.1 at 2 p.m. It is still 101 at 6 p.m. I am worried.

Rod needs to be a lot better than he is. The continual asthma attacks will kill him. Doctor Holman from Derby suggests we try cortisone, a drug I have not heard of. It has side-effects that concern us but, as nothing else is working, we have to try it. Gradually, the cortisone starts to take effect; the asthma attacks are less frequent, less violent, until Rod can control them with Ventolin. The side-effects are evident, but we can live with that and, as his health improves, they disappear. However, he will never be completely free of asthma.

Kevin tells me he has "that pain" again, and he must see a doctor. I do not think there is anything wrong with him, but I cannot be sure. I have Jim Ruck drive him to Halls Creek. They return three days later, both gloriously drunk. They have also brought drink out with them. So much for Kevin's pain. Jim sobers up in two days; it takes Kevin a week. I could kill him. You simply cannot depend on an alcoholic.

Messrs Rowell, Fletcher, and Robinson, Demco directors, flew in this morning, looking for cattle for Derby Meatworks. Rod, a little better, enjoys their company. They try to get him interested in aerial mustering. Rod will have none of it, saying it is impossible to muster cattle from a plane.

John Roulston, in his own single-engine plane, successfully mustered sheep on his property further south. Thinking that, if he could muster sheep, he should be able to muster cattle, he moved to the Kimberleys and proved it. He pioneered aerial mustering, to the great benefit of all Kimberley cattlemen.

Mining companies continue to come and go. They need to repair vehicles or they want fuel. An Army survey helicopter flies low over the station, and round the run; sometimes they land here. Meat buyers call almost every day. They stay for smoko or lunch; some stay overnight. They are all welcome. I am grateful to Kevin; with all his faults, he always has smoko and meals prepared on time. Ray Buckley, a buyer from Broome, arrives in time for lunch today. He stays the night.

It is a very busy time for us. Rod depends on me to keep the boys busy with mustering, breaking in, or whatever has to be done. He tells me what needs doing, and I do the rest. Although he is much better, he is still not well enough to do the things he wants to do; but as long as I have a cook, I can cope.

The children are home for the school holidays. Tommy goes into the camp for three weeks and Meldie is a big help to me. I am able to spend more time with Rod.

All the material for our new home is here and Norman Bruce, a carpenter from Derby, has started to build. There are many hold-ups. Western Australia and Queensland do not have uniform building standards. What is accepted in Queensland differs from what West Australian carpenters can do. Norman has to work his way round these problems, but he is making steady progress.

Jimmy Johnson has a badly burnt arm. He came to me to dress it. It is a mess. I don't know how he did it but I wish he had come to me sooner. Using the whistle, I call the Wyndham doctor. He says I must cut away all the dead skin, clean the wound up and start him on penicillin. I will never make a good nurse.

A dear old family friend, Paddy Le Levire, died in Derby last night. This has upset Rod and he is wheezing again. He cannot have any more cortisone; we will just have to make the Ventolin control the wheezing before it turns into an asthma attack.

Jimmy Johnson is back with his burnt arm. It looks terrible. The bandage is stuck to a pus-filled, weeping sore, and there is more dead skin. Getting the bandage off, I am clumsy and I know I am hurting him. I ask him if he would like a nip of rum. "Ar! Gawd! Missus, yeah." Jim's nip is a quarter of a glass. I fill the glass and give it to him. He downs it without water. It helps him but it does not help me. Perhaps I should have taken the rum.

* * *

I will have to get Rod to a hospital. His health is deteriorating fast and I am unable to help him. I call Wyndham for a medical. Doctor House comes on the air. He is more than pleased to have Rod in hospital. The medical plane, already on a call to another station, is unavailable. Doctor House arranges with Peter Reid, who has a charter service in Wyndham, to fly out. I tell Peter he can land on a strip that Rod has had cleared in front of the house and maintained for small aircraft.

Peter flies over and round the station buildings but he will not land on the small strip. He drops a note to say he will go to the main strip. I will have to drive Rod there. We bump over the 18.5 km to the main strip to find Peter landed and waiting. Rod won't get on the plane unless I go with him. Oh heavens! I had not expected this. I am not prepared — I have nothing with me; I have not told anyone at the station I would be leaving. Rod is very distressed; I will have to go with him and try to send a message back from Wyndham. I will have to depend on Dick and Jim Ruck again. I am concerned about an old saddler who is repairing our stock gear. He has only been here nine days, but in that time, the cranky old man has caused considerable discontent among the staff. What mischief will he do while we are away?

Rod, in Wyndham Hospital, is still no better, but I, at least, have the consolation of knowing he is in good hands. Long days and nights pass. I spend so much time at the hospital and I worry about what is going on at home.

Doctor House tells me he thinks it best if Rod is transferred to Derby, where they have a better-equipped hospital. I agree to the move. An ambulance drives us to the airport. A nurse will fly with us to Derby. Once at the hospital there, Doctor Holman immediately puts Rod in an oxygen tent.

Mother Damian is the hospital Matron. I first met Mother Damian at Balgo Mission, when we were on our way across the desert to meet the children at Alice Springs. A dear, kind, St. John of God nursing nun, dedicated to her career and her religious vocation, she has a mischievous sense of humour that surprised me. I love being with her. There are also several Irish nuns nursing here. They are so friendly and cheerful, and some are beautiful. They are not allowed to discuss the 'Troubles' in Ireland, but it must be on their minds all the time.

I spend all day, and hours into the night with Rod. He seems to be slipping into a coma. Doctor Hollman warns me he is very low; I must accept that he might not get well. I am so worried, so helpless. I have my meals with the nuns at the convent, and we pray together in their little chapel. They are, no doubt, praying for loved ones so far away on their glorious green isle. I pray for Rod — to St. Jude, help of the hopeless, to St. Theresa, who had promised to let roses fall back to earth, to our Lady of Perpetual Succour, to Our Lady of Lourdes, who has performed so many miracles. I ask help from all and every saint I can think of; I beseech God not to take Rod from us. I can no longer worry about what is happening at home. Jim Ruck sends daily telegrams. I start a novena to Our Lady of Lourdes.

Late in the afternoon of the sixth day, Doctor Hollman came to me and said I must prepare for the worst. Such cold, terrifying words, but how else could he say it? He is Rod's friend. He told me to prepare the children. I phoned Mother Superior at Loreto and the Principal at Aquinas. I do not want the children to know, yet, that their father is so dangerously ill, but I want Mother Superior and the Principal to have them ready to leave if necessary. Two hours behind Queensland time, I phone Rod's mother in Brisbane. She will be in bed and does not like night calls, but this is a call that must be made. She is a deeply religious woman who, already having lost one son, is devoted to Rod. I have kept in touch with her during Rod's illness. She says she knew the call was from me as soon as she heard the phone ring. I think I am crying. I do not know how to tell her. Every time I start to say something, she talks over me and I do not know what she is saying. I must listen to her, then I will tell her. She is saying, "I know you are going to tell me Rod is dying, but you are wrong; he will not die. I know he is very ill, but he will not die. I have prayed too long for him. God is merciful; my son will not die." I must believe as she does. O, ye of little faith!

I sit in a reclining chair beside Rod's bed. I pray and doze and pray again. Sometime in the night, Mother Damian comes and whispers that she will sprinkle Lourdes water over him. At five o'clock, Doctor

Hollman comes and tells me to go to the convent. Afraid to go, afraid to stay, I go. At the door, I look back as Doctor Hollman removes the oxygen tent. Rod seems to be breathing normally. Perhaps I imagine it because I want to. I go back and put my rosary beads in his warm hands, then I leave.

The nuns are all up and in their little chapel. I join them there. Father Lorenzo comes and gives us Communion. I ask him if he has seen Rod. He smiles and says, "God is not ready to take a tough old ringer like Rod yet."

I have a cup of tea with the nuns, then settle down on one of their beds to wait. It is just past 6 a.m. I have a dreadful headache. I do not remember slipping into sleep.

I wake slowly; everything is so quiet. I cannot remember where I am. There is a jug of water and a glass on a small table close to the bed. I sit up and pour a glass of water. I am thirsty, and the water, so cool and refreshing, feels good. I look at my small wristwatch, almost 3 p.m. Then I remember! My headache is gone but I am desperate to get back to Rod. I see a note on the little table. I pick it up; I read the beautiful, copperplate writing, "God is surely merciful. Rod is over the crisis. Damian." Mother Damian would not lie to me, and Doctor Hollman would not have let me sleep the day away when I should have been with Rod. I go to the washbasin in the bathroom, wash my face and comb my hair, then I go to the chapel. I need to pray, to offer up thanksgiving. It is hard to explain how I feel. I move freely. I have no idea how I will find Rod, but he will be alive, and that is all I can ask for now.

Sister Benedict meets me at the end of the hospital corridor. I can almost see a halo shining round her beautiful face. She says, "He has been asking for you." I hurry to his room, but quietly open his door in case he is asleep. He is awake, looking towards the door, pale and thin but very much alive. I hope he will not see my tears as I get close to the bed. I phone his mother that night to tell her the wonderful news. She says, "God is good. I knew he would not take my son. Give Rod my love."

I phone Mother Superior at Loreto and the Principal at Aquinas. Meldie and Tommy are due home for the Christmas holidays on 1 December. This is their last year at school. Doctor Hollman arranges for Rod to stay in hospital until the children arrive. Dick Robinson, of the charter service in Derby, will fly us to *Lansdowne*. Each day, Rod grows stronger and more impatient. There is a cyclone hovering over the west coast between Cape Leveque and Broome. It is stationary, but could go in any direction. I hope the children arrive safely. Strong winds and rain are buffeting the little town of Derby.

* * *

Rod and I, with Dick Robinson, are at the airport when the children's plane arrives. Dick quickly gathers their luggage from MMA and loads it onto his Push and Pull; Rod and I have a small overnight bag which I carry. Just as well, because Meldie and Tommy certainly fill Dick's luggage compartment. I see the air hostess, April Rose, carefully and gently hand Meldie a shoe box as she gets off the plane. I think there must be something very fragile in the box. April's parents own *Quanbun*, southwest of Fitzroy Crossing. Her aunt, Lex Jones, is a dear friend. I would like to know April better, but we do not come Fitzroy way often. As lovely as her name, she is indeed an April rose.

There is movement in the shoe box. Although the lid is tied down with a string, Meldie has trouble holding it. Tommy goes to help her, and I also move towards her. Rod calls that Dick is ready to leave. Meldie hands the box to Tommy as she climbs aboard, then he passes it in to her. I get in beside her and Tommy flops into the seat next to me. Rod sits up front with Dick and we are off. It is a rough ride home. Winds toss us round; we rise and drop. The children concentrate on the shoe box. I can't think about it, I am so afraid, but Dick is a competent and experienced pilot. Rod is enjoying himself.

Lansdowne at last! Dick loses no time in getting us off the plane and unloading the luggage. He must get back to Derby before more bad weather sets in. Jim Ruck is at the big strip to meet us. I had sent a telegram from Derby to let him know we were coming.

Everything seems normal as we drive up to the station. Rod and I have been away three weeks, a long time to leave a full complement of staff alone at this time of year, but they have done a good job. I am proud of them, especially Dick and Jim who bore so much responsibility. There is Montie, standing proudly on the front lawn, Zachady waving from the back. The girls gather round, Liddy, as usual, giving orders. They rush to help get the luggage off and up into the new house. Norman Bruce has finished and returned to Derby. Petersons' men have done what had to be done to put the final touches on. The new house is ready for us to move in.

Meldie, still clutching the shoe box, runs into the old house. My faithful alsatian, Silver, jumping up, nearly knocks the box out of her hands. The piccaninnies gather round as she puts the box on the table and unties the string. Before she takes the lid off, I want to know what is in the box: a pet snake, a rat, a bat, what? Before she can answer, the lid is off and out shoots a small black and white kitten. Good heavens! Not another cat? I am so relieved to know it is not a snake, a rat or a bat, that I accept it. "Sooty" had travelled all the way from Perth with them.

* * *

We pay off our white and half-caste staff late in December. We pay our blacks, and give them rations. Those who want to, go off on walkabout. A few of the very old stay. Kevin Brady left us on 20 December. He had made a huge Christmas cake before he left, icing it with "Happy Christmas Mrs Q" on top. I do not know where he will go. He is a lonely, bitter man with a drink problem. I pinned a small Saint Christopher medal inside his hat. He might find it; if not, I hope it will protect him on his wanderings.

Christmas is quiet. We get very little rain from the cyclone. It rushes down the coast and our skies clear. Excellent rain in 1969, twenty six inches (660 mm), carried us through 1970. Just as well, because only eight and a half inches (215 mm) fell in all of 1970. We hope the rains come early in the New Year.

We do not move into our new home until January, 1971. I want to spend my last Christmas in my old home. It holds so many memories for me. I am leaving nineteen years of my life here. From an old, long, empty, ex-army tin shack, to a comfortable home; it is not easy to walk out.

Meldie and Tommy, happy to have their school days behind them, settle down to everyday life at *Lansdowne*. They are now a permanent part of the workforce. The New Year starts well. Rod continues to get stronger. He never goes anywhere without his Ventolin sprays, one in his pocket, one in the glove box of the utility. The rains we hoped for come early, seventeen and a half inches (449 mm) between January and March, then they ease off. The country is picture postcard beautiful, the air, pure and uncontaminated; breathing deeply, I think of how lucky we are. Slow and easy, the weeks pass.

* * *

We have made the move into our new home, Meldie and I deciding where this will go, and where that will go. We are a happy family. Our blacks dribble back from walkabout. Rod and Tommy leave to pick up staff from Wyndham and Halls Creek. Dick, Hilton, and Jimmy Johnson are back; there are some new faces, black, half-caste, a few whites. Jim Ruck, back with Nellie — friend, companion, de facto — who cares? She does not work for me. Fat and slow, I sometimes see her sitting, cross-legged, outside Jim's quarters, crooning to herself as she gently taps her knees to the rhythm.

Fences are checked, flood gates repaired, horses are mustered and foals branded, work horses and colts are drafted off and held, the rest are sent back to the paddocks. Rod, Tommy and Little Mick start to break in the colts. Each stockman has his allotted number of horses, then the shoeing begins. They must shoe their own horses, but not all are able to. The experienced shoers help the inexperienced.

There are a lot of hungry men to feed. Meldie and I are flat-out, cooking. Liddy, back from walkabout and very ill with the 'cold sick', has been flown to Derby Hospital. I miss her, especially in the kitchen, but Meldie is very good; the girls work well with her. Our vegetable garden is a wonderful asset. Heaps of beautiful, fresh vegetables every day. We have all the meat we need, but I am always behind with the bread. Coming out of the oven, the fresh bread smell whirls all over the station. It teases the appetite. Sixteen double loaves is the limit I can make daily; the oven will not hold more.

Because of late heavy rain, it is mid-April before our stock camp can go out. The mining companies, who had left early in December last year, are starting to drift back.

Rod is getting wheezy. Oh, dear God! Please don't let it happen again. Working in the dusty yard with the colts is bad for him, but he insists he will finish the job. At last the horses are shod, the colts broken, and we are ready to move out for our first muster for the year.

Meldie has her own horses. She will ride with Rod, Tommy and the boys. I have Troy and my cunning little Angel, but for the most part I will simply drive the jeep, Mary with me. Thank goodness, Rod is feeling a little better.

We have arranged with John Roulston to meet us at Piantas in his plane. He will aerial muster with us through to Bend Yard, where we will camp for the night.

I was amazed, in the old horse mustering days, at the number of cattle we got, but now I can hardly believe what I am seeing. Cattle pour out of the hills in their thousands — John hot on their tails — bulls, big old pikers that have been getting away for years, cows and calves, strong young mickies, so many! John can see and go where man and horse cannot. I see riders and horses galloping everywhere. Some completely undisciplined, with no idea of how to block-up, or get the cattle in to the coachers. John would bring them out from the west, and they would chase them off to the east, Rod yelling blue murder. I hear him above the roar of the plane, over all other sounds, "You useless, bloody yahoos. Block up there! Hold them!"

Our first aerial muster is not the success it should have been. Of the thousands of head that John brings out, we lose over half. Rod is not pleased, and the yahoos are sullen. Some will give trouble; most of them will pull out. If they want to be paid before they leave, they will have to wait until the end of the muster. I won't be going back to the station before then.

I worry about Rod. I would like his health to be a lot better than it is. Tommy is nearly seventeen years old now, and the sooner he is capable of taking over, the sooner I can ease Rod out of the heavy work. I let Tommy gradually take on more responsibility, but Rod does not want to let go. It is going to be a battle, but Rod cannot go on as he is. His health is bad, there are few good stockmen round, and he has no patience with the inexperienced.

* * *

Little Mick with cattle at Piantas Yard.

Stockboys branding cattle at the bronco panel, Bakers Hole.

Little Mick riding the bronco mule at Bakers Hole.

Leopold Range, as seen from upstairs at the new homestead, *Lansdowne.*

CHAPTER SIXTEEN

Childhood to adulthood

The years ahead, I fondly pray,
Upon your brow may lightly weigh,
And leave no lines of sorrow there,
But keep you always young and fair.

Easter Saturday, 1974, is our darling daughter's 21st birthday party. The years have slipped away. I remember her eighth birthday, the little party on the lawn with the piccaninnies. Meldie loves *Lansdowne*, but I sometimes wonder what the Kimberleys have to offer her. At least her memories of our hard years would be very vague, if she remembers them at all. Rod and I are determined she will remember her twenty-first birthday. We want it to be as happy as possible.

Lists are made and invitations sent out. I get in touch with Pat Glossop, who has a catering business in Subiaco, Perth. During Meldie and Tommy's school days, three women had more to do with their growing-up years than I did. My sisters, Dadie and Coral, and Pat Glossop. I will be forever grateful for the love and care they gave them; now Pat will help me again. She is a good, kind friend. She will do the catering.

Two days before the party, Pat and her helpers arrive. Not expecting her to have her own assistants, I had organised Liddy, Nora, Mary and Rosie to help her. No, indeed, she will manage. I suggest that, perhaps, the girls could wash up? Absolutely not; they have everything, they will do everything; I am just to keep out of their way. It surprises me, to see the way they accept the conditions under which they work; everything is so perfect, so under control. They are a well-organised team. Besides catering for the party, Pat feeds our blacks while she is here. She prefers to do that rather than have me pottering round the kitchen while she is working.

Rod says he will meet our mail plane at the main strip and pick up our mail and freight. The beer for the party will be on this plane. I have no idea how many cartons of beer Rod has ordered. He said we would need a lot — Kimberley men have huge thirsts. I left the beer and hard drinks in his capable hands.

Mail and freight delivered to me, he stacks the beer cartons in our freezer room. Relaxed and happy, he makes several trips up the road to check that it is in good order for the vehicles that will soon drive over it. As the day wears on, he becomes more relaxed; in fact, there are times when I think he is almost floating. I am pleased to see him so happy. However, as he drives off the next day to check the road again, I am a little suspicious, especially when he returns. He is on top of the world; well and truly floating, he looks almost...drunk, but I am sure I am wrong. The beer is in the freezer, locked away, the key in my pocket.

Guests start to arrive early. They come by road and air, with swags and sleeping bags; they toss them down on the lawns and verandahs. There are some strangers I do not recognise, not on the guest list. They apologise and hope we do not mind. Friends of friends, or friends of Rod's. No, we do not mind, but as the crowd grows, I wonder if Pat can manage. We seem to be well over the number I gave her. I rush to tell her. No problem; she can cater for an extra twenty or thirty.

Heavy demands are put on showers and toilets, but bush people know how to cope. While Pat is setting up the long trestle tables on the lawns, Meldie and I try to do a head count. It is not possible; there are too many people. Our best estimate is between 120 and 135 guests. Drinks flow freely — Rod sees to that. With the catering taken care of, I am free to move among our guests. Meldie and Tommy are thrilled that their Julia Creek cousins, Pat and Mike Dawes are here. I check the tables — white tablecloths, crockery, plates, silver cutlery and serviettes; the cups, saucers and glasses are on a separate table. Taking pride of place, on another small table, is a beautiful, big birthday cake. Pat supplied everything, except the lovely crocheted cloth on the birthday cake table. The food is set out. I could not have imagined it possible that such a variety of delicious food could be served at an isolated cattle station, in one of the most remote areas of Australia. Pat has excelled — but there is more to come.

People sit round eating, talking, singing, and drinking. Some of the men are not sober from the time they arrive until the time they leave, but they are all happy. At 3 a.m., Pat comes to tell me that they are finished for the night, and going to bed, but they will be up early to prepare breakfast. Meldie and Tommy are still enjoying themselves, not ready for bed. Neither is Rod. However, I am tired and I turn in. Men sleep where they crash, the women find beds, swags, or sleeping bags, and settle down for what is left of the night.

The party goes on for three days. The young, the sober, and the not-so-sober ride the iron horse or go swimming. Bakers Hole, a great swimming hole, is full. Some of the men play two-up. I am relaxed and enjoying the company of the women I like so much. There are people everywhere. I have to find Liddy. I have not seen any of our blacks since the party started. I go to their camp. They greet me with happy faces. Pat is feeding them well.

On the fourth day, people start to leave. Most of the men are a sorry lot. Their wives have to drive home. Small aircraft roar down the airstrip in front of our house, and take off. Rod drives others to our main strip to catch bigger planes. By four o'clock, everybody but Pat and the helpers have gone. It is time to sit quietly and enjoy Pat's company. I am so grateful to her. They will all fly back to Perth tomorrow.

Some time later, while mustering the area between the airstrip and the homestead, the boys found neatly stacked beer cans in burnt clumps of spinifex. Rod had forgotten his cache when burning off. I learnt that Rod had not delivered all the cartons to the freezer room. He had hidden several cartons along the road. When he drove out each day, it was not to check the road, as he had told me, but to sit quietly under a shady tree and enjoy his beer. I could have said, "Serves you right," but I did not. He was so contrite.

* * *

Things settle back to normal, but the rush is on to get the stock camp out. We are very late this year. Rod and Tommy plan the musters. Drums of avgas are left at the stock camp landing strips, horses are mustered and shod, stock camp gear is checked and made ready and tracks are graded to make it easier for me to drive from camp to camp. Dates and numbers are set with the meatworks; road trains are booked. No matter how many times we go through this routine, it never ceases to thrill me.

199

I am satisfied to sit by and watch, but Rod insists on taking an active part in the musters. Tommy depends on him. Nobody can read cattle like Rod. The father-and-son partnership is improving, but it will never really be good. Tommy is eager to please; Rod is quick to criticise. A friend once said to me, "You should not put two stallions in the one paddock." Perhaps she had the same problem or knew something I did not. It was rather crudely put, but I think I understand what she meant.

It is with a great deal of sadness that we hear Fred Ryle has died at Maylands on 28 April. Dear, kind Fred, with his wife, Pat, had been the shining light that had guided me through my early, lonely, troubled years in the Kimberleys. He had been a ship's wireless operator who, along with Pat, a nurse, moved to the Flying Doctor Base at Wyndham, and became the voice of the Kimberleys. It was not until 1955 that the Flying Doctor Service received the Royal Charter and became the Royal Flying Doctor Service. We will miss Fred, and I feel so sad for Pat and their children.

* * *

Meldie and Tommy have a good healthy life. They have friends in the small towns, and there are a lot of young white jackaroos in the area. They go everywhere together, to cricket at *Moola Bulla*, Halls Creek, and Wyndham, as well as rodeos and race meetings. They are happy. They have both done a few stints with John Roulston and are keen to have their own plane, but first they have to have their pilot's licences. I am not sure how Rod will take this. He is happy to let John chase the cattle from the air while the horsemen do the ground work. I approach him but he is not interested.

After four days of hard aerial mustering with John Roulston's plane, and tireless ground work, we have 800–1000 cattle in hand. We yard them at Wooley Yard, which is really only a temporary yard, consisting of barbed wire running from tree to tree. Tommy and the boys light fires outside the corners of the yard. We all know it is going to be a hard night. With watches worked out and night horses tied up, Rod has the campfire built up high. The cattle are quiet — not a good sign.

Midnight; so far so good. Rod is not asleep. Tommy and Compass move out to take over the watch. Compass is a young, inexperienced, white stockboy — given his nickname for having no sense of direction.

The boys put more wood on the fire; the cattle jump. Rod and Bob Skeen call to the cattle to settle them; they ring round the yard — but do not rush.

Rod and Bob, two old friends, sit by the fire. I hear Tommy singing, "Old MacDonald Had a Farm", loud and clear. I hear Compass too, but do not know what song he is singing.

I think I hear the bulls fighting in a corner of the yard. Compass gets off his horse; as he gets back on, the horse crow-hops into the light of the corner fire, which frightens the mob. They take the yard.

Cattle are rushing madly, wildly snapping the wire and knocking down everything before them; I hear nothing but the thunder of the rush. Tommy and Compass are out there somewhere! Rod and Bob call the boys. Quickly pulling on boots, they pick up their bridles; some go for the horses. Little Mick and Rodney take the remaining night horses. In the melee, some of the boys are gasping in great grunting breaths; some are sobbing. Rod wants to go, but Bob will not catch a horse for him, out of respect for Rod's health. Rod wants me to help but it is so dark, I do not know if I am walking into the backs of the colts, or if I am close to their heads. They could kick me. I actually have no intention of helping Rod catch a horse, but I have to pretend to help him until it is too late for him to go. Bob saddles up and is off. The boys follow. Compass rides into camp; he is so afraid, he is shaking. I understand his fear. I am terrified of the rushes. I fear for the boys because of their inexperience; I do not know what they will do. They could be killed, or they could get lost. In the early years, when the cattle rushed, I was afraid for all our stockmen, both white and black, but the whites were men, not boys, and the blacks have a natural instinct that protected them.

Rod gives up trying to catch a horse. I help him build up the fire and put the billies on. We want the fire to burn high and bright, to guide the lost back to the camp. Some, seeing the fire, come back. They are sensible. They do not know where the cattle are, or where the rest of the boys are. They tie their horses up and sit round the fire. I look out into the dark, in the direction where I think I hear voices, and the sound of animals galloping. The cattle would be well scattered by now. Only Tommy, Bob and Little Mick, being experienced, will know how to wheel them. I pray that the boys who have not come in are safe. I am always praying for something; broken Hail Marys and aspirations. I learn later that Rodney's horse fell.

Rod and I go over to the yard. There is very little of it left. We join the boys and wait. The boys shiver, although they are huddled up in their warm cardigans; they drink tea and talk in whispers. I look at my watch. The cattle must have rushed soon after midnight; it is now a little after

201

two o'clock. We can only wait. Time drags on; some of them should have been back by now. Bob and Little Mick are old men — excellent stockmen, but old. I wish they would just let the cattle go, rather than keep trying to block them. This is a particularly wild area, and it is so dark. It is cold too. I stay close to the fire with Rod and the boys. If I had any whisky I would give Rod a nip because it would help him now.

Rodney rides back to us and tells Rod of his fall. He says that the cattle are blocked up about one and a half miles away. Rod is pleased. As day-break approaches, Rod and the boys ride out to relieve the men with the cattle.

Daylight shows that losses are not as bad as we had feared. John Roulston arrives to start mustering and we head for Mud Springs — it was to be a long, long day.

* * *

One warm October afternoon, Brian Smith from Rossair, Alice Springs, flies over from *Mt House,* where he has been visiting. A good salesman and a good friend, he has a plane to sell, and we are in the market for one, or at least, I am, with Meldie and Tommy. Brian comes up with all the right reasons why a plane will be an asset: time saved mustering, money saved travelling, perhaps a tax deduction... He gently works on Rod, his persuasion perfection. Rod agrees to Meldie getting her licence, and then the plane will follow. Brian makes all the arrangements. Russell Williams, an experienced Rossair instructor, flies from Alice Springs to *Lansdowne* to get Meldie started. He teaches her to fly, and she returns to Alice Springs with him. They take a commercial flight to Adelaide, where, under Russell, she finishes her flying hours and exams. She flies back to Alice Springs with Russell and his fiancée. Arthur Hughes flies her home.

Not long after Meldie arrives home, Brian sends word that he has a good second-hand, single-engine, fixed-wing, 172 Cessna, call sign, WTQ. Jan Styles will fly it to *Lansdowne.* Jan, small and frail-looking, has no trouble on the way. She flies for Rossair, and is an excellent pilot.

Financially, WTQ is a big saving. Meldie flies as a spotter for the musterers, using her two-way radio to keep in touch with Tommy and the boys on the ground. She is in the air from first light until about nine o'clock, a time when our winds are at their most fickle. Strong winds and draughts toss her around. The plane rises and falls, down low in the valleys, up and over the ranges. I am so afraid for her. She some-times guides small mobs of cattle towards the musterers. Rod is as worried as I am. He says WTQ is not powerful enough — we will trade it in for a 182.

Meldie is not well. Like Rod, she is asthmatic. She was wheezy all day yesterday and last night, now the wheeze has developed into full-blown asthma and I can't help her. I blow the whistle for an emergency medical. Derby Hospital comes on the air — the doctor will send their plane out to pick her up. She is in hospital for six days. The rest is good for her. Although this attack has been checked, there will be others. Asthma has plagued her all through her school years. I want to keep her out of the stock camp, but she loves the life. I just have to watch over her.

* * *

Some of the boys having fun on the 'iron horse'.

CHAPTER SEVENTEEN

Accidents and illness

The rigours of the Kimberleys
Take their toll again,
To break the spirit and snap the bones
Of those who dare remain.

We stop Meldie flying for the musterers. John Roulston will fly for us until Tommy gets his licence next year. The musters go well. We load fifty-four head onto an E.K.T. road train late in June. Our musters are shorter, as we bring small mobs into the station for the road trains. By the end of the season, we will have trucked the same number that would have been walked, in the old days. Things move at a more hectic pace now. Rod is finding it hard to keep up, but, thank goodness, Tommy is taking on a lot of responsibility.

There are times when Rod prefers to truck bigger mobs and we need more road trains. E.K.T. arrives the night before we load. The cattle are yarded in the new yards that Rod and the boys have built; the yards are ringed by beautiful, shady poinciana trees. The drivers shower and join us on the lawn for a barbecue tea. They are all good friends. Then it is early to bed for everyone.

Liddy and I prepare breakfast: steak and eggs or steak and onions for the whites and half-castes, thick warm porridge with lots of sugar and milk for the blacks. Meldie cuts sandwiches for the drivers to take with them.

After breakfast, we join Rod, Tommy and the men at the yards. The sun is just rising. Cattle are bellowing; dust, heavy in the air; men are shouting, road trains revving up and getting into position to load. Rod puts me close to the race to keep count. Meldie joins the boys to keep the cattle moving towards the ramp. Tommy is working the gates, easing cattle through without bruising them. As each truck is loaded, it moves out to make way for the next. Most times, the bullocks move freely. Some bail-up and cause lost time. Others become jammed in the race. They also horn and bunt each other in the yard. All this causes bruising that never happened in the old horse and droving days.

* * *

Mustering round The Lily, Meldie has another asthma attack. John Roulston flies her back to the station. She will stay there until the camp goes in. I go again, with Rod, to muster. My saddle is back at the station. I ride Meldie's horses, and in Meldie's saddle. I do not like it. There are no knee pads, and no stirrup leathers. The irons are on the end of the flap. It is a very comfortable saddle, but I have to ride with my legs at full stretch all the time. I get very tired.

Tomorrow, Rod and I will drive back to the station to get ready for a christening party that Rod's brother, Mick and his wife, Cherry are having at *Ruby Plains* for their son, Henry. Rod and I are the godparents of their eldest son, Jim. Tommy and the boys will take the cattle into the station. They will muster a fresh plant of horses and shoe until we return.

On the drive back to the station, my back starts to ache. There is so much pain, I would rather not go to the party, but Meldie and Rod are looking forward to it. I will go.

Meldie flies us to *Ruby*. I spend the entire party in bed. Meldie goes into Halls Creek to get painkillers from the hospital. They help a little — until we get back to *Lansdowne*. Meldie calls Derby Hospital. The medical plane, on the way back from *Koongle Park* with a patient, deviates to *Lansdowne* to pick me up. We fly to Fitzroy Crossing, where a third patient is picked up. My fellow patients, a male and a female, are black. The woman is in pain and moaning a lot. The injection I had at our airstrip before we left *Lansdowne* has made me very drowsy. I have no idea what time we get to Derby. I only know it is dark. Pilots, doctors and nurses never hesitate when a call comes to fly out and pick up the wounded and the sick. Their own safety is secondary. They are a very special breed of people, and we are so grateful to them.

I have been in hospital for three days. Nobody seems to know what is wrong. I wish Doctor Hollman and the nuns were here. Mother Damian and her nursing sisters no longer nurse in the general section of the hospital. They are confined to the children's wards only. What I am doing here, I can do at home — I am simply resting. John Henwood, from

Fossil, has been in hospital. He will fly back to *Fossil* tomorrow. I arrange to be discharged and will go with him.

I am only home a few days when Tommy has a serious accident. He is kicked by a horse, Billy Boy — a beautiful chestnut, but a bad horse. Tommy had hoped to gentle him. None of the boys will ride him as he is quite treacherous and will bite and kick.

Tommy is flown to Wyndham Hospital in the afternoon. We spend an anxious night, knowing that we will not hear anything until morning. I think Tommy's hip is broken. I call the doctor early for his report. It is not good; in fact, it is alarming. Tommy has broken ribs and suspected internal haemorrhaging. His ribs will heal, but internal haemorrhaging is something else entirely. We want him to go to Perth or Brisbane, but the doctor says it is best if he is not moved. We check with the hospital daily.

Rod and Meldie are drafting meatworks cattle close to the station, watched by some government mapping boys. Nobody actually sees what happens, but Noble, one of the native stockboys, rides close to Meldie and tells her, "Boss bin fall of 'orse and sid under tree." Meldie quickly finds her father. She thinks it is a heart attack. She is very upset. The mapping boys gather round, but there is little they can do. As soon as Rod is resting a little easier, they drive him back to the station. Meldie stays with the cattle.

* * *

Healthwise, things are not going well for us. Tommy is in hospital; Rod has had a bad turn, whatever it was; and I am handicapped with my back. I have a medical on Rod. He won't go to hospital and it is impossible for the doctor to diagnose without examining him. In 1958, when I first hurt my back, I had complete rest. I barely got out of bed until the pain had cleared. I know now, unless I rest, or have treatment, the pain will stay with me. We decide that, as soon as we have turned off the last of our meatworks cattle, Rod, Tommy and I will go to Brisbane for check-ups and tests. Tommy has been in hospital eighteen days and there are still no positive results. I wonder about the haemorrhage, but I know absolutely nothing about medicine. The doctor says there are signs of damage and bleeding from his liver.

Brian Smith, aware that Rod wants to trade our 172 in for a 182 Cessna, calls in to discuss the deal. He flew to Wyndham yesterday, to pick Tommy up. He will fly Rod, Tommy and me to Darwin in the morning, to connect with Australian National Airways (ANA) for our flight to Brisbane. Meldie will have enormous responsibility while we are away, but she is sensible and will cope. However, I wish we did not have to leave her.

207

We quickly contact our doctors in Brisbane. Rod and Tommy trudged round the city, having X-rays, heart checks and blood tests. I stayed with Rod's friend, Michael Gallagher. We waited for the results — Tommy's ribs are healing. Certainly, there was a lot of damage to his liver and a little bleeding, which was contained. The doctor did not prescribe any treatment. Whatever had to be done, was done while he was in Wyndham Hospital. We are pleased indeed with that report. Tommy is free to go home. We saw him board Trans-Australian Airlines (TAA) for the return trip.

Rod's report is not so good. High blood pressure, and yes! a mild stroke — a warning. He will have to take care, break down his workload, and try not to worry. Rod is a worrier; this aggravates his blood pressure.

My X-rays show an old injury and a curve in my spine which will get worse as I grow older. The long hours riding, with my legs at full stretch, put severe strain on my back, causing more damage to the old injury. Michael sends me to a physiotherapist. Rod borrows his sister's car, and regularly drives me for treatment for five weeks. We stay with my sister, Meldie Holmes, and her family. I think the treatments will never end. I am conscious of a soreness in my back now, but the pain has gone. We fly ANA to Darwin, MMA to Kununurra, then Peter Reid's charter plane flies us to *Lansdowne*, arriving late in November. Meldie had done an excellent job while we were away, but was pleased to hand over to Tommy when he arrived home. We pay our staff off, the whites and half-castes go to town, our blacks go walkabout and we settle down to spend a quiet Christmas, the weather humid and overcast.

* * *

From left: Elsa and Rod McLeanan with son, and Rod and Basil Quilty at *Ruby Plains*.

208

CHAPTER EIGHTEEN

Next generation

Be good to him,
Because of me.
If he be hurt,
My heart shall break.

The news about Cyclone Tracey and the destruction of Darwin comes through on Boxing Day. The city has been utterly devastated; 62 people have been killed and about 1000 seriously injured; nine out of ten homes are destroyed, leaving 45,000 homeless. How very sad for the people of Darwin; it was not built to bear the force of a cyclone — and Tracey was savage.

Sean Murphy flies out from Halls Creek to spend New Year's Day with us. Commonly called "Spud", he is a good friend, a stock inspector who immigrated from Ireland and took well to Australian life. We are surprised to see Paddy and Big Mick at the station; they can't be camped too far away. They want Sean to fly them to Halls Creek to pick up a car that Big Mick had bought when he was in town for the Races. We suspect he has spent all his wages on a bomb some smart aleck has sold him. Sean flies them in. Five days later, Bedford Bob walks into the station and tells us that Big Mick and Paddy have broken down at Gordon Springs, and asks us to help them. He says, "Alla dime, bruk down." (All the time, break down.)

Rod and I set out with tools, tow chain, petrol, water, bread and meat. Bob hops on the back of the utility. We meet Little Mick at the horse-paddock gate. He comes with us. Paddy and Big Mick are in a bad way. They have not eaten for days. I give them the food while Rod puts petrol in the empty tank and tinkers with the engine; it kicks over. They quickly gather their belongings and toss them onto the back of the utility. With Big Mick driving, Paddy beside him, and Little Mick and Bedford Bob in the back, they are off. Rod gives them about an hour's start. We catch up about half a mile down the road, Big Mick still behind the wheel, Paddy, Little Mick and Bedford Bob pushing. Little Mick is yelling, "Gibit da duce!" (Give it the juice!) Nothing works. Rod tows them back to the station. He parks the car in front of Big Mick and Rosie's house. They are all so proud of Big Mick's car. To them it is a symbol of ... what? I do not know. The fact that it is a worn-out, broken-down bomb does not upset them all that much. It is a car, Big Mick owns it, and they are all proud of it. I am so annoyed with the smart aleck who sold it to him.

In time, we get used to seeing broken-down vehicles, rusting away beside roads in the Kimberleys and the Northern Territory. Not all bombs, some had been new vehicles when handed over to the blacks.

* * *

We are still waiting for the rains; it is getting very late in the season. There are lots of dry storms about, with thunder and lightning, bushfires and hot winds. Static is very bad over the Traeger radio. It makes it hard to receive and send traffic. We are concerned that Tommy's twenty-first birthday party will have to be postponed or held early. We decide to hold it early. Invitations go out for 29 March. There is not much time. My friend, Pat Glossop, will again cater. The catering is the biggest problem, but, thank goodness, Pat has that under control.

We had given Meldie a piano for her birthday, hoping she was musical and would enjoy playing. She can belt out "John Brown's Body" and that is it. We get a billiard table for Tommy. Maxine McDonald keeps it at *Fossil* until the day of his party.

Meldie and Sean Murphy do several runs to fly guests in. Some come in their own planes and others arrive by car. As with Meldie's party, there are strangers. They are made welcome — it is open house. After four happy days, people begin to leave. We say goodbye to Pat and her crew, and the station settles back down into work mode.

* * *

Tommy's Aquinas school friend, Des Lavendar, came to the party. He and Tommy plan a working tour round Australia. I do not agree to

Tommy going. We cannot carry on without him. I have looked forward to this time for so long, when he and Meldie would be home for good, for them to be here to take over some of the responsibility of running *Lansdowne*. I don't think I can carry on much longer. If Rod was in better health, things would be different. Without Tommy, I will have to go back into the stock camp full-time. I am not sure that I can face that. Rod would like to sell and get out. I cannot agree to that. I know Tommy is bitterly disappointed. I will try to make it up to him some other way.

Des stays with us for twelve months. He does all and everything. He is stockman, handyman, offsider, and he is Tommy's friend. His parents must be proud of him.

* * *

Earlier this year, we bought Brahman bulls and heifers to improve our herd. Brahman blood, crossed with Shorthorn, should throw a bigger beast, but I doubt the meat will be sweeter.

The plane certainly is an asset. Flying to town, to pick up staff or parts or whatever, can be done in a matter of hours; road vehicles take days. Meldie does a lot of flying, but I am always afraid for her. Tim Emanuel, of Gogo Station, an experienced pilot, was reported to have said that he would not fly a single-engine plane in the Kimberley area. Should WTQ's engine conk out, there is no second chance, and very few places to put down. We fly to Kununurra, Batchelor or Darwin for the plane's one-hundred-hour service, depending on where a service is available.

* * *

I like to plan well ahead, but there is always the unexpected. After Tommy's party, I think we will have a clear, uninterrupted work year, but an invitation from my sister Dadie, to her daughter Mary's wedding on 17 May, causes us to make some quick changes to our plans. Mary wants Meldie to be her chief bridesmaid and Dadie wants us all to be there. Of course, we all want to go, but it will take some organising. I leave that to Rod, and he does splendidly.

A friend, Peter Murray, flies Meldie and me to Mt Isa. My nephew, Mike Dawes, meets us and drives us to Julia Creek. From there we fly by TAA to Townsville, where the wedding will be.

Tommy has saved for and bought a second-hand yellow utility. Jack Dalzell, a buyer for Wyndham Meats, flies Tommy and his friends to Wyndham, where they pick up the utility, and then Tommy drives it to Townsville.

211

Rod is the last to leave. Jan Styles flies Rod, in WTQ, from *Lansdowne* to Townsville, staying overnight at *Inverway*, in the Northern Territory. Rod leaves Bob Skeen to brand while we are away and Liddy and Zachady are to look after the station.

By 15 May, we are all in Townsville. There are lunches, parties and happy gatherings before the wedding. Mary and Rod O'Neill leave for their honeymoon in New Zealand, and we return to *Lansdowne*, some flying, some driving. The cost of a commercial flight from Townsville to Mt Isa is $61.90 at this time.

It takes a while to settle back to work after such enjoyable interruptions. Maree, a little New Zealander who has been with us for two years, is a big help. She gets meals cooked quickly, and on time.

* * *

My darling mother died on 4 September, this year. The anniversaries of the deaths of Rod's mother and my father are close together on the calendar, but not in years — my father died before Rod's mother. These dates are always very sad times for us.

In mid-November, Meldie flies Tommy to Lake Gregory, then Brian Smith takes him on to Alice Springs, where he starts his flying lessons. Ossie Watts, a hard, no-nonsense instructor, will supervise. Tommy quickly learns that who he is, and what he is, cuts no ice with Ossie. He learns to grin and bear it when Ossie tells him, "Just because your father owns a bit of dirt called *Lansdowne*, does not mean you have the right to take off and land wherever you like in Alice Springs. Get back onto the tarmac!" as Tommy desperately tries to remember not to treat the controls as he does those of a car. He finishes his flying lessons at Alice Springs and does his exams and flying hours at Adelaide. It is good to have him home again.

A message comes from Brian Smith, saying he finally has a new 182 Cessna ready for delivery. He will be at *Lansdowne* this afternoon. He flies in with Sue, his attractive young wife, who is pregnant with their first baby. They are to stay the night. Contracts and forms have to be signed. All goes well until Rod realises the new plane will cost more than he is prepared to pay. He starts to look for a way out. He mixes his before- and after-dinner drinks — beer and whisky. A happy drunk, he is now happily primed. I could kill him... I will kill him... He is too drunk to sign anything! Brian says he has an ace up his sleeve, but will keep it until last. Rod dithers round; it is getting late, and I am getting madder by the minute. Brian has to leave at first light tomorrow, and Sue has had a long day; she should be in bed.

212

My temper snaps; I rush at Rod. I run into a wall of people. Meldie and Tommy, knowing my temper, are expecting something like this. They move quickly to protect their father. Brian is not slow to move either. They form a ring around Rod, and I can't get near him. My temper fizzles out, and Rod is a little less drunk, a little more sober.

Brian produces his ace — the call sign of the new plane is RTQ, Rod's initials. Surely he cannot resist this. Rod signs all the forms and we are the proud owners of a new Cessna, more powerful and, to me, safer than the 172. Later that night, before he goes to sleep, Rod wants to know if I really would have hit him.

* * *

We have a Quilty family Christmas at *Lansdowne*. Basil and Lesley, from *Bedford*, with their little family; and Mick and Cherry, with their children, are with us. Rod is close to his brothers, Basil and Mick. *Mt House* also has a big Christmas party. Dick Northcott and his staff are there. On his way back to *Moola Bulla*, on Boxing Day, with his bookkeeper, Wendy Wagstaff, Dick calls into *Lansdowne* for morning tea. Tommy is very impressed with Wendy.

We receive beautiful rain from January to March. I can still hear the storm birds calling, so I hope there is more rain to come. Late in March, we hear that Russell Williams has been killed in a plane accident at Parafield, in South Australia. Such a sad, dreadful tragedy. Meldie and Tommy are very upset. They knew Russell so well.

Olive has invited us to *Springvale* for Grandfather Quilty's eighty-ninth birthday party. Although I often argued with my father-in-law, and did not always approve of him, he is a great man who has done great things; he is generous to a fault, a good friend, and a forgiving enemy. His great love for Olive is returned tenfold. Since her early teens, she has been in love with Tom Quilty, a man twenty-odd years older than her. He is proud of her good looks, as well he might be. He says, "I was born on April Fool's Day and I've been a fool ever since." Another favourite saying is, "Live long and die happy." He certainly has had a long life.

* * *

Tommy is seeing Wendy whenever he can. Dick is not about to let his bookkeeper go gallivanting round the country, so the sightings are not all that often, but I begin to wonder if the friendship is serious when Tommy asks if he can invite Wendy for the weekend. He picks her up at *Moola Bulla* late on Friday afternoon and flies her back on Sunday evening.

The friction between Rod and Tommy continues. It could be an ideal and happy setup if only Rod would let up on Tommy. He is proud of his son but he simply cannot show it. He haggles Tommy at every turn.

* * *

SHIRE / PROPERTY	NO. OF CATTLE IN PRESENT HERD	NUMBER OF CATTLE MARKETED							METHOD OF TRANSPORT		ACCESS	
		1972	1973	1974	1975	1976	1977	1978	ROAD TRAIN	DRIVEN PART WAY	Yes	No
BROOME												
Anna Plains	17,535	3,733	3,759	3,987	3,193	5,066	2,908	5,228	*		*	
Country Downs	600				100					*	*	
Mandora	3,000	336	763	374	400	947	596	364	*		*	
Waterbank				160	50	20	50		*		*	
HALLS CREEK												
Bedford Downs	14,000	1,515	2,054	2,037	1,154	1,850	1,694	1,289		*	*	
Flora Valley	)		289	1,148	2,718	2,075	3,534	983	3,783	*		*	
Spring Creek	)												
Gordon Downs	)		808	260	74	48	700	865	1,202	*		*	
Sturt Creek	) 71,698												
//Kirkimbie/Mistake Creek	)	2,378	1,808	879	684	1,495	1,207	1,469	*		*	
Nicholson	)	1,274	569	364	414	334	513	445	*		*	
Landsdowne	11,480	1,338	1,707	782	701	987	1,040	1,584		*	*	
Moola Bulla	41,000	8,000	8,000	7,000	5,000	5,000	4,800	4,800	*		*	
Osmond Valley		70	55	65		75		45	*		*	
Spring Vale	10,000	980	2,050	1,323	1,035	1,204	1,207	1,059	*		*	
WEST KIMBERLEY												
Beverley Springs	4,000					300	320	340	*			*
Cherrabun	21,000	2,991	3,162	2,697	1,564	2,507	3,867	4,713	*		*	
Christmas Creek	20,000	3,214	3,206	2,668	1,604	3,923	3,302	3,337	*		*	
Myroodah, Luluigui Kalyeeda	23,000	3,247	3,748	1,753	820	1,819	2,643	2,555	*		*	
Mt. Anderson	2,500	200	500	200	200	200	200	200	*		*	
WYNDHAM/EAST KIMBERLEY												
Doongan	9,351	228	190	401	209	233	Nil due to road	1,136	*		*	
Lamoreaux	290	28		90			44	36	*		*	
	249,454	30,629	32,979	27,412	19,360	30,315	26,209	33,635				

// Kirkimbie/Mistake Creek is technically in the N.T. but markets its cattle at Wyndham as part of the Vestey Group and is therefore included.

214

Table showing size of herds, numbers of cattle marketed, methods of transport to market and state of access roads across four shires from 1972 to 1978.

CONDITION OF ACCESS ROAD	IMPROVEMENTS REQ.	ADD'N ACCESS RD. REQ.	APPROACHES FOR ASSISTANCE		RESULTS	
			SHIRE	M.R.D.	SHIRE	M.R.D.
Fair; some potholes	Grading and filling		To upgrade rd. each year and maintain		Was started but never finished	
Deplorable	Flat grade every year				Broome Shire has promised to upg. in Feb.	
Fair					Shire and M.R.D. repaired road last year	
We service own	Was poor at beg. of year				Only time ever done, there was river to front door	
Rough; bad crossings	Re-aligning and low-level cross's		Maintenance and upgrading		Requested to submit proposals for consideration	
Problems due Negri Cross'g at Dun. Hwy			Restore to orig. condition			nil
We service own			Restore to orig. condition			Temp. repairs to cross'g and surface
Cartage prob's on Dun. Hwy due Negri Cross'g			Restore to orig. condition			Temp. repairs to cross'g and surface
We service own				Repeatedly		Temp. repairs
Poor to Terrible	Bulldozer for most of stretches		3 yrs run'g		Lack of Money Not enough use of road	
Very Poor	Gen. Upgrading		Inspected road letter sent for 79 programme		No action	M.R.D. preferred
Bad	Cut drains to stop wash outs					
Fair			Maintenance and upgrading		Some assist.	
Grading after wet conditions	Gravelling to make weather-proof		Shire grade annually; is usuable			Main Gibb Rvr Derby Cross'g add. concrete
Fair; needs perm cross'g at Christ. Crk	More gravel and perm cross'g		Repeatedly		Very little; Main grade once yr.??	
Rough	A compl. new access road	8-10 mile	Repeatedly	Mn. Rd. was shifted; they would cut line	nil	nil
Poor; Kalyeeda is inaccess'le	Extensive grading		Every year with varied success		Forced to repair with contract grader	
Very Poor	Washed out in heavy rains not repaired		Several		Road was graded	
4wd only; no access dur'g wet	Gravelling of sandy & swampy areas		77 and 78	Letter to Company	Every effort to open; never do	No reply No evid'c
Bitumen road; good condition						

Bob Skeen, August 1979.

CHAPTER NINETEEN

Happiness and misery

No one knows what Fate
Awaits them on the morrow.
Some are granted every wish,
Others, pain and sorrow.

This has been a good year — good rain, good brandings, good turn off. Winter is over and spring is here again. The wild bush wattle is in bloom and my garden is a riot of colour — oleander, frangipani, hibiscus. The sweet perfume of flowers fills the air. The big poinciana tree is a mass of bright red flowers; bougainvillea vines climb to the sun, brilliantly colourful and scentless; the tamarind and ghost gum trees cast their cooling shade over everything.

We have so much to be thankful for — endless clean, fresh water, abundant meat, our own vegetables, fruit trees, a life our children love, wonderful friends, and the purest air on earth. Free of town and city restrictions, we do not fear to sleep out on our lawns, or leave our doors and windows open. It is the best of all lives, but this country has also taken so much from me. I am tempted to go looking for our babies' graves. I think about it a lot, but just cannot bring myself to go. All the old lubras, who know where the graves are, have gone. I would have to go alone.

Blacks drive out from Halls Creek to visit their "'lations" at *Lansdowne*. Town-wise and cunning, they come, not out of love, but to fleece their working relations of whatever money they can get — or, at walkabout, to con them into parting with some of their walkabout rations. The girls are as bad as the boys. Non-workers, living on their wits, they quickly spend their "sid down money", mostly on liquor, then they move out to the stations, knowing their working relations will have money. They have become a general nuisance.

* * *

Dick Northcott and Wendy fly Rod and me to Halls Creek for the Council Elections. Ernie Bridge, of mixed blood, is the Council Chairman. He is a very ambitious young man. I never knew his father, but his mother, Sarah, is a lady — a gentle woman devoted to her family, and proud of their achievements. Ernie's Uncle, Bert Sharpe, was a carrier in Wyndham when I was there with Rod and my sister Coral, in 1951.

We call in to have a cup of tea with Sandy and Libby Taylor, business owners in Halls Creek. The tea party goes on for the rest of the day, and long into the night. The tea doesn't last long. Kimberley men are not tea drinkers. It is a boisterous party. Beer and spirits flow freely. Rod, Dick and Sandy are well and truly drunk. Wendy is drinking Coke® and Libby and I drink tea until we can no longer look at a cup. Torrence MacMicking and a few town men join our happy drunks. They drink, then stagger off home. Late at night, our happy drunks get hungry. There is nowhere to buy food, so Libby, Wendy and I have to hustle something up for them. The men eat, then crash. I can't wake Rod. Libby drives me to the hotel to get ready for mass. We are all very tired. I think Wendy drives Dick out to *Moola Bulla*, then back to town later. Dick then flies Rod and me to *Lansdowne*.

* * *

Tommy is now doing all our aerial mustering while Rod and the boys do the ground work. Meldie is always close to her father, on the ground. I never thought it possible for a plane to have so much control over cattle. It herds small mobs into bigger ones. Quick as a flash, Tommy is onto anything that breaks out.

Early in November, Brian Smith comes to give Tommy experience in crosswind flying and to endorse him for aerial mustering. He also puts Meldie through a few aerial tests. Rod and I appreciate what Brian has done for Meldie and Tommy. Although the plane makes things a lot easier and more convenient for us, we are always aware of the dangers.

Our blacks are quarrelling among themselves over Big Mick's car. Liddy seems to be the one causing the trouble. She claims Little Mick put money into buying the car and that it should be parked in front of her house, not Rosie's. The fact that it is broken down and will never go, no matter how often they push it round the flat, does not change her mind. Liddy and Rosie have never been the best of friends.

In December, Tommy flies Wendy to Queensland for her holidays. This confirms what I have gradually come to accept; the relationship has developed into something more serious than friendship. I am pleased; so is Rod.

The McDonald family fly from *Fossil* to spend Christmas Eve with us, a lovely surprise. We want them to stay longer but there are storms around, and they have to get back. Although I spend a lot of time at *Fossil*, this is Maxine's first visit to *Lansdowne*.

It is very hot. Lightning strikes from dry storms start bushfires. There is a cyclone further down the coast, but we get no rain, certainly not before Christmas.

Early in the New Year, Rod, Meldie and I drive to Brisbane, for my nephew, Jim Dawes' wedding. Tommy and Wendy meet us there. Jim's bride, Rosemarie, is the daughter of an old and dear friend from my Julia Creek days, Pat Collins. Rosemarie is a strikingly attractive brunette; they certainly make a handsome couple. We do not stay long after the wedding. Without rain, the bushfires on *Lansdowne* are a worry for us now, with so many yards and fences to protect. Tommy, Wendy and Meldie leave in RTQ; Rod and I book out of Lennons Hotel a few hours later.

At Julia Creek, we hear that the Georgina River is in flood — we could be held up at Camooweal. We spend three days at Julia Creek. As soon as we hear that the Georgina is down, we leave, but as fast as we move, the river is faster — it is up again before we get to Camooweal. The crossing is well and truly under water. We spend the night at the Camooweal Hotel.

There is still water over the crossing the following morning, but Rod is anxious and impatient. He takes the fanbelt off, covers the engine with a tarpaulin and we tackle the crossing. There are potholes and wash-outs; the river is strong and swirls around us. I am afraid; water comes in under the doors, but the far bank is getting closer. At last, we are across. Muddy water drips from our car. We dry it out, take the tarpaulin off the engine and put the fanbelt back on. We are on our way, up the bitumen, sheets of water all along the highway and big rain clouds building up.

At Renner Springs, we stay at Jack Chambers' Hotel/Motel. Jack and Rod are old friends. The night's rest is good for both of us, especially for Rod. We have another long day ahead of us; we will go right through to

219

Katherine. Another big disappointment awaits us at Katherine — The King River is up. Notorious for its low-lying bridge, we know we could be held up here for days. We book into the Crossways Motel.

Heavy rain all night and again today does not make our prospects of crossing the bridge look too good. Meldie and Tommy set out to fly to Katherine. The weather is bad and they must turn back. Rain continues to pour down and the King continues to rise. Rod starts to drink. He drives down to check the bridge. A bus load of children ahead of him and a police car close behind him; they want to pass. Rod weaves all over the bitumen, and comes close to running them off the road. He is arrested for driving under the influence of alcohol, and tossed in jail. He spends the day there and gets out this afternoon on $300 bail. He has had a terrible fright and I am very upset. We decide to take on the bridge tomorrow, and get out of Katherine.

Although we are packed and ready, the wretched river is higher this morning. We will just have to wait another day. We do not leave the motel room.

Just before four o'clock, the police knock on our door. Rod has to go with them again. We ask why, but they will give us no reason why they are taking him, or when he will be back. Young, arrogant, intimidating, they take our car and drive off with my darling husband. I could cry.

I phone the Police Station several times, but cannot find out where Rod is or when he will be back. I pace the small room, saying the rosary over and over. About ten o'clock, there is a knock on the door — it has to be Rod! I rush to open it. Another young, arrogant policeman stands there. I feel faint. I can hardly understand what he is saying. When I get over the shock, I am so mad, I could sue the entire police force.

"I want Rod out immediately."

"Impossible."

"He has been locked up again. Why?"

"I can't answer that, Madam."

"Don't dare call me Madam, you know my name."

"Yes, Mrs Quilty."

"Why are you here now, without Rod?"

"He must spend the night in jail. He wants his spray."

"He is having an asthma attack?"

220

"Yes."

"You have got to let him out. I must go to him."

"That would not be advisable."

"Then get a doctor for him."

"You are wasting time; he needs that spray now."

I give it to him. He says, "Be at the Court House at nine o'clock tomorrow morning. Your husband will be released then." I spend a miserable night, but I know Rod's misery is far greater than mine. Our friend, Trevor Christensen, comes early to find out if he can help. I ask him to drive me to the Court House. He stays with me until Rod receives a $500 fine and a restriction from driving in the Northern Territory for eighteen months. I do not have $500 in cash, and a cheque is not acceptable.

Rod is taken away again. Trevor goes off to get the money from his bank. I sit on a long form in front of the Court House, the only white there. There are three male blacks and an old lubra sharing the form with me. The lubra sits beside me; she has a terrible rattle in her chest and is hawking and spitting mucus everywhere. A great blob lands on my leg. I feel the warm slime slip down to my ankle. I jump up. I am so disgusted — I'll whack her one, or push her off the form! She has deliberately done this! But then I see her poor, old ravaged face. She puts her hand on my arm and pats the seat beside her. She moves to wipe my ankle with her dress. I am no longer angry with her or with anyone.

Trevor comes back with the money and we are free to drive away with Rod. At dinner tonight, with Trevor and Jill Christensen and Bob and Bryce Napier, we decide that, tomorrow, we will drive back to Dunmarra, turn off the highway there, onto the Top Springs — *Wave Hill* road and get home that way. We just have to get out of Katherine. The Christensens and the Napiers are truly good friends. We all have an early night.

The King River rose again after we left and the bridge was closed for sixteen days. We called into *Inverway* on the way home. It was good to see Peg Underwood again.

* * *

For all the water we have seen while on our journey home, there has been very little rain at *Lansdowne* while we were away. It looks like it is going to be a bad year. It started badly; I just hope it will end well. My faithful old dog, Silver, is dead. Rod says he will get me another alsatian.

221

Not long after the stock camp goes out, Meldie's horse bolts and she has a bad fall. She is unconscious. We get her back to the station, and the medical plane flies her to Wyndham. We spend a worried night. Tommy flies Rod, Wendy and me to Wyndham to see her this morning. She is hallucinating; we are very concerned. I speak to her doctor. He says she has concussion. I want to take her home, but the doctor says that will only harm her.

Five days later, and Meldie's condition has not changed. Tommy flies me to *Moola Bulla*, to phone Bob McInerney in Sydney. Bob says to get her to Sydney as soon as possible. We pick her up at the hospital and Tommy flies us to Alice Springs where we board a plane for Sydney. Bob and Betty Rose meet us at the airport. Bob takes Meldie straight to the hospital, where a brain specialist is waiting to see her. I go with Betty Rose.

Meldie has extensive scans and checks; whatever the problem, Bob says it has been isolated and contained. A week later, we fly home.

* * *

It is taking Rod a long time to get over the Katherine affair. I simply put it out of my mind. David and Suzie Bradley arrived this morning. David, a good vet, has his own plane. He looks at some of our horses; pink-eye, walkabout disease and worms are becoming big problems. Suzie is good company. They stay the night.

Kununurra Council has organised aerial dingo baiting with the deadly 10-80 poison. It is understood that they will not drop baits inside our horse paddock. Tommy, mustering long hours for *Lansdowne* and *Tableland*, over the range, keeps well out of their way.

Meldie, completely over her accident, settles down to the station routine, and the happy social life she enjoys with Tommy and the boys. But, where before it had been Tommy, Meldie and the others it has become Tommy, Wendy, Meldie and the others, and her nose is a little out of joint. She flies, with me, to Darwin for RTQ's one-hundred-hour checks. We shop and relax for the few days we are there.

The plane makes a wonderful difference to my children's social life. We all fly to *Bradshaw*, in the Northern Territory, for a weekend party. Dick Gill, working for Rolley Walker, is a fearless pilot. He does a lot of aerial mustering and is a big help to Tommy. *Bradshaw* used to be an old Quilty property, but it has been many years since Rod has been here. He takes me for a walk along the banks of the Victoria River. He shows me where his father and Olive had lived, and where he and his brother, Pat, had their dongas. The gallows, where they hung their meat, is the only thing still standing; there are a few stumps, a few paving stones, nothing else. It is a sad place. The new, modern homestead is some miles away.

I keep hearing a strange sound, like dogs barking, coming from the river. I know it is not dogs. I ask Rod what it is. He says it is crocodiles — they lie on the sand. Oh, dear God! I could walk right onto one and not know! I panic. "Let's get out of here! Quickly — move, MOVE!"

Rod says there are many stories to be told about *Bradshaw's Run* and the Brothers Bradshaw. It was the wish of one brother that, when he died, he be placed in a lead coffin and taken to the top of the mountain on *Bradshaw*, so that his spirit could look down, for ever more, on the place where he died. Later, a bushfire came burning over the mountain and melted the coffin. True story or false, Rod believes it to be true, and so do I. We fly over the mountain, on our way home, so that Rod can point out where the coffin was.

* * *

There has been very little wind for days; we are pumping at all our bores, engines going day and night. Our old pensioner blacks are camped at the bores to keep the engines refuelled and running.

John and Annette Henwood often fly in for the day. We are always pleased to see them.

Rod and I have been flying to all the race meetings from Halls Creek to Broome, sometimes for Cup Day only, for the last two years — a far cry from our driving days. Now we have to slow down. Our little old bush meetings have changed; thoroughbred horses, big money, imported jockeys, and drunken blacks have gone a long way to spoil our simple pleasure.

When the Tom Quilty Grandstand was first built at Halls Creek, we whites sat up high, in all our splendid grandeur, watching drunken blacks stagger by; now, drunken blacks loll up high while we, the whites, sit on our garden chairs, down in front, where drunken blacks once staggered.

Wendy is leaving *Moola Bulla*. Dick and the staff are giving her a farewell party on Sunday night. We will all go. Her mother is on her way to *Lansdowne*. At a small 'family and friends' party at *Lansdowne*, on 23 September, Tommy and Wendy's engagement is announced. A few days later, Wendy and her mother leave to drive back to *Thornleigh*, the family property at Blackall, Queensland.

223

Strong night winds get our windmills going and our old pensioner blacks come back to the station. Mid-October storms give a little relieving rain, but not enough. Bushfires around Coral Springs and The Lily are bad. Lightning strikes the dry grass and fires are springing up all over the run. The smoke haze is heavy.

Our wet season stores have left Fremantle on the "Nyanda". Rod will pick them up, off the ship, at Wyndham.

Tommy flies Rod and me to Darwin for a hundred-hourly on RTQ. It is Melbourne Cup Day. Rod has a win on Gold and Black but Tommy loses on Reckless. I do not bet.

* * *

Our original storeroom, now much dilapidated, with original vegetable garden over-grown behind.

CHAPTER TWENTY

Politics

Politics are the foundation of modern society.
Let us not forget, however, that it is also a type of warfare,
Sometimes more bloodthirsty than the real thing.

Matthew Quilty

The State Election, to be held on 17 December, is on everyone's mind. The Liberal Party, worried about the black vote, has Alan Ridge, the sitting Member, approach Meldie to see if she will stand as an Independent candidate, to try to stop the all-out flow of black votes to Ernie Bridge, the Labor candidate. Blacks outnumber whites, so it is a big thing to ask of Meldie.

Nominations close today, 25 November. Meldie's nomination was announced yesterday. A member of the Archer family, of Derby, has also nominated as an Independent.

I go with Meldie, as she starts her campaign in Halls Creek. She gets a good door-to-door reception. The names Ridge and Bridge are seldom mentioned, or if they are, it is by-the-way. We meet friends we are pleased to see, but it is very hot, and I dread the trudge through the blacks' camps this afternoon — there will be no cups of tea or cool drinks.

This is Ernie's home town; the blacks are friendly, but loyal to Ernie. Most of them are at a public meeting that Ernie is holding at the Civic Centre. It has been a long day for all of us. Tomorrow, Tommy will fly us to Fitzroy Crossing, to campaign there.

The Fitzroy people are wonderful. Maxine McDonald lends us her air-conditioned car; Cameron and Liz Bell are marvellously supportive, as are Morgan and Nina Neilson. Mr. Ruse offers to scrutinise for Meldie, and Jim and Joy Motter say they will hand out how-to-vote cards. We are so grateful, but we must concentrate on the blacks. We have to try to win their vote.

There are so many all-black camps here; they are all set-up with electricity, running water and septic systems. The Court Government has certainly spent a lot of money here. The camps are crowded. No-one seems to be working. I suspect they are all on "sid down money" — child endowment, pensions of all and any name — whatever; they have a glorious life. We drive from camp to camp, carefully steering Maxine's car between and around the camp 'bombs'. The blacks are happy to see Meldie. Most of them have known her since she was a baby. White teeth flashing, they laugh and joke with her, but are confused when she mentions the election. They talk about the apple and the banana — or is it the apple and the orange? Now we are as confused as they are. Everything goes smoothly until we come to the Windmill camp, where we meet Bennie. Bennie is quite hostile; brother or half-brother to Essie, the witch doctor, we are told, "Beware!" We are not welcome at Windmill. Bennie smartly sends us on our way.

Painstakingly, we continue from door-to-door, through the blacks' camps, and at all our little towns. The whites that we know are supportive and encouraging, offering help in any way they can. The blacks, as a whole, are pleased to see us but we are not always welcome at some white and half-caste homes. The blacks ask if we "zabby de happle an de 'nana?" (savvy the apple and the banana?). They are going to vote for the "Happle, 'im proper good tucker."

We begin to see a little light. Meldie asks, "Who is the happle?"

They reply, "Dat Hernie Bridge, 'im de happle, proper good fella, proper good tucker."

We laugh with the blacks, and wonder whose ingenious brain thought up the apple and banana symbols to differentiate between the similar-looking names, 'Bridge' and 'Ridge'.

What started out as an amusing, happy campaign, gradually turns spiteful and nasty as it moves into the second week. We hear at Turkey Creek that Paddy Quilty was the father of Trooper Bedford. I know this to be a lie. Paddy, due to a boyhood accident, was sterile — never able to have children. It was the reason he never married. A good Irish Catholic, he

226

believed a happy marriage produced children; if he could not father a child, he would never marry.

Meldie and I are amused; could the Labor camp be hurting? Trooper's mother, as far as I know, had been a *Bedford* lubra. Trooper took his surname from the station, as blacks often do, and 'Trooper' from the police force. If, as I suspect, the lie is to discredit or discourage Meldie, the storyteller failed miserably. But, we wonder, who could be so vicious?

We call into *Springvale* on our way home. At lunch, we repeat the story that Meldie and I found so funny. Rod, there to meet us, and Olive, are hurt and horrified. To them, it is malicious, spiteful, and completely untrue. In their anger, they talk of legal action. They want Meldie out of the campaign, but she is enjoying herself — she is not going to give up. It is best to ignore the lie.

There were many times during the campaign, and on Election Day, when I regretted that we did not pull out that day, as things got more vicious. Our poor old blacks were terrified. Liddy whispered to me, at night, that the "gidarchie" was about.

On Election Day, at Halls Creek, long lines of blacks slowly move towards the polling booths. They go in and painstakingly place their mark beside their favourite fruit — "Dat propper good fella, Hernie Bridge." In all our small towns, on this day, the scene is the same.

Ernie fought a hard and clean campaign. That is more than I can say of some of his helpers, but we should have been more aware of what was involved before we went into it. His party did nothing illegal. We learnt a bitter lesson: politics is a dirty, no-holds-barred business. Sir Charles Court and his Liberal Party were returned to power and Alan Ridge retained his seat.

* * *

Chapter Twenty-one

Turbulent years

What is in the lonely bush
That calls us from our home?

Tom Quilty

This will be our last Christmas together as a four-member family. In January, we leave for Queensland — for Tommy and Wendy's wedding in Toowoomba.

They are married in the beautiful old Catholic Cathedral on 3 February, 1978, and honeymoon in New Zealand. Flying over *Lansdowne* in RTQ on our way home, Meldie confidently handling the controls, and Rod sitting beside her, I look out the window and see lush green valleys, waterfalls gushing out of the range, rivers and creeks running high, full lagoons — and cattle everywhere. We have a lot to be thankful for. This is a gloriously beautiful country. We land on the strip in front of the house.

Things move smartly. Wendy, after returning with Tommy from their honeymoon, settles happily into *Lansdowne* life. She goes everywhere with Tommy. Neither flying nor camp life frazzle her. There is a lot of movement and excitement. Meldie and Tommy have RTQ in the air for long stints. They must keep an eye on the total air-time it has up. The plane starts to run a little roughly. We have come to depend on it so much, but it would be unwise to fly it unless it is in perfect flying order. Alice Springs is the only place where we can have it serviced now, as Darwin and Kununurra are booked out for weeks ahead.

Meldie and I fly to the Alice. Rod tells Meldie that she must call the Department of Civil Aviation (DCA) at Kununurra, every hour on the hour, until we land at Alice Springs.

It is a blessed relief to sign in and hand the plane over to the mechanics at the airport. They estimate that it will take two to three days to find and fix the problem. Meldie and I book into the Territorian Motel. We decide to give them two days, then call at the airport to check their progress. They haven't even started! Snowed under with work, they promise they will get onto it tomorrow. Rod is not pleased with the news. He wants us home; the plane is needed for musters. We get a phone call Saturday afternoon to say RTQ has been checked, the fault found and repaired. Meldie asks that they refuel both tanks, for an early take-off on Sunday morning.

Doing her routine check before take-off, Meldie notices that the gauges indicate one tank is full, but the other is barely three-quarters full. She goes to find someone to fill it up. It is Sunday morning, there is no-one available, and a big passenger plane, en route from Sydney to Darwin, is approaching to land. We cannot wait any longer. Meldie gets her clearance from the tower, and we are on our way. We will make only one landing — at Rabbit Flat Roadhouse — to refuel.

Sitting quietly beside Meldie and enjoying the flight, it is some time before I realise that she is uneasy about something. Something is bothering her. I ask her if there is a problem with the plane. She says, "No. We are off course and low on fuel." A smoke haze restricts visibility and it is hard to recognise any landmarks. Looking out and down, all I can see is desert. There is nothing I can identify as a landmark. Meldie says, "I haven't much fuel left and I think I am too far south. I should be able to see Rabbit Flat now, but there is no sign of it." She calls DCA at Kununurra. They suggest she flies round in a tight circle, increasing the circle until she finds a landmark. I scramble desperately in my handbag for my rosary beads. God will have to move quickly; we are in big trouble.

I am too busy praying to notice how long it is before Meldie says, "There it is!" Sure enough, just ahead and off to the north-east, is the little settlement of Rabbit Flat. A white family living in a few tin buildings in this vast wilderness. I say, "God is good to us, Mell."

She replies, "Don't thank Him yet, Mum, I still have to land." I start to pray again.

We come in low over the airstrip. Air pockets drop us and wind currents pick us up and buffet us from side to side, threatening to tip us over.

230

The windsock is blowing and flapping around. It is rough. Meldie is straining to keep the plane steady. We hit the ground, but we are forced off the strip. We career wildly, past huge ant beds and short, stumpy trees, before she is able to get back onto the strip. I want to close my eyes, but that would be silly, if we have to get out quickly.

Bruce Farrar, the owner of Rabbit Flat Roadhouse, checks our tanks — barely any fuel left! Meldie has done a marvellous job. Bruce invites us in for a cup of tea, just what we need. He must realise what we have gone through, especially Meldie. To give her time to get over the fright, he starts to tell us stories of his life at Rabbit Flat; how blacks would arrive demanding beer, whisky, or plonk. When he would not, or could not, sell to them, they would stone his buildings and abuse his family. He told of how his French wife had delivered their twin sons there herself, because there was no medical help — they were too far from a hospital.

Bruce told us how the blacks claimed Rabbit Flat as their own sacred ground. Native welfare officers came with tribesmen to prove their claim. Some said, "Yes! this is our sacred ground. Our sacred rabbit ran that way."

"Which way is that?" The blacks pointed north and south. Others come to back up the claim.

"Which way did your rabbit run?" they were asked. They point east and west.

"You all belong same tribe, same sacred rabbit?"

"Yar all-a same belonga, 'nother fella brudder longa me, same sacred rabbit."

Bruce was very sceptical. After all, hadn't rabbits been introduced to Australia by the white man?

I wonder if the only interest the blacks have in this so-called sacred ground is the attraction of the buildings and the bore that pumps water. Hundreds of rabbits run in all directions here. As far as Bruce knows, blacks have not lived in this God-forsaken place for many, many years. They drive out from settlements and towns to get here.

Meldie is relaxed and over her fright. Time to go. With full tanks, we say goodbye to this kind man and leave. His wife is in Adelaide with the twins. She will be back.

* * *

Tommy is mustering for *Ruby Plains* and *Tableland* as well as *Lansdowne*. It keeps him hopping but he loves the work. He is well-organised and

231

carries a great deal of responsibility. Ever ready to ask Rod's advice, and striving, always striving to please Rod, he would dearly love to hear Rod say, just once, "You have done well, my son." Rod will tell me, but he cannot tell his son — it is not the Quilty way. I remember the arguments I used to have with my father-in-law when he would tell me how he considered Rod to be the finest cattleman he had ever seen; how he could not have carried on without him. I would say, "Tell him, tell your son."

"No!"

Rod longed to hear a simple word of praise from his father, but it never came. Now history repeats itself. Meldie is close to her father, but he will not let Tommy get close.

Tommy introduces many changes at *Lansdowne*. Rod clings firmly to the old ways and there is a lot of friction. These are turbulent years for us. Rod admits, to me, that the changes Tommy makes are all for the better, but his Irish pride will never let him admit it to his son.

At Tommy's suggestion, we bring in portable yards and great rolls of hessian to string along the wings — to guide the cattle into the yards. Rod thinks it is a fool's idea. He resents Tommy's interference, but I back Tommy.

The years when our stockmen turned their hands to fencing or any other station job during the off season are gone. Things are moving too fast to cling to the old ways. We must move with the times. We buy heavy equipment — graders, tractors, Toyotas, post-hole diggers. All this benefits Rod more than anyone, especially the bulldozer — his favourite.

I am concerned about Meldie. Her days are full. She flies here, there and everywhere, does her share in the stock camp and at the station; but she has changed. I know it is hard for her to see Wendy taking what she thinks is her place. I would like to get her away from the rough camp life she is settling into here. I suggest she goes to stay with her relations, the Dawes, at Julia Creek, for a while. She loves *Lansdowne*; she does not want to go.

Her Aunt Dadie writes to see if she would help them out, for six months, in their newsagency. With all her cousins married now, and off on other jobs, her Aunt Dadie and Uncle Peter are short-staffed. Reluctantly, she agrees to go, "But only for six months, Mum." She leaves in September. It is hard, parting with her. Her letters come; she likes being with her cousins again, but she does not like Julia Creek, and

232

she misses *Lansdowne*. We also miss our darling daughter. Rod and I decide we will drive over and bring her home for Christmas.

* * *

Rod's father, now ninety-one years old, does not take kindly to the wheelchair that moves him about. Irritable, and in failing health, he is not easy to live with. He is a proud man who, I think, would prefer death to living as he is now. Olive has decided to move with him to Capel, south of Perth, where they have a farm. On a weekend in October, Tommy flies Rod, Wendy and me to *Springvale* for a last family gathering. Basil and Mick are there with their families. It is a very sad occasion. We all try to be cheerful, but my heart goes out to Olive and my father-in-law. It must be tearing them apart to be leaving. They belong here. Olive's mother, father, and brother Jim are buried here. Possibly the happiest years of Tom and Olive Quilty's lives have been spent on *Springvale*.

I remember all the happy days and nights I have spent here. My father-in-law, big and robust — the life of all parties, Olive, quietly keeping an eye on him. I keep trying to think of them like that. Dinner over, we all retire early. They are leaving tomorrow. It is sad for me, but for Rod, Basil and Mick, the parting is almost unbearable. Rod knows he will not see his father again.

The Flying Doctor's plane, with a doctor and a sister aboard, lands at 7 a.m. on Sunday morning. We are all at the airstrip. Half an hour later, it is airborne again. They have a long flight ahead of them. We have said our goodbyes. I wonder what thoughts are going through their minds as they fly, for the last time, over their beloved *Springvale*.

* * *

Passing through the Northern Territory, on our way to Queensland, we are approached by Roy Edwards, owner of Newcastle Waters Station, to see if Meldie would be interested in flying for him. He says he will arrange to have her endorsed for a 210 if she will be his pilot. We are doubtful, but Meldie will have to decide. Calling into *Brunette Downs*, we again meet Ken and Sally Warriner. Ken is looking for a secretary; would Meldie be interested? While Rod and I are hoping she will refuse both offers, we will have to leave the decision to her.

Meldie is not interested in Roy's offer, but, to our surprise, she does not hesitate about *Brunette*. Most of the *Mt House* stockboys are working there now. She knows and likes all of them. She will go to *Brunette*.

233

Although I knew our 1977 Christmas would be the last time we would be together as a family of four, I have a strange feeling that our 1978 Christmas will be the last time we will be together as a family of five. Meldie, with mixed feelings of sadness and excitement, gathers her things; not as she packed for Julia Creek, but on a large scale now. She will need her saddle, and jeans, and riding boots and her stock hat, but very few of the fashionable clothes she took to Julia Creek. I think, like me, she feels that this is a major change in her life, more permanent than the three-month stay in Julia Creek.

It had rained almost every month in 1978. We had bought twenty Santa Gertrudis bulls from *Brunette*, and scattered them round the run. *Brunette* had an almost perfect Santa Gertrudis herd, the deep red colour uniform. Rod had decided to try them, although we both still thought they were lazy bulls. Our herd is strong, brandings and turn off good. It has been a good year, but we no longer call in to *Springvale*. Rod misses his father and he cannot face not having him there.

Rod and I drive Meldie, and all her gear, to *Brunette*. We spend a few days with her, then we leave to drive to Queensland for our holidays. Tommy and Wendy stay at *Lansdowne* until we return, when they leave for their holiday.

* * *

Tommy is at Top Lily, to peg and clear a landing strip, when Doug Oliver and Angus Adnam fly out from Kununurra. They are looking for export cattle for Australian Rural Exports Ltd. Rod and the pilot fly over Top Lily and drop a note, telling Tommy to come into the station. Rod wants him there while we discuss numbers, dates and deliveries with Doug and Angus. We agree to sell 620 steers, with delivery on 21 April. Tommy will have them ready. Having been caught once, selling cattle on trust, we ask that a contract be signed and witnessed before Doug and Angus leave, for payment within twenty-one days of delivery. With our contract in hand, we are happy with the deal.

The cattle are delivered on the due date. Twenty-one days come and pass; no money has been banked to our credit. When another week passes and still no money — and no word from Angus — Tommy and I fly to Halls Creek to phone our solicitor, John Lemonis, in Perth. It seems the words, 'time is of the essence' were not included in the contract. That made all the difference to when the payment would be made. 'Payment within twenty-one days of delivery', which we thought covered us, was of no consequence whatsoever. We wondered, did Angus know

234

the significance of those all-important words not being included in the contract? We certainly did not. We will now have to await the convenience of the Australian Rural Exports Company. They will pay, we hope, in their own good time — three months? three years? Did Angus know? Doug said he did. This is another hard lesson, but we are learning.

We arrange with Jack Dalzell to sell our bullocks to Wyndham this year. Prices there are exceptionally good, and they would get better.

* * *

Kerry Slingsby flies his helicopter from Kununurra to *Lansdowne*, to introduce us to helicopter mustering as against fixed-wing aircraft. With his team of experienced, young ex-stockmen turned pilots, Kerry can show us where the helicopter has the advantage. He takes Rod up for a muster round Bluff Yard. Rod is impressed. They return to the station and Kerry flies Wendy to Bluff, where Tommy is doing the ground work. Having convinced us, Kerry leaves to fly to *Mistake Creek*.

We are now into helicopter mustering, and things move smartly. Helicopter pilots, landing at last light, stay overnight for an early start in the morning. They muster all day, then wheel their machines around and head for their next job. There is no time to be lost. Tommy spends some time in the choppers with the pilots. Sean Murphy comes to see if we will lend him $10,000. He wants to buy a helicopter. We decide to go guarantor, and also give him some good strong heifers. He can choose them from our herd.

Rod, Wendy and I drive out for the musters. All our old blacks are here, and a few of the young black stockboys are still with us — but they are restless and not interested in their work. I wonder how much longer they will be with us. We pick up staff where and when we can, but it is getting harder to find anyone.

* * *

I speak to Meldie, on the Codan two-way wireless, three or four times a week. We will see her soon. In October, on our way to Queensland for our holidays, Rod and I spend a week with her at *Brunette*. She is happy. My nephew, Jim Dawes, and his wife Rosemarie are also at *Brunette*. Jim is the company vet.

We holiday at the Gold Coast. With my sister, Meldie Holmes, and an estate agent, we start to look at homes at Burleigh Heads; we are after a place for Rod and me to semi-retire to. Finding nothing suitable in the way of a house, we look at units. Rod tags along, but is getting further behind. At the third unit, he has had enough; he disappears. I am getting desperate. I find him sitting on the beach, with a little bundle of fish and chips. He looks so lonely. I want him to be happy, but I know he will buy here if it is what I want. He tells me he does not like the Gold Coast. I do not push him.

The agent suggests we look at the Sunshine Coast, where his brother, Les Peters, has units for sale at Caloundra. Les went to Nudgee College with Rod. I know, as soon as we see *Croxley*, that it is just what we want, but I must know that Rod feels the same way. He smiles at me. We both want to retire beside the sea; this is it — we buy! A three-bedroom unit with glorious unrestricted views of the ocean on three sides and a perpetual park at the back. Les Peters has the top unit, we have the middle one and Billie Ross, widow of the late Johnny Ross of Tennant Creek, has the bottom, or ground floor unit.

We are at Julia Creek, on our way home, when Tommy phones us from Kununurra to say his grandfather, Tom Quilty, died this morning, 24 November, 1979. Rod is in shock, and Meldie is still very upset when we meet her at *Brunette*. It is hard to accept that this great man is dead. Rod starts to drink. We have a sad, miserable trip home.

Rod mopes around, drunk and indifferent. His father's death has affected all of us, but Rod is devastated; I don't know how to help him. He has to pull himself together; there are so many people and so much depending on us.

Paddy tells me that the few young black stockmen that we still have will not come back after walkabout. He and the old ones will return, but not the young ones. He is upset and angry that they want to leave. He says, "Town is bad for them. They will get sid down money, get drunk and fight. Not good! Not good!"

Against our better judgment, we advertise in Queensland and West Australian papers for 'Young men, 18 to 23 years of age, in good health and willing to work.' Asking for experienced stockmen is stretching it a bit too far, for what we consider to be a long shot. We do not know how many, if any, will reply.

The year is slowly coming to an end. I look back as I always do. My sister Dadie and her husband Peter come for a visit. They enjoy themselves but I know they will not come again. My sister thinks that *Lansdowne* is "way, way beyond all civilisation".

We were lucky with our bullock delivery. We missed the industrial strife at the meatworks. I do not know why the meat workers went on strike, I only know what it cost the stations. In May, there were eight hundred cattle in the yards at Wyndham. Basil was holding *Bedford* bullocks at *Springvale*, waiting for road trains that did not come. Stations everywhere were holding cattle. It cost them dearly.

Rod and Tommy start to grade the *Lansdowne–Bedford* road. We owe it to the road train drivers to keep it in order. It is beyond the means of Halls Creek Shire Council, both financially and time-wise, to maintain it. Wayne Rivers, from Halls Creek, has been with us for a while. It would be interesting to know his opinion of the road.

On one of our visits to Wyndham, we had dinner with Charlie and Dot Prideaux, at the Flying Doctor Base, before they left for Derby. It was a happy little dinner party. They are dear friends. It was good to know they are only going as far as Derby.

Tommy and Wendy went to the Kununurra Rodeo. Wendy was proud of Tommy's saddle ride, on a horse that had never been ridden before. The horse had tossed every rider who tried. Dick Northcott was yelling, "Ride him, Possum, ride him!" Possum was Dick's nickname for Tommy. Tom's best friend, Reg Underwood, won the bullock ride. So much for the shortcomings of the present generation!

* * *

Early in the New Year, replies to our advertisement start to come in. We are amazed at the number of applicants. Some reply by letter, some by telegram. We choose four from Queensland, two from Perth, and three from Wyndham. Some come from good homes, some from broken, unhappy homes. None are over eighteen years old, and some are much younger; they lie about their age. I look at these boys, for they are surely not men yet. Rod looks them over and walks away in disgust. Tommy says, "Don't worry, Mum, by the end of the season, they will all be good men." I hope you are right, Tom. You will have to train and work them. We accept that some will not last, but even if only two or three turn out to be good stockmen, we will be satisfied.

I get used to seeing so many teenagers moving round. Rod is starting to take an interest in them and that is good. They get on well with each other and do all and everything that is asked of them, but all admit they are looking forward to the day they can ride. Although I see the loneliness in some, none want to leave. City-bred, there is much that will surprise and frighten them here. They give Rod the respect due to him, but

Tommy is their boss. They learn to roll their swags, put aside their city clothes, squeeze their feet into stock boots — and walk in them without wobbling.

The blacks come back from walkabout. Paddy was right; there is not one young stockman in the group. The blacks are natural stockmen; it will be years before these white boys will be in their class, if ever. I am pleased to see my old lubras again.

Tommy, Paddy and Little Mick muster the horses. Foals are branded and the males cut, colts drafted off to be broken-in, and seasoned stock horses are drafted off to be shod. The mares and foals are treated for eye problems or sores before being sent back to the paddock. Tommy shoes Rod's horses and he and the old blacks shoe horses for the white boys. The boys hover about, sorting out horseshoes and nails, learning to put bridles on horses — learning as they go. They climb the rails to watch the breaking-in, wondering if these were the horses they would have to ride. Tommy drafts off old pensioner horses for them. They learn quickly. The horses are old, but well-trained.

Wendy supervises the cook and domestic help. Liddy and Mary potter around. I do not think Liddy is about to take orders from Wendy, or from anybody for that matter.

Bob Skeen and Ted Bolton are back. We are pleased to see them. Garry arrives a few days later. Garry says he is nineteen years old, he looks much older. He has never done stock work, but wants a job and will do anything as long as he can stay in the bush. He is friendly, but does not mix freely with the other boys. He takes a bad turn during the night. I have no idea what is wrong with him, but he frightens me. The medical plane picks him up in the morning and flies him to Derby. The doctor says that Garry has a drink problem and he is also on drugs. He advises us not to have Garry back. We let it go at that; Garry would not want to return, or so we thought. He turned up on our next mail plane. He is desperate. He thinks that if he can keep away from drink and his supply of drugs, he will be cured. Rod and I feel so sorry for him. Perhaps there is a chance for him if he cannot get the drink, and we will make sure no drugs are sent to him here. We will have to watch his mail carefully. It is the drugs that worry us.

Our old blacks stay loyal to Rod; he will always be their boss, though they work well for Tommy. "We bin grow dat young fella up. 'E tell us what to do, but old man Rod our boss." Not so the boys, Tommy was definitely their boss.

238

There are accidents, mistakes and tears, but Tommy is patient, and the boys help each other. Ted is there to tell funny stories when things go wrong, and Bob and the old blacks are there when they need them. By the end of the season, they are "all good men", as Tommy said.

Tommy and the boys formed a very strong friendship. One of the boys wet the bed. It was a terrible embarrassment and humiliation. In the stock camp, Tom would wake him during the night, and get him to go to the toilet. It was never spoken of outside their little circle. Only Tommy and Wendy knew, and they covered for him. It was their secret.

* * *

Every year brings more changes. Father Peile is no longer our parish priest. He worked in the desert, out from Balgo Mission, trying laboriously to record native dialects. It was a cruel life for a white man. He had to live alone in a black man's world. Balgo was his base, but his visits there were rare. He missed the warm welcome of Father McGuire's days as Principal of Balgo.

Father Kreiner is our new parish priest. Father Kreiner, a German, struggles to understand us and we are hard-pressed to understand him. He tries to say with his hands what he cannot say with his mouth. English, a hard language, coupled with good Aussie slang, presents a formidable barrier for our New Australians.

Leo Wills and Bob Wainright of E.K.T. are easing down their workload to make way for a takeover. Noel Buntine buys E.K.T., and the new drivers complain about the road, and the long hours that they have to drive to *Lansdowne*. Loaded with cattle, it then takes 10 hours to cover the 175 kms back to the bitumen. We miss our old drivers.

Mining companies are still flying in and out constantly. One company camps at Gordon Springs for weeks. Maureen, the young woman in charge, either from England or South Africa, often invites us to the camp for a barbecue. She later moves on to *Argyle*, south-east of Kununurra, where they finally find the famous Argyle diamonds. We hear she would have liked to call the mine after her little son, Nicholas, but this might only be a rumour.

It is with relief that we finish our last bullock muster and have the cattle safely yarded at the station. The boys have done well. They help water the yards down, and put sprays out before they knock off. Road trains start to arrive.

239

We are all going to the Halls Creek Races and Rodeo. Some of the boys who are not interested in the races, enter for the bull ride. Much as they want to enter for the saddle ride, Tommy is against it, and advises them not to. They have been riding strong young mickies in the stock camp, but a saddle ride is far too dangerous for them. Maybe next year, if they are here. Some of them, no strangers to drink, get drunk. The sober ones cover for them until Tommy can bundle them onto the Toyota and get them out of town.

We had high hopes of winning the Visitor's Cup with our little stallion, Eckquil. He had top weight and ran second.

Flying home, we run into bad weather. Flying through and under great black clouds frightens me, but Tommy is a good pilot. We land safely and call DCA Kununurra for a weather report. I had arranged to meet a friend of Betty Rose McInerney at Kununurra. She was touring the Top End and wished to visit *Lansdowne*. I had met her at one of Betty Rose's dinner parties in Sydney. Her husband was Jimmy Bancks, the creator of *Ginger Meggs*, the popular cartoon figure. I had found her very interesting and was looking forward to having her stay with us.

The weather closed in more. It was too dangerous to fly from *Lansdowne* to Kununurra, with cloud masses so low and heavy over the high ranges. I got in touch with Suzie Bradley. Could she meet our friend? Suzie could and would. I was very disappointed that the visit to *Lansdowne* never came off.

Jim and Norma Kiesey, of the Royal Flying Doctor Service (RFDS), are relieving at the Wyndham Base. They meet a lot of old friends but they also notice the changes. Although the Victorian Section supports our RFDS handsomely, local bodies also contribute. Last year, the Turkey Creek Gymkhana donated $2000 from their Easter Carnival. Charlie Prideaux, while based at Wyndham, was a member of the Turkey Creek Club. He said that, in two days, a total of 10,276 cans of drink, both beer and soft drink, were consumed at the Gymkhana, an average of 40 cans for every man, woman and child — a worthy entry for the Guinness Book of Records. Copies of a Pro Hart painting are for sale in Melbourne, proceeds to the Victorian Section. We are grateful.

Guy Henry, working at *Springvale*, breaks his leg. He comes to *Lansdowne* while his leg is mending, and stays. Guy, who came from Perth, finds *Springvale* lonely, he is the only white boy there. Tommy gives him a job. All the boys have nicknames. With his head of fiery red hair, Guy got 'Louey'. I do not know why, maybe it is because it rhymes with 'Bluey'.

The boys learn a lot in a remarkably short time. They are dependable and we trust them, but with the season almost over, they will soon return to their homes and probably not come back. We will have staff problems all over again.

Jim and Norma Kiesey hand over to Everett and Laurel Bardwell in mid-November. After almost 18 years in the RFDS they say a sad goodbye. They are retiring.

* * *

Our lifelines, the radios. On the bottom is the original Traeger two-way radio; on top, the modern Codan two-way radio with its battery charger beside it.

Meldie and Tommy near the front verandah of the old homestead, *Lansdowne.*

Cattle coming out of Bluff Yard, *Lansdowne.*

243

Meldie and Tommy sitting in a tyre on the dirt verandah of the old homestead, *Lansdowne*.

Steven (ex-Balgo Mission) with a mule carrying water canteens, *Lansdowne*.

Jack Vitnell, Tommy, Meldie and Rod with our old Willys Jeep.

Tommy, aged 3, on Hunt, with Meldie 'driving' the Willys Jeep.

The old homestead at *Lansdowne* in the mid-1950s.

Tommy riding Fat-Fat, Rod riding Skyline at *Lansdowne*, 1957. You can see the homestead on the left and the Leopold Range in the background.

245

Meldie riding Tommy's "colt".

Johnny Ray and Tommy, dressed by Peggy for a corroboree, *Lansdowne*, 1957.

Tommy drinking tea and eating damper, and Meldie (obscured), *Lansdowne*, 1957. Tommy is wearing a coat I made for him from saddle serge; Meldie is wearing a shirt I made for her from an old chenille bedspread.

From left: Doreen Carne (Rod's sister), with her sons Peter and Paul, me, Tommy and Meldie at *Bedford Downs*, 1958. The coats the Quilty children are wearing I made from saddle serge, and lined with bits of Rod's old Nudgee College pyjamas.

246

From left: Johnny Ray, Tommy, Meldie and Maggie, eating rib bones at dinner camp (at Poison Camp) on the way to Halls Creek Races.

Front garden of the old homestead, *Lansdowne*, 1960.

Three generations of Quiltys: Grandfather Quilty, Tommy and Rod at *Springvale*, 1959.

Native quarters at *Lansdowne,* showing flood damage.

Rod at the old bronco yard, *Lansdowne.*

Corroboree at *Lansdowne.*

248

Tommy, Peggy and
Johnny Ray in the
goat yard.

Tommy, Meldie and
me with the Holden
station wagon Rod
gave me for my
birthday, at the
gorge on the
Ord River between
Springvale and
Bedford Downs.

The new homestead at *Lansdowne*, 1971, soon after it was built.

In the box: Glenda Marshall, Dick Northcott, Meldie, and Brian Fielder. Standing: Andy Martin, Sally Warriner, Tommy. Kneeling: a rodeo rider (unidentified) from New Zealand.

Rod playing two-up at Meldie's 21st birthday party at *Lansdowne*.

New cattle yards at *Lansdowne*, built by Rod and the boys, showing the lights installed for night loading. The Leopold Range is in the background.

CHAPTER TWENTY-TWO

Old ways, old days are gone

Down memory lane,
There is no returning.

Early in December, Rod and I leave for our holidays. We spend time with our relations, then, with my sister Coral, we head for Caloundra. How I love it here. Tommy and Wendy will join us later, and, some time in February, Meldie will come. She is now at *Newcastle Waters*. When Roy Edwards sold *Newcastle Waters* to Baillieu and Chisholm and Warriner, Ken moved there as manager. Meldie and some others of the *Brunette* staff went with him.

Rod and I look to invest in Caloundra. We buy a nest of flats in Mackay Street. The bottom flat is rented to Sir Zelman Cowen's staff. Sir Zelman has a holiday house next to the flats. The bottom flat brings in a steady return, whether it is occupied or not. The other flats are, more or less, holiday rentals. Although we consider them a good investment, they are a worry. I buy a three-bedroom brick house at Wurtulla. I call it the Bougainvilla House, because of the colourful bougainvillea vines there.

Tommy keeps in touch with the boys. To our surprise, they all want to return to *Lansdowne*. This is wonderful news. Our staff problems are over for another year, at least. Most of them return with Tommy and Wendy late in February. Rod and I do not plan to drive back until the end of April.

Rod buys Meldie a second-hand Holden sedan. She proudly and confidently sets out to drive back to *Newcastle Waters* in March. We are not so confident. She phones back to us along the way, but we worry until we know she is safely at *Newcastle*.

Rod is listless. I persuade him to have a general check-up before we return to *Lansdowne*. The results alarm me. His heart and lungs are in a very bad way. He will have to be very, very careful. He has always been a heavy smoker. From his 'roll your own' to 'tailor-mades', he smoked his way through the years. Asthma has weakened his heart. It makes me sad to remember how hard he worked and deprived himself in those early years, and now that he is in a position to relax and enjoy himself, he has such a serious health problem. My dear old Rod.

In March, Coral and I fly Henbery's Air Service to Brisbane for the opening of State Parliament. We meet our sister, Dadie Dawes, and Suzie Katter there and thoroughly enjoy the garden party that follows the opening. Coral returns to Julia Creek shortly after that. Rod is still not well enough to travel. We will not leave until he is.

One night, not long after her return to *Newcastle Waters*, Meldie phones to say she would like to become engaged to Bruce Wreford. This has taken me completely by surprise. I had no idea she and Bruce were friendly. I keep asking her to repeat it. I had met Bruce at both Meldie and Tommy's 21st birthday parties. He came with the *Mt House* boys. Rod is all for the engagement; he says Bruce is a good man.

During the last week of May, Rod and I leave to drive back to *Lansdowne*. We will do it in easy stages. We have been away nearly six months. Wendy has written to say that all is well, all the old blacks are back, and the stock camp is out. Nora has the vegetable garden going, and Liddy continues to boss everybody.

* * *

Rod is pleased with the way Tommy is handling things. There is harmony in the camp. Musters are going well; road trains arrive and cattle are loaded. Strong, cold winds are blowing from the east. Empty double-deck road trains, on the way out, turn back with engine troubles. The cattle have to be held in the yard until other road trains can be sent out. There are long delays. We don't like the double-deck road trains. Narrow, winding roads, with overhanging tree branches along the way, make the driving dangerous — and rough on the cattle. A lot of bruising means lost revenue for us. But that is the way it is now.

252

One night at the station, Paddy and Montie come to see me. They look ill-at-ease, so I know that whatever they are about to tell me will not be good. Paddy says that they will all be leaving soon, no-one will be coming back after walkabout. I can't believe him — I do not want to believe him. Montie puts his hand out, white man fashion. He does not speak, but I know it is his way of saying goodbye. I put my hand in his; he gives a gentle shake and lets go.

I appreciate Paddy telling me. It is not their way, to say goodbye, or to let their white bosses know if they plan to leave — but twenty-nine years is a long time, and we have been through so much together. Paddy says that they are all old now, and they must go to their relations. They can do no more for us. Tommy has a good stock camp of young white boys, and old man Rod will go soon, too. I just look at them, as they disappear into the dark.

* * *

Meldie and Bruce left *Newcastle Waters* for *Lansdowne* a few days ago. They will stay with us until Meldie and I leave for Brisbane to shop and make arrangements for the wedding in January. Bruce will help out in the stock camp. Bill Banton, a clever electrician from Kununurra, will fly out to check the 240-volt lighting plant he installed in 1978 — more progress, progress Rod does enjoy. Meldie is busy gathering her things. She knows she is leaving home, and I know how much she loves *Lansdowne.*

There is little joy in my days. I am losing my darling daughter; Rod's health is a constant worry and I know I am going to miss our faithful old blacks. I know I will never see them again.

We go to the Kununurra Races. Bob, Ted, and all of the white staff go. None of our blacks want to go. I wonder, can this be when they all up and leave — none here when we return? But no, Paddy said they would go at walkabout. They will be here when we return from the races.

It is on the Saturday of the races that Tommy tells me that Wendy is pregnant. This is absolutely wonderful news. With her cousin, Mary O'Neill, as her Matron of Honour, Meldie had asked Wendy to be her bridesmaid. Wendy would be six months pregnant in January. We receive a letter from Dadie, saying that Mary O'Neill is expecting, and would be eight months pregnant by the time of the wedding! Rosemarie Dawes would have to be Meldie's Matron of Honour and Anna Underwood, a childhood friend, would be her bridesmaid.

253

Everything seems to be moving so fast at *Lansdowne*. It will be the same at all the stations now; the old relaxed days are gone. We are so lucky to have Tommy. I know Rod could not possibly keep up this pace. I also know our plane, RTQ, is one of the best assets we have.

* * *

A typical week on *Lansdowne*.

We still rise at 4 a.m. for a 5 a.m. breakfast.

Sunday

Ian Petherick and Dave Swanson are up bright and early. They landed their choppers at dusk last night. Tommy drives in from the stock camp. He must have left very early, but he wants to fly back to the camp in one of the choppers.

Wendy gives the cook instructions, then she leaves, with Rod and me, for the camp. Meldie and Bruce are in the camp. The old blacks will potter round the station until we get back. The muster has started by the time Rod, Wendy and I get there. Rod joins the boys in the bull catcher and does the ground work while Tommy gets in the helicopter with Ian.

Both choppers are moving fast. Sometimes we see them, sometimes we only hear them. There are cattle everywhere. From time to time, the choppers land to refuel from the drums of avgas carried to the site on the truck. Eleven o'clock; Ian lands, close to the truck. Tommy jumps out and waits for Douglas Tassie to bring his horse over. Ian moves off. Tommy joins the musterers.

The cattle move, and we move with them. A late dinner camp; mustering goes on all afternoon. Ian and Dave return to the station. Tomorrow, they fly to *Lissadell*. Rod and Tommy are pleased with the muster. Rod drives Meldie, Wendy and me back to the station. Tomorrow, Tommy and the boys will draft and bring bullocks and bulls into the station to be trucked.

Monday

Meldie flies RTQ to Halls Creek to pick up the mail. She then flies to Kununurra to pick up parts for the tractor. There is a delay with the road trains; they will be late. Rod contacts Tommy — we always carry a portable two-way radio in the camp now. The cattle will still have to come into the station. Peter Morell, a vet, is here to do a blood test our little stallion, Eckquil. Rod drives out to bring Tommy in. He will have to go to Joe's Paddock to catch Eckquil and help Peter. Tommy drives our big truck back to camp to shift our portable yard. Bulls and bullocks are yarded at the station. We wait for the road trains. They arrive during the night, very late. Expecting an early morning loading, we are surprised when the drivers want to load before then. They want to be gone before daylight. Fortunately, our yards are wired for electricity, but it has only been used for pre-dawn loading before. There is no more sleep for anybody this night. Everybody is up and over at the yards. Rod calls me at midnight to keep tally. The last road train pulls out at 3.45 a.m. I go back to bed, but nobody else does. They shower, have breakfast, roll their swags and go back to the camp. Meldie goes with them. Our old stockboys also go. Like Rod, they are too old for this work now.

Tuesday

Tommy drives back to the station at 10 o'clock to help Rod put the new parts into the tractor. An hour later, he flies to *Fossil* to discuss attending a boundary muster. Our stock camp moves, mustering onto the next camp. Tommy joins them. A road train's trailer has turned over at Emu Point, on *Lansdowne*. Rod and I drive out to the camp to pick up Tommy and a few boys. They drop me off at the station, pick up some gear, and drive to Emu Point. They do not get back to the station until eleven o'clock at night. Tommy and the boys drive back to the camp. Tomorrow, Wednesday, they will muster again. Rod says we had heavy losses at Emu Point. Some of the cattle were dead, mostly bulls; he had to shoot some, the rest he had to let go bush. The driver left the trailer behind.

Wednesday

Bruce has a bad back problem. Meldie flies him to Kununurra to make plane connections to Ballarat, Victoria, where he will see a doctor recommended to him. It is a long way to go, but no one else has been able to help him.

Rod and I do a bore run. The stock camp is at Bakers. Meldie is grounded at Kununurra for a few hours while a faulty radio is fixed. We hear the Russ family have sold *Gibb River*.

Tommy brings the boys in from Bakers to cut and cart wood for the station. He takes some boys out to strain the bullock paddock fence.

Thursday

The camp moves to Coral Spring; there will be another big muster there tomorrow. Meldie flies me to Wyndham to phone Andrew McPhail, our accountant in Perth. We are home for lunch. Early afternoon, Meldie flies bread and vegetables out to the camp. Rod and I go with her. We return to the station before last light.

Tommy bulldozes a clearance through a gap to make it easier for us to drive through tomorrow. Rod will fly out.

Friday

Rod leaves very early in Foot's chopper. Meldie drives Wendy and me out, then she joins the musterers. It is a long, exhausting day, but the cattle are turning up and that is all that matters. Wendy flies back to the station with Foot. She will come out with him tomorrow.

Saturday

Another long day. The boys are tired but happy. The old blacks move slowly, but they can still outride any of the young white boys. Our muster over, Foot turns and flies to *Fossil.*

Someone has accidentally started a fire. A match or cigarette, dropped unnoticed during the muster, has now caught on and a bushfire rages. Rod burns off every year before the storms, and he always burns a break around our stock camps and yards, but it is getting late in the year, and the grass is long and dry.

We keep a close watch on the fire. So far, it is burning away from us. Hopefully, it will burn out on the hills. If the wind changes, it could turn towards Lily Yard. Tommy and Bob drive back to the station to get the plane. They will fly over the fire to see where it is heading. He drops a note — the wind has changed and the fire is now burning down the valley towards Lily Yard. There will be little sleep for the boys tonight.

Tommy has brought drums of water and lots of old bags back to the camp. He fills up even more drums with water. Bob, Ted, and all the white boys go with Tommy to fight the fire. Rod wants to go with them, but it is best that he stays here. We have a lot of restless cattle in the yard; he is needed here. The old blacks stand with us awhile, as we watch the glow of the fire. Then they drift off to their swags.

We build up the campfire and sit round. There is nothing we can do about the bushfire, and very little we can do if the cattle rush. The hours pass. Propped up beside Meldie, against her swag, I doze. I see Wendy, trying to stay awake near Tommy's swag. Rod moves around. It is a long night. The glow from the bushfire is not as bright; it is either burning low, or it is further away. I think of the boys; fire-fighting is a treacherous, dangerous job. They will have to clear around the yard with shovels and hoes and with their hands, continually beating the flames with wet, heavy bags. It will tire their young arms. They have had two long days mustering, and tomorrow, Sunday, Tommy will cut out and brand. There are a lot of cleanskins. It is not an easy life, especially for city boys, but they stand up well. We are proud of them, and they are proud of themselves.

* * *

The weeks continue to pass, long and tiring but never boring. Our pleasures are simple. We have a TV, set up for videos. I do not know how it is done; suffice to say Tommy has set it up and it works. I look forward to the videos as much as the boys do.

Bruce is back. Meldie and I are to leave for Caloundra in a few days. The afternoon before we leave, I go down to the blacks' camp. They have been waiting for me and they gather round. I see them all. Liddy, very subdued, puts her hand in the pocket of her dress and pulls out a red-striped zebra stone. She gives it to me. No-one speaks; even their dogs are silent. They do not want me to stay long. We stand together for about a minute, then they turn and walk away. It is time for me to go. They will not be here when I get back.

John Bickton, in charge of Jay Row Helicopters based at *Lansdowne*, arranges for one of his pilots to fly Meldie and me to Halls Creek. We pick up her car there and drive to Queensland. Like her father, Meldie believes in early starts; four o'clock every morning sees us well on our way. Six days after we leave Halls Creek, we arrive at Caloundra. It has rained all the way and I have a cold. Meldie is a whirlwind; we get a lot done in a short time. The church, priest, reception, invitations — everything that has to be done is done.

I would like Meldie to be married in Brisbane, but she does not want to be married from a motel or hotel, so Caloundra it is. Satisfied that everything is under control, and she can do no more at Caloundra, she returns to *Lansdowne*. I remain at *Croxley*. A few sunny days and I feel a little better. The rain pours down again and my cold comes back, worse than ever. I go to the outpatients' section at the local hospital. The doctor admits me with pneumonia. I am there for two weeks. It is still raining when I get out.

Rod is on his way over. He phones me from Winton. He has driven through rain all the way. Wonderful news for the graziers.

Rod arrived last night but he is very wheezy. Travelling, cold and wet, has not been good for him, and the Caloundra climate does not help. We take long drives — Roma, Rockhampton, Emerald — to anyplace where the air is dry. It helps a little, but not much.

It is late December, and Tommy, Wendy and Meldie are at Caloundra. The wedding is on 8 January. Rod is very ill. Tommy and I drive him to the local hospital and he is admitted. They will not let us stay with him. This upsets Rod, and he gets very agitated. This will only worsen his condition. We call in again at 7 o'clock, but again we are asked to leave. We leave a message, and pray that he will have a good night.

Meldie is not allowed to see him when she calls in this morning. I phone, and they tell me that he is as well as can be expected — but he is not allowed visitors. We decide we will have to move him. However, it is midnight before we sign the final discharge paper; the ambulance drives him to Prince Charles Hospital at Chermside, in Brisbane.

We see him on New Year's Eve. He has had a restful night; his breathing is easier and he looks a little better but he is going to be in hospital for a few days. With Meldie's wedding so near, he worries that, as the father of the bride, he will not be able to give his daughter away.

The doctor says, all going well, Rod should be able to leave hospital the day before the wedding, but he warns us that Rod will never be really well again. He has to give up smoking entirely, among other things. It seems that he will have to give up all the things he likes most.

Meldie and Bruce fly to New Zealand for their honeymoon. They travel in a modern plane. Thirty years ago, Rod and I, on our honeymoon, flew to New Zealand in a seaplane. Rod's sister Irene and her husband, Frank, live in Auckland. They have entertained Rod and me, Tommy and Wendy, and now Meldie and Bruce.

The rain continues to fall at Caloundra. We hear reports of good rain at *Lansdowne* — there is a cyclone down the west coast.

Tommy got his private helicopter licence at Caloundra early last year. His instructor was Barry Coster, an ex-Navy man. Tommy now flies whenever the rain lets up.

With Wendy due to go to Sydney soon, for the birth of her baby, and Meldie and Bruce on their honeymoon, I think it would be good to get

Rod away from Caloundra. I ask him if he would like to drive back to *Lansdowne*. He tells me that he does not want to go back. This is a shock; but there is a bigger one coming. He has already spoken to an agent about finding a buyer for *Lansdowne*.

We have always discussed our problems. This was not like Rod. He told me, a long time ago, that he never wanted to stay in the Kimberleys after his father had gone. He has been very happy at *Lansdowne*. Does he really want to leave because he misses his father so much? I suggest that we just retire, and hand over to Tommy and Wendy, and Meldie and Bruce; divide it equally, land and cattle. He will not agree. He says the Kimberleys are moving into very unhappy, troubled times and he wants no part of it. He wants us all out now. I think, "We have been going through troubled times since 1960, so we should be able to face whatever comes now." I know that the state of his health has a lot to do with it. I decide not to tell the family just yet. Perhaps Rod will change his mind.

Meldie and Bruce arrive back late in February. They fly to Perth, then up the west coast to Kununurra, Darwin and on to Katherine. Tommy returns to *Lansdowne* and Wendy flies to Sydney with her mother. Rod and I leave Caloundra to drive around. We pass through Gympie, Mundubbera, Springsure; taking the days slowly and easily, always travelling west to dry air. Rod is very ill, but he is enjoying himself. We return to Caloundra and fly to Sydney. Our first grandchild is to be born soon. Tommy, who flew to Sydney early in the week, meets us at the airport. Matthew Thomas Quilty, born 3.10 p.m., Friday, 26 March, 1982, is a healthy baby, and, thank God, Wendy is well; Dr. Bob McInerney can guarantee that. There is great rejoicing. We return to Caloundra, Tommy returns to *Lansdowne*.

Rod and Robert Coleman, one of our young stockboys, load the Toyota with Meldie and Bruce's wedding presents and things I want taken back to *Lansdowne*. They leave Caloundra early one morning. I do not go with them. I have been away seven months, but I will wait until Wendy returns from Sydney. Rod is upset that I am not going with him. He phones me along the way; at every night stop, I know my phone will ring.

* * *

Wendy is a sensible mother and Matthew, a happy healthy baby. They quickly settle down at *Lansdowne*. Tommy, with his family, move into the big house and Rod and I move into their caravan, parked close by.

259

Rod is 'dozing the road to Arthurs Stock Camp, but the dust is choking him. Reluctantly, he hands the 'dozer over to Tommy and works on the vehicles. He won't rest. I am so worried about him. Tommy has to fly RTQ to Darwin for its 100-hourly check. I want Rod to go with him; the high, thin air will be good for him. He won't go without me. I go.

Tommy takes the camp out; Rod insists on riding with them. I wish that he would ease up. Sick, cranky and irritable, he never lets up on Tommy and the boys. They still show him respect, but they dodge him whenever they can. He still drives the bull catcher. To me, that is more dangerous than riding, but Bob tells me it is safer than mustering.

Much as I was against selling, I have become all for it. I will have to tell the children. I would still prefer to hand over to them, but my only concern is Rod. He will kill himself here. I don't really know if Caloundra is the answer either.

* * *

Tommy riding Billy Boy at Arthurs Yard, 1981.

Mt Laptz, November 1981.

261

CHAPTER TWENTY-THREE

For Rod's sake

The writing is on the wall,
Read <u>between</u> the lines.

Tom Quilty

Reg and Janelle Underwood visit. Janelle stays at the station with Wendy while Reg goes out to the stock camp. He does a stint in the bull catcher with Rod. Tommy flies to *Bedford* to see if his Uncle Basil will sell him *Bedford* or *Springvale*. Unfortunately, Basil has given Bruce Crowson, a prospective buyer, first offer, and I do not think that Bruce will turn it down.

Grandma Griffin Quilty told me once that she never wanted *Bedford* to go out of Quilty hands. She considered it the best investment they had ever made.

Bruce Crowson buys both *Bedford* and *Springvale*.

We do short, quick musters on *Lansdowne*. Road trains load and leave. Tommy is very capable and handles it well. With so much water available at the moment, the cattle are scattered but the helicopters quickly gather them together.

Rod and I charter a plane and fly to Timber Creek, in the Northern Territory, where we inspect Fitzroy Station for Meldie and Bruce. We meet Meldie there. *Fitzroy* is run down; the buildings are a disgrace. The sale price is $400,000. Rod does not like the country. He knows it well

263

from his days on *Coolibah*. He says that the price is too high but he is prepared to make an offer. We are told it is to be auctioned in Darwin. Meldie and Bruce are no longer interested.

* * *

Although it is still mid-winter, I am always pleased when we pass the shortest day of the year; the lengthening days show the promise of spring to come. I miss our old blacks. For the first time in thirty years, their camp is deserted and silent at this time of year. I do not know where they all are. I only saw Peggy once after she left *Lansdowne*; living on the fringe of Wyndham, old and frail, she was slowly dying of some sickness she did not understand. "More better we stay *Lansdowne*, Yumman. Town no good for black people."

I know, I know, Peggy. Those interfering, heartless fools. You should have been given a choice, not empty promises.

Tourists, brave enough to take on our rough bush roads, call in. They stay for morning or afternoon tea or a meal. Most of them need repairs to their vehicles. They look round the station and admire our vegetable garden. Bless them, they should learn a lot on their tours.

An RFDS party of six flies in for morning tea today. They are so welcome. Because they want to visit as many Flying Doctor stations as possible, and their time is limited, they do not stay long before flying on to their next stop.

Back in the camp, Rod, Tommy and the boys muster from Piantas to Pyra Gorge. I want to go with them but Rod says I am to drive the Toyota back to the station. It is not easy for me to camp out now, but I do not like leaving Rod.

All our bores are pumping good to adequate supplies of water, but Fontaine's bore needs new buckets. Tommy and the boys will have to pull the bore column after the Pyra muster.

We are doing a lot of night loading now. Very few road train drivers stay overnight. They drive in late, load up and leave, going before sunrise. Rod sends Tommy and some of the boys to follow them until they are over the worst of the road.

I start a novena. There is so much I want for my family; Rod's health is at the top of the list.

While in Wyndham for the Races and the Rodeo, John and Reg Underwood, Dick Northcott and Tommy take their first bi-annual flying tests. They all pass.

264

Also, Matthew Thomas Quilty is christened at the Catholic Church in Wyndham. He is hot and irritable, and his yells almost drown out the priest. There is a gathering of our friends for the christening party at the town hotel after the church service.

Two days after the races, all our staff are at home and it is work as usual.

* * *

Rod and I are getting ready to leave on our annual holiday. Tommy will fly us to Kununurra. I always wish that I had just one more day to get ready. We fly from Kununurra, via Darwin, Mt Isa and Brisbane, to Sydney. Once again, we stay at the beautiful old Wentworth Hotel. Rod will be in St. Vincent's Hospital for a few days. Six days later, we fly back to Brisbane. Rod's sister, Doreen, drives us to Caloundra. Tommy, Wendy and the boys spend Christmas at *Lansdowne*.

Meldie and Bruce drive down in their Toyota to stay with us while Bruce learns to fly fixed-wing aircraft at Redcliffe. We are all thrilled when he gets his licence. They intend to buy a second-hand 182 plane. Tommy and his little family arrive early in the New Year. Rod buys a new Holden Commodore as a surprise for me. We all gather at *Croxley*, to discuss selling *Lansdowne*. Bruce Crowson wants to buy it. He also wants to sell us *Kianna*, a property he owns in the Northern Territory.

Towards the end of February, we all drive to Mt Isa, where we charter a plane and fly to the Territory to inspect *Kianna*. Rod suspects that the purchase of *Kianna* is part of the *Lansdowne* deal. He is suspicious, and not interested in such an arrangement. Although Rod goes with us as Bruce Crowson drives us around, I know we are not going to buy. Meldie and Bruce are prepared to give it a go. Tommy is disappointed, I think, that Rod will not buy but I agree with Rod. We return to Mt Isa and Rod, Meldie and Bruce drive back to Caloundra. Tommy picks Wendy and Matthew up at Blackall and flies back to Mt Isa in a chartered plane. I leave with them and we fly to Darwin and down the west coast to Kununurra. There are wild storms and heavy rain. Our plane, RTQ, has been parked at the Kununurra airport while Tommy and Wendy have been away. Tomorrow, we will fly to *Lansdowne* in RTQ.

* * *

We have had excellent rain at *Lansdowne*, all from Cyclone Clem. This cyclone has come further inland than any I have known and has blown the tail off Fontaine's windmill!

265

Bruce and Lyn Crowson fly in. Bruce has his own plane and is a good pilot. We discuss the sale. Things get a bit hot, and Tommy and I tell them that the sale is off. They leave in a huff.

Tommy drives me around the run. There are places where we cannot go; because it is too boggy, but there is good rain everywhere.

It is still raining when Tommy and the boys muster the horses. All the horses are shining and frisky. Tommy is kicked in the face by a young colt. Guy and I fly with him to Wyndham. He must be in a lot of pain. The doctor stitches the great gash over his eye. We book into the Town Hotel. Tom had a bad night; his eye is black and swollen this morning. We hire a car and Guy drives me to Kununurra to make my connections to Caloundra. Tommy and Guy spend another day in Wyndham before flying home to *Lansdowne*.

Meldie and Bruce leave for Alice Springs. They phone from Newcastle Waters to say that heavy rain and floods have cut Alice Springs off. A telegram from Tommy at *Lansdowne* says it is still raining there.

Bruce Crowson comes up with a new proposition which is more acceptable than the first. Meldie phones again from Newcastle Waters; she is not happy with the deal. I know she does not want to sell *Lansdowne*. Bruce Crowson and Tony Edwards, the manager of Bennett & Fisher of Alice Springs, inspect *Lansdowne* late in March. With so much rain, the country must have looked absolutely beautiful, water everywhere.

The grass, both imported and native, is fresh and green and the cattle are all in good condition; *Lansdowne* is at its very best. Discussions for the sale, to be held at *Lansdowne*, put a lot of responsibility on Tommy and Wendy. They keep in touch by phone from Kununurra. I think that Rod and I should be there, but Rod does not want to be personally involved. He prefers to phone his instructions to Tommy, who is to pass them on. We make an appointment with our solicitor, Jim Byrne, in Brisbane. I have great faith in Jim. He is Rod's cousin and a very good solicitor.

Bruce Crowson cannot meet our price. He makes an offer — so much cash down, and *Dunrobin*, a 1200 acre property he owns on the Fitzroy River near Rockhampton. He values *Dunrobin* highly — too highly, according to Jim. Tony Edwards suggests we inspect *Dunrobin*. I am impressed, very impressed. It is just right for Rod. The climate will suit his asthma; it would be kind to him. It is a small place to run, without staff problems or any big hassles.

I meet an old friend, Nancy McCullagh, at *Dunrobin*. Nancy is Lyn Crowson's mother. I first met Nancy many years ago, when she and her husband Harry were on *Alice Downs*, out from Halls Creek.

Although we are impressed with *Dunrobin*, we are not prepared to accept Bruce's valuation. *Lansdowne* is worth more than he is offering. There is also a tax valuation on the ⊢ Q2 cattle that is causing a problem. We become suspicious when Bruce continues to push for the inclusion of *Dunrobin* in the sale. He will not move from his offer; and we will not accept it. We decide we will only accept a straight-out sale of *Lansdowne*; we do not want *Dunrobin*. Bruce is hopping mad. As far as he is concerned, *Dunrobin*, heavily mortgaged, must be part of the deal or everything is off. Negotiations fall through a second time.

* * *

All is quiet; no more phone calls. Tommy carries on at *Lansdowne*. It is still raining there. About two weeks later, Tony Edwards phones to find out if we could all meet in Jim Byrne's Brisbane office. The meeting is set up for Wednesday, 13 April. Rod is not well. I am worried that he will not be able to make the meeting. Tommy flies down. Bruce Crowson, Tony Edwards and the Crowsons' accountant arrive, on time. Rod does not attend. It is a very heated meeting; it goes on and on. Tommy and I know that we are not to say anything unless Jim asks us a direct question. Things get very nasty; Bruce shouts; Jim remains calm — and Tommy and I remain silent, but uneasy.

Bruce, Tony and the accountant decide they would like to take a walk to talk things over. As soon as they are out of the office, Jim relaxes. He says, "They are going to agree to our terms when they come back."

I wish I was as confident as Jim. Tommy looks doubtful. We enjoy sandwiches while we wait. On their return, Bruce looks much calmer; Tony and the accountant look relieved. They agree to everything — our value of the cattle, more money for *Lansdowne*, less for *Dunrobin* — on one condition: Tommy is to muster and deliver 1000 bullocks to a place they will nominate. Jim looks at Tommy and asks, "Can you do it?"

Yes, he can, but he will nominate the place of delivery.

I return to Caloundra, and Tommy flies back to *Lansdowne*. Three weeks later, Rod and I fly from Brisbane to Kununurra, where Tommy meets us. We are only home for two days when Bruce Crowson flies in from *Springvale* to see us. Tommy and the boys have the muster well in hand. A helicopter lands at last light, for an early morning muster. Winter is not far away, and the days are getting shorter,

Bruce returns, with Lyn and their son, Jim, and Tony Edwards, bringing the contracts for our signatures. Meldie calls, on her portable wireless, from Jasper Gorge in the Northern Territory, to say she is on her way to pick up her things. She is very unhappy. It nearly breaks my heart to see her so upset. She always wanted to call *Lansdowne* home. Rod drives back with her when she returns to *Humbert River*, where she and Bruce now live.

I meet Rod in Halls Creek, on his way back from *Humbert River*, and we drive to Alice Springs to say goodbye to some friends. We do not stay long. Blacks are everywhere; drunk and abusive, they clutter the footpaths. We cannot pass through them. We get off the footpath and walk in the gutter. They spread out and follow us for nearly half a block, spitting and hurling abuse in pidgin English and in their own language. They tell us they do not have to work anymore. They do not work and they do not hunt; too drunk to corroboree, they will drink themselves to death. We are pleased to be on our way home.

* * *

I am not sleeping well; my nights are disturbed and restless. My thoughts go back and pictures form, sometimes in my dreams, sometimes so real that I live those scenes all over again: Peggy and I climb high up the range and the whole world opens up below us. We see for miles: north, south, east and west. Hills, creeks, rivers, and valleys. Dust rising, horses, riders and cattle. Nothing can harm us here. I sit and watch as the helicopter runs cattle into the coachers; there are bulls in the mob. One breaks out and Chuck, one of the new boys, goes after it. I want to call a warning, "Go wide, Go wide!" but I cannot. Inexperienced, he rides right behind it; the bull turns, swift and dangerous; his horns pierce Chuck's horse behind the front off-side leg and rips through to the back leg. The horse staggers but does not go down; its stomach hangs out. Tommy and the boys gallop over. Tommy chases the bull away, Chuck jumps off his horse, and Bill Banton runs for the rifle. The horse is shot. Cruel and upsetting, I am to remember that scene for a long time. No wonder it comes back to me at night now. So many thoughts ring round in my mind. I cannot sleep.

More forms have to be signed and witnessed. Tommy finishes the muster. It is our last muster on *Lansdowne*. Cattle buyers will be here tomorrow to inspect the bullocks; only Jack Dalzell turns up. He offers Bruce $330 per head for 1035 ⊢ Q2 bullocks. His offer is accepted. Tommy and the boys walk the mob to Fish Hole Yard on *Bedford*. He drops two lame bullocks off and picks up four others, delivering 1037 head to Bruce's men on 4 June, Tommy's birthday.

Jim Byrne advises us that the Minister's Consent has not come through yet. Things are moving slowly. We ask Meldie and Bruce if we can borrow their big truck to help cart some of our things to Queensland. They agree, but Meldie will have to drive it.

Wendy holds a little birthday party for Tommy. In a way, it is a farewell party for some of the boys. They leave Halls Creek, by bus, the next day for Perth. It is a sad little party. The boys have grown close to each other. For some, it is the only family they have known.

Meldie arrives and we start packing. Horrible, cold, windy days; sad days.

* * *

Lansdowne from the air, 1976.

CHAPTER TWENTY-FOUR

Farewell

The past is mine
For I remember everything.

I ask Rod if he will drive me round the run. He does not want to. I know it will upset him, but I really want to go. We take our time. There is so much to remember. Every camp has its own special memories: the creeks and water holes where we would sometimes swim; the hard times, the sad times, the good and happy times; the great changes. As the old timers in the past had left signs that they had been here — rusty old horseshoes, a broken bridle bit — we now found signs of the times we had spent here. I feel so sad for all of us. I wonder if anyone will ever pick up a rusty horseshoe or bridle buckle that we have left at any of our stock camps.

Rod sends Bob Skeen to *Moola Bulla* with the horses not included in the sale. They will be picked up later and taken to *Dunrobin*. Meldie left early this morning. Robert went with her. She has my alsatian, Sparkie, on the truck. She has a long, tiring trip ahead of her.

I go over to the yards, the garage, horse stalls, saddle shed, and wander around. We all have to say goodbye in our own way. Rod is busy preparing his Toyota. He wants to leave tomorrow. Some of the boys, still with us, will go with him.

Rod left at 12.30 p.m. today, Tuesday, 21 June. Everything is so very quiet. The sooner we leave now, the better. We receive a message from Jim Byrne to say CitiCorp have not released the mortgage on *Dunrobin*, and we must not leave *Lansdowne* until it is cleared and the money in. Tony Edwards says there could be a week's delay.

Rod and Meldie arrive at *Dunrobin*. That is one worry out of the way, thank goodness. I take long walks in our horse paddock, after dinner at night, and almost always get lost in the dark. I have no sense of direction. Time drags by. We are sleeping on the floor. The takeover date, 1 July, comes and goes. Jim Byrne phones a message to the Flying Doctor Base — we should be able to leave on 19 July. Still a few more days to wait, but at least we have a definite date now.

* * *

The night before we leave, I go down to the blacks' camp. It is a cold night filled with emptiness, silence, and ghosts. I shiver in the cold. Night winds stir up small puffs of dust. I see the gunyahs and campfires as I slowly move round; I hear the happy laughter of the piccaninnies, and the snarl and snap of dogs. There have been births and deaths here, and a lot of happiness. The gunyahs make way for the two-room huts with the lean-to verandahs, running water and electric lights, but always the campfires. The spirits of my long-departed friends drift round and past me. I can feel them but when I call their names, there is no answer.

On my first night here, I could not sleep; now this, my last night, is just as disturbed, but for a different reason. In memory, I hear again the mournful cry of the curlew, the distant howls of dingo packs as they call to each other, the throb of the didgeridoo, stomping feet, and voices raised in song. I wonder again why Rod would never take me to Pyra Gorge, the only place on *Lansdowne* that I have never been. I think of the three babies I am leaving here; they will forever bond me to *Lansdowne*. I must stop. Now is not the time for memories. I wish Rod was here.

Dawn comes, cold and gloomy. We are all up. Everything we want to take, or can take, has already gone with Meldie, or is loaded on our cattle truck. Tommy flies Bruce round, to show him the *Lansdowne* boundaries. We pack our few personal things and wait for final word from Jim. It comes at 4.15 p.m. this afternoon. Tommy quickly gets Wendy, Matthew and me buckled up in RTQ for our flight to Kununurra. Shadows are lengthening, but we will land before last light. A quick pass down our small strip and we are in the air. We fly over the homestead once. No time for more. It is just as well. I look down as we fly over country I have flown over many times: Tullewa Hill, Tableland Station, the mighty Chamberlain River winding its way to join the Pentecost, the Salmond and the Durack Rivers, before flowing into the Cambridge Gulf; the Durack Range casting huge shadows, *El Questro* off to our left. Beautiful, wild, untamed land. Matthew will never know *Lansdowne*. I doubt any of my grandchildren will ever know *Lansdowne* as I knew it.

* * *

This taken from my diary, written the afternoon as we were leaving:

Left *Lansdowne* this afternoon, Tuesday, 19 July, 1983. Cold and windy. I feel so terribly, terribly, sad and lonely. It will take me a long time to get over this. I must do it myself. We had to sell for Rod's sake.

* * *

273

Epilogue

My thoughts drift back
To scenes long past
And I feel the strength
Of the love that bound me
To those cherished times
That could not last.

Tom Quilty

Rod found it hard to accept the changes that came in the late 1960s and 1970s. It was not a gradual thing. The changes came with a bang; they followed quickly, one after the other.

Rod moved, reluctantly, with the changes, but he was not happy.

I remember my life in the Kimberleys with happiness for the years I spent there and sadness that those years have now passed. I remember, with affection, the people, both white and black, too numerous to mention here, who were part of my life there. Some I knew in all the thirty-one years I spent on *Lansdowne*, others called in, stayed awhile, then left.

I think of them and wonder where they are now, and if we will ever meet again.

Rod and I moved to Caloundra. The *Croxley* unit was going to be our retirement home, but this was not to be. Rod was miserable. He missed his bush connections, got tired of listening to town talk, and the climate was bad for his health.

The move to *Dunrobin*, Rockhampton, was to his liking. He had his cattle, greatly reduced compared to his *Lansdowne* numbers, and no staff problems; he happily pottered round his small run.

Three years after we left *Lansdowne* Rod died of a heart attack. My beloved husband was gone. He is buried at Rockhampton, but I think his free spirit still roams the Kimberley Ranges.

I loved him; I miss him; I will always miss him. It is very lonely, one without the other.

* * *

Glossary

A
ant bed: termite mound

B
bandicoot: term meaning to dig up tubers (e.g. sweet potatoes), steal the root and replace the leafy top back in the soil, making it look like it has not been disturbed
banker: river in flood, flowing right up and over its banks
Bend Yard: name of a *Lansdowne* stock camp
bomb: an old car
bough-shed: rough shelter, with boughs thrown over frame to form the roof; some of these were more permanent structures, with a roof of spinifex grass between two layers of chicken wire; these could be 'air-conditioned' by pouring water over the spinifex
box them up: in the absence of a yard or pen, to put frisky cattle (or other animals, such as horses) in amongst quiet cattle (coachers) to settle them together
brackish: slightly salty (water)
breakaway: eroded gully; also, an animal that breaks away from the herd
brumbies: wild horses
bully beef: boiled, corned or tinned beef
bulwaddy: tree in northern Australia, *Macropteranthes kekwickii*, stands of which form impenetrable thickets

C
carpenter's trestle; sawhorse
chock-a-block: jam-packed; full to capacity
cleanskin: an unbranded animal
coachers: docile cattle used to attract frisky or wild beasts — cattle will run to cattle
colour bar: barrier (social and political) separating whites and non-whites
colt: (1) male foal; (2) freshly broken-in horse
coolum/coolamon: an oval all-purpose curved wooden carrying object, usually cut from the bark or outer layer of a tree trunk (Aborigines carried their babies, food, etc. in them)
cradle: framework used to hold a calf firmly for purposes such as marking or branding
cut: castrated
cut out: to separate individual animals from a herd

D

dieldrin®: highly toxic organochlorine compound used as insecticide
dinner camp: drovers' midday meal; also the place where this meal is taken
displaced person: one who, through no choice of their own, must live outside the boundaries of their native country
dodge: to be evasive, or sneaky; also a sneaky trick
dogger: one who hunts dingoes and wild dogs to obtain a bounty
donga: (1) a tent or shelter, in or beside a gully; (2) a shallow gully or dried-up watercourse
dressed out well: good-quality carcass, after removal of hide and offal

F

finger-talking: using the fingers to hold secret conversation
Flaming Fury: toilet made over a pit, its contents regularly covered with oil, then burnt
flood gate: a flap-like gate which hangs from wire stretched across a river or creek, forming part of a fence, allowing the passage of water and debris during minor flooding
form: a long, wooden, backless bench seat

G

gentle: to quieten or tame
galah session: radio session where far-flung neighbours chat to one another
gidarchie: witch doctor; maker of magic; in the Arrernte language: gwerdayje; also: goditcha, kadaicha, kadaitja, kaditcha, kurdaitcha
gin: (derogatory) a female Aborigine
gossip session: see **galah session**
greenhide rope: rope plaited from strips of raw, uncured hide
gunyah: an Aborigine's hut, usually made of boughs and bark

H

humping their blueys: carrying bedding and belongings over the shoulders in a rolled bundle

I

iron horse: a 44-gallon drum on ropes; used to practise rodeo riding

J

jitterbug: energetic dance, popular in the 1940s
junket: sweet custard-like pudding made from flavoured milk and rennet

K
kapok trees: *Cochlospermum* trees of Northern Australia, whose flowers yield a cotton-like silky down or floss; used as stuffing for bedding
kicked over: started (e.g. an engine)
Kimberleys: the East and West Kimberley Ranges; a lightly-populated area of north-western Australia, bounded by the Northern Territory border in the east, coastline in the north and west, extending south as far as 19 degrees S latitude
konkerberries: bush fruit like small, very sweet blackberries

L
landed gentry: land-owning class (particularly inherited land)
lean-to: a shelter propped up against a wall or building
lifted: picked up from point of departure; taken delivery of (refers to livestock)
lubra: an Aboriginal woman

M
man-maker: one who performs the Aboriginal male initiation ceremony
micky: young, unbranded bull
myall: Aborigine still living in the traditional manner

N
narga: Aboriginal male's garment, like a loincloth
near side: the left-hand side, particularly of a horse
New Australian: immigrant (generally one whose first language is not English)
nobby micky: young, hornless bull
novena: nine days of special prayer

O
off side: right-hand side
open broncoing: roping cattle for branding, etc. while on horseback, in the open (without a yard or pen)

P
Piantas: name of a *Lansdowne* stock camp
piccaninny: small child (generally refers to a small Aboriginal or coloured child)
pikers: old wild bullocks
plant: horses for all men in a stock camp
plunge: a bath

poddy-dodging: the theft of cattle (the term originally referred to the theft of poddy calves, just old enough to be weaned, but soon came to mean theft of cattle of any age)
polio: poliomyelitis, acute viral disease which attacks nerve cells of the spinal cord, often resulting in paralysis and muscular atrophy of a permanent nature
punka: a swinging screenlike fan, hung from the ceiling and often operated by a servant
Push and Pull: an aeroplane with engines mounted forwards and backwards

Q
quart pot: tin vessel holding one quart of liquid (approximately 1200 mL); it has a lid which can be used as a cup

R
red water fever: cattle disease transmitted mainly by *Babesia argenta* tick, characterised by red-coloured urine in affected beasts
ring round the yard: move restlessly about in a circle
rush: cattle stampede

S
septic: a sewerage system using a septic tank where organic matter is decomposed by anaerobic bacteria
sked: an arranged or scheduled time for a radio contact
smoko: tea-break (from work), usually mid-morning
spray: a slender shoot, twig or branch with leaves attached
stint: period of time at a particular task
stirrup clogs: 'trainer' stirrups, which enclose the foot in a leather clog
sugarbag: honey from native bees

T
TB: tuberculosis
The Lily: name of a *Lansdowne* stock camp
traffic: telegrams and messages via the Royal Flying Doctor Base radio operator
turkey nest: a tank or dam built in flat country, its walls above ground level look like a turkey's nest; a windmill pumps water from a nearby bore to fill it
turn off: to sell or dispose of stock

V

Vestey: English peer, Lord Vestey; managers ran his many Australian holdings

W

waddy: heavy wooden stick or club
walkabout: annual holiday period when Aborigines return to their traditional lifestyle, visiting sacred sites, holding ceremonies and
 corroborees
walkabout disease: fatal liver disease of horses, possibly caused by eating some forms of crotalaria bush; also known as Kimberley disease
wet season/the wet: monsoonal rainy season between December and March in the Top End of Australia
whirly winds: spiralling winds, often collecting dust and debris, also known as a willy-willy

X, Y, Z

yahoo: someone who is undisciplined, uncouth or coarse

⊢ **Q2**: lazy T Q two, the *Lansdowne* brand (Take you 2)

* * *